Non-signatory States in International Refugee Law

International Refugee Law Series

VOLUME 22

The titles published in this series are listed at *brill.com/irls*

Non-signatory States in International Refugee Law

Edited by

Maja Janmyr, Özlem Gürakar Skribeland
and Arjumand Bano Kazmi

BRILL | NIJHOFF

LEIDEN | BOSTON

The open access publication of this book has been funded with the support of the European Research Council (ERC) under the European Union's Horizon 2020 research and innovation programme (Grant agreement No. 851121).

European Research Council
Established by the European Commission

Library of Congress Cataloging-in-Publication Data

Names: Janmyr, Maja editor | Gürakar Skribeland, Özlem editor | Bano Kazmi, Arjumand editor
Title: Non-signatory states in international refugee law / edited by Maja Janmyr, Özlem Gürakar Skribeland, and Arjumand Bano Kazmi.
Description: Leiden ; Boston : Brill Academic Publishers, Inc, 2025. | Series: International Refugee Law Series ; volume 22 | Includes bibliographical references and index.
Identifiers: LCCN 2025032126 | ISBN 9789004710290 hardback | ISBN 9789004710306 epub
Subjects: LCSH: Refugees--Legal status, laws, etc. | Convention Relating to the Status of Refugees (1951 July 28) | Convention Relating to the Status of Refugees (1951 July 28). Protocols, etc. (1967 January 31) | Emigration and immigration law
Classification: LCC KZ6530 .N66 2025 | DDC 342.08/3--DC23/ENG/20250725
LC record available at https://lccn.loc.gov/2025032126

Typeface for the Latin, Greek, and Cyrillic scripts: "Brill". See and download: brill.com/brill-typeface.

ISSN 2213-3836
ISBN 978-90-04-71029-0 (hardback)
ISBN 978-90-04-71030-6 (e-book)
DOI 10.1163/9789004710306

This book is printed on acid-free paper and produced in a sustainable manner.

Contents

Acknowledgments

This edited collection is an integral part of the research project *Protection without Ratification? International Refugee Law beyond States Parties to the 1951 Refugee Convention* (BEYOND), funded by the European Research Council. The genesis for the collection is two workshops held in 2023 and 2024. An exploratory workshop was held virtually in May 2023. This was followed by an in-person authors' workshop in August 2024, where preliminary chapter drafts were presented and discussed. We wish to thank all participants at both workshops for engaging discussions. A special thanks, of course, to the contributors of this volume for sharing their knowledge, and for their enthusiasm and commitment throughout this book process.

The publication of a project such as this depends not only on the dedication of its contributing authors, but on the sustained support from a larger team. We want to thank David Cantor for paving the way for this book to see the light of day. At Brill, we also want to especially thank Lauren Danahy and Akiko Hakuno, who have provided us with unwavering support and diligently addressed all our queries throughout the process. We feel tremendously fortunate to also have been able to draw on the meticulous copyediting skills of Susannah Salle, whose professionalism and eye on detail greatly improved the outcome of this publication.

A special thanks goes to the Department of Criminology and Sociology of Law at the University of Oslo. Head of Department Helene Gundhus and Head of Office Eivind Roll have followed the BEYOND book project with genuine enthusiasm. Additional funding to ensure that this book can be read open access has also been provided by the Department. For this we are grateful.

Finally, during the course of this book project, we have been fortunate to work alongside three outstanding research assistants. Nora Milch nourished the growth of this volume in its early stages, assisting also with the virtual workshop that was held in May 2023. Maisie Fitzmaurice supported our work ahead of the in-person authors' workshop held in Oslo in August 2024. During and after this workshop, Hanna G. Berg offered crucial editorial support. Her sustained efforts kept this project afloat across the finish line in early 2025, coordinating with contributors, editors and copy-editors in an exemplary fashion. Hanna's positive outlook and stamina kept us all going even on the most challenging of days.

Maja Janmyr, Özlem Gürakar Skribeland and
Arjumand Bano Kazmi
Oslo, February 20, 2025

Figures

CHAPTER 1

Studying Non-signatory States: A Shared Ambition, Complementary Approaches

Maja Janmyr and Özlem Gürakar Skribeland

1 Introduction

We are at a critical juncture in the development and application of international refugee law. On the one hand, the continued relevance of the 1951 Convention relating to the Status of Refugees[1] and its 1967 Protocol[2] ("the Refugee Convention"[3]) has come under doubt, and political and scholarly debates about "the end" of the global refugee protection regime are ongoing.[4] On the other hand, major refugee-hosting countries in several regions of the world are not party to the Refugee Convention, leading some mainstream scholarship and practice to view them or their regions as an "exception" to international refugee law.[5] This chapter and the wider volume seek to challenge these rhetorics. We argue that the Refugee Convention not only continues to be relevant, but that it also plays important roles in shaping responses to refugees in many non-signatory states.[6] Furthermore,

1 Convention relating to the Status of Refugees (adopted July 28, 1951, entered into force April 22, 1954) 189 UNTS 137.

2 Protocol relating to the Status of Refugees (adopted January 31, 1967, entered into force October 4, 1967) 606 UNTS 267.

3 The 1951 Convention and the 1967 Protocol are technically two separate treaties with very similar but not identical states parties. We use "Refugee Convention" when speaking more generally about one or both of those instruments.

4 David J Cantor, 'The End of Refugee Law?' (2017) 9(2) *Journal of Human Rights Practice* 203.

5 Martin Jones, 'Expanding the Frontiers of Refugee Law: Developing a Broader Law of Asylum in the Middle East and Europe' (2017) 9(2) *Journal of Human Rights Practice* 212.

6 For an overview of this research agenda, see Maja Janmyr, 'The 1951 Refugee Convention and Non-Signatory States: Charting a Research Agenda' (2021) 33(2) *International Journal of Refugee Law* 188; and Maja Janmyr, Special Feature on 'Non-Signatory States and the International Refugee Regime' (2021) 67 *Forced Migration Review*. "Non-signatory states" is used in this volume and more generally in the literature to refer to states that are not parties to the Refugee Convention, whether by way of ratification, accession or succession.

DOI:10.1163/9789004710306_002

the fragmented but rich body of international refugee law (ie with the Refugee Convention at its center and comprising much other hard and soft law that is relevant and essential for refugee protection today) manifests itself in dynamic ways in non-signatory states, and those states in turn contribute to its development.

Since its adoption, the Refugee Convention has been central to scholarship on refugee and asylum issues. Yet, at the end of 2024, 46 United Nations (UN) member and observer states were not party to either the Convention or the Protocol.[7] These non-signatory states are found predominantly in the Middle East and in South and Southeast Asia. In the Middle East, only Iran, Israel, Egypt, and Yemen are party to the Convention, while major refugee-hosting states such as Iraq, Lebanon, Jordan, and most states in the Gulf region are not. Non-signatory states in South and Southeast Asia include India, Bangladesh, Pakistan, Sri Lanka, Malaysia, and Indonesia. Non-signatory states are found in other regions of the world as well, and include, for example, Eritrea, Libya, Mongolia, Cuba, and Guyana. Furthermore, we argue that Türkiye can also be framed and analyzed as a non-signatory state due to its geographical limitation to the Refugee Convention: Türkiye has undertaken to apply the Refugee Convention exclusively to Europeans while the big refugee population in the country originates mainly from Syria, as well as Afghanistan, Iraq, and Iran.

Non-signatory states' engagement with international refugee law has only rarely been considered worthy of examination, a point increasingly observed in recent years by critical scholars. David Cantor, for example, has criticized "the international and Western bias" in the study of international refugee law, pointing to its overwhelming reliance on the practices of a handful of "Western" states while the practices of states in the Global South seem to go largely unnoticed. And this is despite the fact that the former group hosts only a portion of the world's refugees and produces only a small part of the global refugee law practice and jurisprudence.[8] It indeed seems, as argued by Georgia Cole, that there exists a "methodological nationalism" in which "only certain nations count" in academic analyses of refugees and, through their work, scholars perpetuate the normative and geographical parameters

7 UNHCR, 'Rights Mapping and Analysis Platform' <https://rimap.unhcr.org/refugee-treaty-legislation-dashboard> accessed December 3, 2024.

8 Cantor (n 4) 203. See also Cecilia Bailliet, 'National Case Law as a Generator of International Refugee Law: Rectifying an Imbalance within UNHCR Guidelines on International Protection' (2015) 29 *Emory International Law Review Recent Developments* 2059.

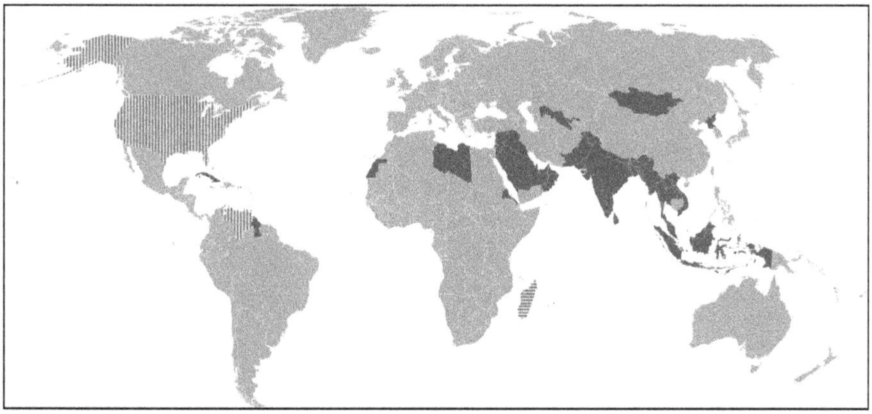

The figure shows the states that are signatories to the 1951 Convention and/or its 1967 Protocol, as well as the territories to which the application of these instruments extend. Highlighted in light gray or grayscale stripes, 149 UN member and observer states have signed either or both of these agreements. In contrast, there are 48 states or territories where neither instrument applies.

FIGURE 1.1 The 1951 Convention and the 1967 Protocol

of the Refugee Convention.[9] B. S. Chimni has similarly condemned the omission of critical Third World perspectives from discussions on international refugee law.[10]

The BEYOND project at the University of Oslo, of which we and this edited collection are an integral part, is devoted entirely to studying non-signatory states in international refugee law.[11] That said, there is a burgeoning scholarship that shares our ambition to disrupt the dominant scholarly focus on signatory states and on "Western" refugee protection. Several important books have been published in recent years with this outlook, and these span different disciplines.[12] When it comes to international refugee

---

9 Georgia Cole, 'Pluralising Geographies of Refuge' (2021) 45(1) *Progress in Human Geography* 88, citing discussions in Andreas Wimmer and Nina Glick Schiller, 'Methodological Nationalism, the Social Sciences, and the Study of Migration: An Essay in Historical Epistemology' (2003) 37(3) *International Migration Review* 576.

10 BS Chimni, 'The Past, Present and Future of International Law: A Critical Third World Approach Feature' (2007) 8(2) *Melbourne Journal of International Law* 499; and BS Chimni, 'The Birth of a "Discipline": From Refugee to Forced Migration Studies' (2009) 22(1) *Journal of Refugee Studies* 11.

11 'Protection without Ratification? International Refugee Law beyond States Parties to the 1951 Refugee Convention (BEYOND)' <www.jus.uio.no/ikrs/english/research/projects/beyond/index.html> accessed December 5, 2024.

12 Just to name a couple of recently published as well as upcoming books: Ola G El-Taliawi, *The Politics of Refugee Policy in the Global South* (MIT Press 2024); Tamirace Fakhoury and Dawn Chatty (eds), *Refugee Governance in the Arab World: The*

Non-signatory states
Andorra
Bahrain
Bangladesh
Barbados
Bhutan
Brunei Darussalam
Comoros
Cuba
Democratic People's Republic of Korea
Eritrea
Federated States of Micronesia
Grenada
Guyana
India
Indonesia
Iraq
Jordan
Kiribati
Kuwait
Lao People's Democratic Republic
Lebanon
Libya
Malaysia
Maldives
Marshall Islands
Mauritius
Mongolia
Myanmar
Nepal
Oman
Pakistan
Palau
Qatar
Saint Lucia
San Marino
Saudi Arabia
Singapore
Sri Lanka
State of Palestine
Syrian Arab Republic
Thailand
Tonga
United Arab Emirates
Uzbekistan
Vanuatu
Vietnam

The figure identifies the 46 United Nations member and observer states that have signed neither the 1951 Convention nor the 1967 Protocol.

FIGURE 1.2 Non-signatory States to the 1951 Convention and the 1967 Protocol

law, the recently published Asian Yearbook of International Law provides valuable insights into refugee protection in several non-signatory states while comprehensive textbooks and handbooks include state-of-the-art insights crucial to understanding this body of law in non-signatory states even if their focus is not exclusively or specifically on them.[13] Several major international research projects and initiatives have set out in recent years to look beyond law and/or the Global North.[14] And importantly, one of the focus areas of the 2025 International Association for the Study of Forced Migration (IASFM) conference was precisely "non-signatory countries and the 1951 Refugee Convention."[15]

Our work intersects with this scholarship and research in meaningful ways. At the same time, the volume we are presenting is unique in its exclusive focus on non-signatory states, and for specifically zooming in on these states' relations with international refugee law. Our aim is to bring non-signatory states into the ongoing debates about the past and future of the Refugee Convention and of international refugee law more generally, and to instigate further debate on the broader workings and impact of international refugee law, beyond treaty ratification. By examining the influence of international refugee law in non-signatory states and exploring how these states engage with, and help shape, this field of law, we can further our understanding of this field.

How does the Refugee Convention impact and inform the relevant laws and practices of non-signatory states? To what extent and how do non-signatory states engage with international refugee law more broadly

---

International Refugee Regime and Global Politics (Bloomsbury 2024); Ria Kapoor, *Making Refugees in India* (OUP 2022); Mitali Agrawal, Cathryn Costello, Luisa Feline Freier, Natalie Welfens and Tamara Wood, *Recognizing Refugees* (CUP forthcoming); and Susan Kneebone, Reyvi Mariñas, Antje Missbach and Max Walden (eds), *Refugee Protection in Southeast Asia: Between Humanitarianism and Sovereignty* (Berghahn 2024).

13 Seokwoo Lee and Hee Eun Lee (eds), *Asian Yearbook of International Law: Volume 28 (2022)* (BRILL 2024). In the latter category, again to name some recent and upcoming books: Cathryn Costello, Michelle Foster and Jane McAdam (eds), *The Oxford Handbook of International Refugee Law* (OUP 2021); Satvinder Juss (ed), *The Research Handbook on International Refugee Law* (Edward Elgar 2019); Cathryn Costello, *A Critical Introduction to International Refugee Law* (Bristol University Press forthcoming); and Stephen Meili and Dallal Stevens (eds), *A New Research Agenda in Refugee and Asylum Law* (Edgar Elgar forthcoming).

14 Examples include ACCESS (<https://site.unibo.it/access/en>), MOBILE (<https://mobilitylaw.ku.dk/about/>), and MIGJUST (<https://hrc.ugent.be/research/global-migration-justice/>) accessed December 3, 2024.

15 IASFM Conference 2025 <https://iasfm.org/iasfm2025/> accessed December 3, 2024.

conceived, and how and what do these states contribute to that body of law? What are the reasons behind non-ratification of the Refugee Convention? How can we understand compliance without ratification: can we talk of different types and degrees of commitment? How does UNHCR carry out its mandate in non-signatory states: is it fundamentally different from or inherently more difficult than the agency's work in signatory states? To what extent are lessons learned from specific non-signatory contexts applicable to other non-signatory contexts – also beyond international refugee law? These and similar starting questions have guided the editors and authors of this volume to explore non-signatory states in international refugee law from diverse, yet complementary, critical perspectives.

Many of the contributions in this volume zoom in on regional and local contexts, empirically informing the discipline from a Global South perspective. This is important for many reasons: technically oriented international lawyers, for example, would appreciate that this brings to light the practices and/or *opinio juris* of some of the key "specially affected states" in this area.[16] Others would appreciate it as a more general contribution toward countering the undemocratic nature of custom formation and the smaller role the "Third World" gets to play in that process.[17] For many, as we will examine in more detail, zooming in on these geographies and their accompanying histories is a necessary first step in the decolonization of international refugee law scholarship. And for the practically oriented, these empirical insights present a valuable opportunity to learn, providing us with concrete examples of what does and does not work in different non-signatory contexts. The list can be expanded.

In the following, we aim to capture and briefly discuss what we consider to be some of the most essential aspects of studying non-signatory states, how these have been addressed by this volume, and why they should be taken into consideration by future studies. To begin with, breaking with the status quo in the study of international refugee law arguably requires, first and foremost, diverse critical perspectives. Section 2 thus elaborates on the markedly different critical perspectives that complement each other

16 International Law Commission, 'Draft Conclusions on Identification of Customary International Law, with Commentaries' (2018) 136–37; and Kevin Jon Heller, 'Specially-Affected States and the Formation of Custom' (2018) 112(2) *American Journal of International Law* 191.

17 George Rodrigo Bandeira Galindo and Cesar Yip, 'Customary International Law and the Third World: Do Not Step on the Grass' (2017) 16(2) *Chinese Journal of International Law* 251; and BS Chimni, 'Customary International Law: A Third World Perspective (2018) 112(1) *The American Journal of International Law* 1.

in forming this volume. This is followed by Section 3's focus on methodology. The methodological approaches employed by the different contributors are as diverse as their critical perspectives but here, too, there is an important connecting thread: the contributions are empirically anchored and richly contextualized, and they go well beyond traditional positivist, doctrinal analysis that has thus far dominated the scholarship.

Moving on, how international refugee law is reshaped when actors in non-signatory states engage with its norms, and how national legal and protection landscapes are reconfigured as part of the process is a question that lies at the heart of our study and is another thread running through this volume. We share our observations on this in Section 4. And in Section 5, we focus on the role of UNHCR in non-signatory states, in its capacity as a cornerstone of the international refugee regime.[18] Finally, Section 6 offers some concluding observations and forward-looking thoughts.

2 Critical Perspectives

The different contributions to this volume intersect in several ways, whether by virtue of their theoretical underpinnings, the methods they employ, geographical focus, or otherwise, but the immediately visible commonality running through *all* of them is a reflective and critical stance, albeit in different ways. To take but three examples: Brian Barbour (chapter 4) applies a critical lens to the notion of perceived "Asian exceptionalism" with respect to the ratification of the Refugee Convention. Jittawadee Chotinukul, on the other hand, meticulously scrutinizes Thailand's recently established National Screening Mechanism (NSM) against international law, showing how the NSM falls short of international standards (see chapter 8). And Georgia Cole reflects critically on UNHCR's strategies in "enrolling" states into the international refugee regime, pointing to how these often result in short-term compromises and pragmatic alliances (see chapter 9).

Some of the contributions to this volume employ postcolonial and/or decolonial argumentation, responding to calls to decolonize international

18 We use "international refugee regime" to refer to the instruments and institutions of refugee protection, which include the Refugee Convention and UNHCR as cornerstones. Martin Jones, 'The Governance Question: The UNHCR, the Refugee Convention and the International Refugee Regime' in James J Simeon (ed) *The UNHCR and Supervision of International Refugee Law* (CUP 2013) 76.

refugee law.[19] Decolonizing international refugee law would involve, among other things, transforming its pedagogy.[20] This in turn makes it important to study if and how the subject is taught in non-signatory states. In their pioneering contribution, Arjumand Bano Kazmi and Sikandar Shah undertake this important task with respect to Pakistan, discussing the promises and challenges of teaching international refugee law in that country and sharing critical insights that can be useful for rethinking the teaching of international refugee law, not just in non-signatory states but more generally (see chapter 11).

The contributors to the present volume represent and present "situated knowledge."[21] Many of them are from or have long experience of conducting research in the Global South. They reflect critically on the social, political, and historical contexts relating to the local level, while also being cognizant of the global imperatives which have shaped and continue to shape those local contexts in myriad ways. The resulting contributions complement each other, both conceptually and methodologically, in challenging the exception rhetoric and unsettling the "international and Western bias" in the study of international refugee law. They also constitute modest contributions toward countering the Global North's domination of knowledge production in refugee studies.[22]

As editors, we are drawn more generally to Third World Approaches to International Law (TWAIL). This school of thought challenges mainstream international law scholarship by focusing on international law in the colonial and postcolonial eras, with its class, gender, and race perspectives, and with an eye to diversifying knowledge production.[23] We are mindful and inspired

---

19 E Tendayi Achiume, 'Migration as Decolonization' (2019) 71 *Stanford Law Review* 1509; Richa Shivakoti and James Milner 'Beyond the Partnership Debate: Localizing Knowledge Production in Refugee and Forced Migration Studies' (2021) 35(2) *Journal of Refugee Studies* 805; Nergis Canefe, 'Decolonizing Forced Migration Studies: Notes from the Borderlands' in Sanja S Petkovska (ed) *Decolonial Politics in European Peripheries: Redefining Progressiveness, Coloniality and Transition Efforts* (Routledge 2024).

20 BS Chimni, 'Three Approaches to the 1951 Convention: The Case for a Dialectical Approach' (2024) *Journal of Refugee Studies* <https://doi.org/10.1093/jrs/feae011> accessed December 8, 2024.

21 Donna Haraway, 'Situated Knowledges: The Science Question in Feminism and the Privilege of Partial Perspective' (1988) 14(3) *Feminist Studies* 575.

22 Chimni (n 20) 2.

23 Obiora Chinedu Okafor, 'Critical Third World Approaches to International Law (TWAIL): Theory, Methodology, or Both?' (2008) 10 *International Community Law Review* 371, 377; Antony Anghie, *Sovereignty, Imperialism and International Law* (CUP 2003); Antony Anghie and BS Chimni, 'Third World Approaches to International Law

by the critique that mainstream international refugee law scholarship has been failing to adequately consider structural and historical factors impacting on refugee protection, and for carrying a Global North-centric position that overlooks the fact that the majority of refugees reside in the Global South.[24] We hear Chimni when he argues that decolonizing international law scholarship would require breaking the "epistemic silence" by bringing in the factors of geography and race within the mainstream discussions.[25] And we think it is crucial to explore the colonial roots of the 1951 Convention.[26]

The colonial context has diverse implications for how states relate to the international refugee regime in a postcolonial and neocolonial world. This includes first and foremost how colonial histories can play into some states' decisions not to ratify the Refugee Convention or more generally distance themselves from the broader international refugee regime. Not as well known but equally intriguing, colonial histories can also play into some states' present lack of choice on the matter. It is with this awareness and perspective that some of the chapters in our volume delve into reasons for non-ratification of the Refugee Convention.

Barbour, as mentioned, challenges the notion of "Asian exceptionalism" with respect to the ratification of the Refugee Convention. Building on TWAIL, he argues that the "resistance" that is perceived among Asian states is not a resistance to human rights or refugee law, but rather to Global North hegemony (see chapter 4).[27] Zooming in on a local context in Asia, Bilal Dewansyah then examines Indonesia's reluctance to ratify the Refugee

---

and Individual Responsibility in Internal Conflicts' (2003) 2(1) *Chinese Journal of International Law* 77; BS Chimni, *International Law and World Order: A Critique of Contemporary Approaches* (2nd edn, CUP 2017); and James Thuo Gathii, 'The Promise of International Law: A Third World View' (2021) 36(3) *American University International Law Review* 377.

24 Chimni (n 20). See also Glen Peterson, 'Sovereignty, International Law, and the Uneven Development of the International Refugee Regime' (2015) 49(2) *Modern Asian Studies* 439.

25 Chimni (n 20) 9–10. See also BS Chimni, 'The Geopolitics of Refugee Studies: A View from the South' (1998) 11(4) *Journal of Refugee Studies* 350; and Walter D Mignolo, 'Epistemic Disobedience, Independent Thought and De-Colonial Freedom' (2009) 26(7–8) *Theory, Culture & Society* 159.

26 Edwin O Abuya, Ulrike Krause and Lucy Mayblin, 'The Neglected Colonial Legacy of the 1951 Refugee Convention' (2021) 59(4) *International Migration* 265; and Ulrike Krause, 'Colonial Roots of the 1951 Refugee Convention and Its Effects on the Global Refugee Regime' (2021) 24 *Journal of International Relations and Development* 599.

27 For more on Asian exceptionalism, see Sara E Davies, *Legitimizing Rejection: International Refugee Law in South East Asia* (Martinus Nijhoff 2008); Sara E Davies, 'The Asian Rejection?: International Refugee Law in Asia' (2006) 52(4) *Australian Journal of*

Convention, exploring the colonial history which shaped the interactions between the state, civil society, and international actors (see chapter 5). In her chapter, Natalie Jones grapples with the colonial antecedents and evolving neocolonial ties in the Kingdom of the Netherlands and its former colonies in the Caribbean. Here it is argued that the colonial legacy has impeded territorial application of the Refugee Convention in the former colonies, resulting in a neocolonial power struggle of "responsibility." Jones's discussion of the intricacies in Aruba and Curaçao's relations to the Refugee Convention draws attention to the not-so-well-known cases of small island states, highlighting the importance of colonial histories in understanding ratification patterns (see chapter 6).

The approach underlying this volume requires us also to address "the endurance of coloniality."[28] Here, one must critically reflect on how colonial legacies can impact the governance and treatment of foreigners in postcolonial states and, as part of this, add to refugees' suffering, whether by continuing to perpetuate colonial logics of control, in an effort to counter colonial immigration policies and protect citizens, or otherwise. In his contribution to this volume, Dewansyah underscores this endurance and its negative impact on refugees with his analysis of Indonesia's selective policy principle (see chapter 5).

Non-ratification is not the only way colonial histories and neocolonial dynamics can fit into the puzzle of how individual states relate to the Refugee Convention. Nauru and Papua New Guinea are interesting cases in this regard. Nauru, and Papua New Guinea's Manus Island were formerly UN Trust Territories administered by Australia, and both countries still rely on Australia for trade and development funding.[29] In their cases, historical and current dependencies[30] seem to have led to an increased formal engagement with the Refugee Convention, presumably to "qualify" to be on the receiving end of Australia's infamous externalization scheme. Indeed, Nauru is one of only two states to accede to the Refugee Convention in recent

Politics and History 562; and Sébastien Moretti, *The Protection of Refugees in Southeast Asia: A Legal Fiction?* (Routledge 2022).

28 Martin Lemberg-Pedersen, Kate Pincock, Clayton Boeyink and Laura Rosanne Adderley, 'Editorial Introduction: Colonialism, Postcoloniality, and the Study of Forced Migration' (2024) 7(1) *Migration and Society* 94, 99.

29 JC Salyer, Steffen Dalsgaard and Paige West, 'It Is Not Because They Are Bad People: Australia's Refugee Resettlement in Papua New Guinea and Nauru' (2020) 32(2) *The Contemporary Pacific* 435, 438–39.

30 Cait Storr, International Status in the Shadow of Empire Nauru and the Histories of International Law (CUP 2020) 257.

years (2011). In 2013, Papua New Guinea lifted its reservation to article 17 of the Convention, but only with respect to those refugees transferred to it by Australia.[31] In this connection, we may question whether Nauru's ratification of the Refugee Convention and Papua New Guinea's partial lifting of its reservation indeed increased protection in the region.[32]

This in turn calls for a more general and critical exploration of the interrelation between protection on the one hand, and ratification and other types of commitment on the other. A crucial question here is whether ratification or formal engagement – or in the case of Chotinukul's analysis of the Thai case in chapter 8, fulfillment of pledges at the global level – always means better protection for refugees. Lili Song's analysis of the genuinely unique non-signatory case of the Republic of China (Taiwan) is also relevant here. The Republic of China is one of the original drafters of the 1951 Convention, but through its exclusion from the UN system in 1971, it is today unable to become a state party to the Refugee Convention while at the same time engaging with it in substantive ways (see chapter 7). In short, several of the contributions significantly enhance our understanding of why some states commit or do not commit to the Refugee Convention, whether willingly or not so willingly, and whether formally or informally.

The in-depth analyses in these contributions constitute valuable additions to the literature, as well as a good starting point for further research: we argue that a more *systematic* mapping and study of patterns of accession, succession, and ratification relating to the Refugee Convention is needed. In addition to helping better understand the international refugee regime, such a study would also provide much valuable insight into how international law functions and why it functions that way. Certainly, the cases to be studied further are plenty.

To take only one example: Mauritius is formally considered by the UN not to be a state party to the 1951 Convention, but in 2003 its Supreme Court concluded otherwise. Upon its independence from Great Britain in 1968, the Court argued, Mauritius had indeed succeeded to the Refugee Convention.[33] Related to doctrinal debates on state succession that date back

---

31 Özlem Gürakar Skribeland, 'Forced Return of Migrants to Transit Countries: A Case of Competing Sovereigns' (PhD dissertation, University of Oslo 2022) 274–75.

32 Özlem Gürakar Skribeland, 'Refugee Protection and Human Rights' in Borhan Uddin Khan and Jahid Hossain Bhuiyan (eds) *Human Rights after 75 Years of the Universal Declaration of Human Rights: Reflections from the Global South* (BRILL 2024) 228.

33 For a discussion, see Nora Milch Johnsen and Maja Janmyr, 'State Succession to the 1951 Refugee Convention: The Curious Case of Mauritius' (2021) *Refugee History Blog* <https://refugeehistory.org/blog/2021/9/30/state-succession-to-the-1951-refugee-con

centuries, the case suggests that the linkages between states and the Refugee Convention are more complex and legally intricate than generally recognized. A closer examination of the processes of state succession would therefore be helpful in explaining how divergent doctrines and practices of state succession leave space for such contrasting conclusions.

3 Empirically Anchored Approaches

This volume brings together uniquely diverse perspectives on the study of non-signatory states. The contributions are legally informed and richly contextualized at the same time, providing empirical, conceptual, and critical insights. By foregrounding bottom-up, grounded, and empirically anchored approaches, we respond to wider calls for an "empirical turn" to the study of international law[34] and for "methodological heterodoxy" with respect to refugee law scholarship.[35] We find this crucial, considering how law generally is shaped by, and shapes, networks of cultural, political, and economic relations that "crisscross local, national, international, regional, and global domains and spatial scales."[36] For the field of international refugee law, this perspective is particularly necessary, given how this body of scholarship has become, in the words of Thomas Gammeltoft-Hansen and Daniel Ghezelbash, "increasingly insulated from other parts of refugee studies."[37]

The privileging of positivist, policy-driven research has among other things served to promote doctrinal refugee law analysis, a hallmark of which is not only the separation of law from politics but also the absence of interdisciplinarity.[38] In their contribution to this volume, Simon Behrman and

vention-the-curious-case-of-mauritius> accessed December 8, 2024. See also Jamil Ddamulira Mujuzi, 'Mauritian Courts and the Protection of the Rights of Asylum Seekers in the Absence of Dedicated Legislation' (2019) 31(2–3) *International Journal of Refugee Law* 321.

34 Gregory Shaffer and Tom Ginsburg, 'The Empirical Turn in International Legal Scholarship' (2017) 106(1) *American Journal of International Law* 1; and Daniel Abebe, Adam Chilton and Tom Ginsburg, 'The Social Science Approach to International Law' (2021) 22(1) *Chicago Journal of International Law* 1.

35 Thomas Gammeltoft-Hansen and Daniel Ghezelbash, 'What Role for Law in Refugee Studies? Towards a Transdisciplinary Agenda' (2024) *Journal of Refugee Studies* 2 <https://doi.org/10.1093/jrs/feae068> accessed December 8, 2024.

36 Eve Darian-Smith, 'Locating a Global Perspective' (2013) 4 *Transnational Legal Theory* 524.

37 Gammeltoft-Hansen and Ghezelbash (n 35) 2.

38 Chimni (n 20).

Dallal Stevens observe how refugee law scholarship was predominantly doctrinally oriented in the 1990s and early 2000s (see chapter 2). When it came to the study of non-signatory states, they note, there was negligibly little focus by refugee lawyers on the treatment and protection of refugees; "any studies undertaken were by non-lawyers, and where there was some coverage of applicable law, this frequently lacked detail and was one issue of many discussed." Likewise, a "myth of difference"[39] between white European refugees – whose contours are set within the Refugee Convention – and refugees from the Global South meant that law often only framed discussions of the former while ignoring the latter.

Several of the contributors to this volume employ legal historical approaches, understood in refugee law to be vital tools not only for comprehending the present, but also for shaping and envisioning "different and better futures."[40] Some focus on the drafting history of the main legal instruments. Jones, for example, spotlights the Dutch Caribbean, governed by colonial powers at the time of the 1951 Convention's drafting (see chapter 6). Her chapter emphasizes the addition of the colonial clause to the Convention (ie article 40), which compelled metropole states to consider to which colonies they would extend territorial application. Similarly, in her contribution, Song demonstrates how, as a founding member of the UN, the Republic of China participated in the drafting of the 1951 Convention and vocally disagreed during that process with Western-centered approaches, including efforts to distinguish between European and non-European refugees (see chapter 7).

UNHCR's archives in Geneva are increasingly being recognized as an invaluable source for understanding the origins and development of the current refugee regime.[41] These histories can have immense explanatory power. One example is Dewansyah's chapter, which combines insights gathered from UNHCR archives with in-depth interviews with Indonesian government actors, to explain the evolution of Indonesia's formal position on accession to the Refugee Convention (see chapter 5). Maja Janmyr, Sanjeeb

---

39 Chimni originally argued that during the drafting process of the 1951 Convention, a "myth of difference" presented non-European refugees as radically different from European refugees and therefore requiring solutions outside of the Convention. Chimni (1998) (n 25).

40 M Sanjeeb Hossain, '"Doing" Legal History in Refugee Law: A Snapshot of Bangladesh's Engagement with Non-Refoulement' (2023) *Journal of Refugee Studies* <https://doi.org/10.1093/jrs/fead025> accessed December 8, 2024.

41 Jay Ramasubramanyam, 'TWAIL, Archives, and Refugee Law' (2024) *Journal of Refugee Studies* <https://doi.org/10.1093/jrs/feae013> accessed December 8, 2024.

M. Hossain, and Lewis Turner similarly highlight the important role of these archives in making available historical agreements between UNHCR and non-signatory host states (see chapter 10). The archives also hold documents and correspondence relating to their negotiation – details which, they argue, are important because such agreements may function as "alternative protection regimes" in lieu of the Refugee Convention.

The study of non-signatory states often requires empirical research in the countries concerned. Behrman and Stevens draw on their work in Bangladesh and Jordan respectively to reflect on the distinct challenges and revelations of doing such research (see chapter 2). In the absence of a clear and justiciable domestic refugee law framework, their research often needed to focus on the complex and sometimes ambiguous administrative and political aspects of refugee protection, where several distinct issues influenced the understanding of refugee law and protection. These included the intricate interplay between state, UN, international non-governmental organizations, law firms, and local civil society; the significance of UNHCR and its handling of asylum and resettlement; and the role of UNHCR's partner organizations in the delivery of services to refugees. In the Middle Eastern context, they emphasize, the protection landscape is also influenced by the developing concepts of "protection space" and "temporary protection."[42]

Finally, empirical studies can shed light on how legal and non-legal norms interact, help explain the transnational circulation of global norms, and enhance our understanding of the local settings where these multiple orders interact.[43] Indeed, international refugee law is implemented in a space where, as Janmyr has argued elsewhere, "bureaucratic, international law and domestic norms typically overlap and sometimes conflict."[44] Norm diffusion emerges as a key issue when it comes to understanding the interplay between non-signatory states and international refugee law, and we zoom in on this in the next section.

---

42 Maja Janmyr and Dallal Stevens, 'Regional Refugee Regimes: Middle East' in Cathryn Costello, Michelle Foster and Jane McAdam (eds), *The Oxford Handbook of International Refugee Law* (OUP 2021).

43 Sally Falk Moore and Martin Chanock, *Law as Process: An Anthropological Approach* (2nd edn, LIT Verlag 2000); Sally Engle Merry, 'International Law and Sociolegal Scholarship Towards a Spatial Global Legal Pluralism' in Michael A Helfand (ed) *Negotiating State and Non-State Law: The Challenge of Global and Local Legal Pluralism* (CUP 2015); Paul Schiff Berman, *Global Legal Pluralism: A Jurisprudence of Law Beyond Borders* (CUP 2012).

44 Maja Janmyr, 'Ethnographic Approaches and International Refugee Law' (2022) *Journal of Refugee Studies* <https://doi.org/10.1093/jrs/feac042> accessed December 8, 2024.

4 Globalizing and Localizing Norms

How is international refugee law reshaped when actors in non-signatory states engage with it, and how are national legal and protection landscapes reconfigured in the process? This enquiry runs as a thread throughout the volume, with authors examining the roles played by domestic courts, UNHCR, national governments, civil society, regional organizations, and national universities and higher education in this iterative process. Most contributions focus on a range of actors, critically examining their roles in what is often somewhat simplistically referred to as norm making and norm taking.[45]

In our thinking, we draw on a combination of scholarship and research focusing on the spread of norms. In international refugee law, scant attention has been paid to transnational norm diffusion in non-signatory contexts, with the focus having been mainly on the Global North.[46] As observed by Satvinder Juss more generally, mainstream scholarship rarely engages with questions concerning how norms in refugee law evolve and who are the actors making the norms of international refugee law.[47] Notable exceptions exist, however, and include the work of Susan Kneebone, Alice Nah, and Dallal Stevens who focus on the contexts of Southeast Asia, the Asia Pacific region and the Middle East respectively.[48] These scholars seek to identify the key actors promoting refugee protection norms and their agenda

45 Jeffrey T Checkel, 'Norms, Institutions, and National Identity in Contemporary Europe' (1999) 43(1) *International Studies Quarterly* 83.

46 Hélène Lambert, Jane McAdam and Maryellen Fullerton (eds), *The Global Reach of European Refugee Law* (CUP 2013); Guy S Goodwin-Gill and Hélène Lambert (eds), *The Limits of Transnational Law: Refugee Law, Policy Harmonization and Judicial Dialogue in the European Union* (CUP 2010); Jill I Goldenziel, 'When Law Migrates: Refugees in Comparative International Law' in Anthea Roberts and others (eds), *Comparative International Law* (OUP 2018).

47 Satvinder S Juss, 'Transnational Refugee Law' in Peer Zumbansen (ed) *The Oxford Handbook of Transnational Law* (OUP 2021) 218.

48 Notably, Susan Kneebone edited a special issue on 'Comparative Regional Protection Frameworks for Refugees: Norms and Norm Entrepreneurs' in the *International Journal of Human Rights*, which included an introductory article with that same title. See Susan Kneebone, 'Comparative Regional Protection Frameworks for Refugees: Norms and Norm Entrepreneurs' (2016) 20(2) *International Journal of Human Rights* 153; Alice M Nah, 'Networks and Norm Entrepreneurship amongst Local Civil Society Actors: Advancing Refugee Protection in the Asia Pacific Region' (2016) 20(2) *International Journal of Human Rights* 223; and Dallal Stevens, 'Rights, Needs or Assistance? The Role of the UNHCR in Refugee Protection in the Middle East' (2015) 20(2) *The International Journal of Human Rights* 264.

setting in regional contexts. Inspired by work such as theirs, we find that examining more closely the interaction between actors on a global, regional, national, and even local level gives us a deeper and more nuanced understanding of the interplay between international refugee law and non-signatory states.

In international law more generally, we find Koh's notion of "transnational legal processes" useful; it allows for a precise focus on the socialization processes relating to legal argument and doctrine.[49] This view sees state behavior as influenced by interactions both within the domestic system and between the domestic and international systems. Of specific interest to international refugee law, this theory counters state-centric accounts of these processes by introducing a different set of actors, fora, and transactions, allowing us, for example, to capture actors as fundamentally different from one another as UNHCR, state diplomats, local non-governmental organizations, legal aid providers, domestic courts, and universities.

In understanding the transnational spread of norms, we also draw on approaches beyond international law, including the rich international relations literature on norm diffusion. That scholarship has historically focused on investigating transnational agents and processes shaping norm diffusion on the international level, with international organizations regarded as playing a key role in this regard.[50] More contemporary studies have emphasized the agency role of norm takers, recognizing that there is a constant back and forth occurring between global and local actors.[51]

Literature identifies *globalization* and *localization* as the two main processes of norm diffusion. The former refers to the process by which international norms and standards are *incorporated* into national standards, while the latter assesses how global norms are *adapted* to domestic contexts. Localization has been defined by Amitav Acharya as:

> a complex process and outcome by which norm-takers build congruence between transnational norms (including norms previously

49 Harold Hongju Koh, 'The 1994 Roscoe Pound Lecture: Transnational Legal Process' (1996) 75(1) *Nebraska Law Review* 181.

50 Martha Finnemore and Sikkink Kathryn, 'International Norm Dynamics and Political Change' (1998) 52(4) *International Organization* 887. See also Thomas Risse, Stephen C Ropp and Kathryn Sikkink (eds), *The Persistent Power of Human Rights: From Commitment to Compliance* (CUP 2013).

51 Sara Hellmüller, 'Meaning-Making in Peace-Making: The Inclusion Norm at the Interplay between the United Nations and Civil Society in the Syrian Peace Process' (2020) 26(4) *Swiss Political Science Review* 407, 409.

> institutionalized in a region) and local beliefs and practices. In this process, foreign norms, which may not initially cohere with the latter, are incorporated into local norms. The success of norm diffusion strategies and processes depends on the extent to which they provide opportunities for localization.[52]

Localization centers the role of local actors – the supposed norm takers – and calls for a "shift in the understanding of norm entrepreneurship from 'outsider proponents' committed to a transnational or universal moral agenda to "insider proponents."[53] Certainly, domestic actors can be more important than transnational actors in the implementation of international norms. And as Acharya has observed, norm-diffusion strategies are more likely to succeed if they accommodate local sensitivity rather than seek to supplant it.[54] Importantly, Leila Brumat and others' recent study on the impact of global norms and standards on the protection of asylum seekers and refugees in six countries, including Bangladesh, Türkiye, and Jordan, provides evidence of localization as the prevailing pattern in the domestic incorporation of international norms and standards, concluding that "it is less likely that states adopt or adapt to the global and more likely that the global is adapted to state and regional level contexts."[55]

That said, there is now also increased acceptance that globalization and localization need not necessarily be separate or opposing processes; they can happen simultaneously and feed each other. And in our examination of norm diffusion, we hear the calls being made for a "critical localism" that rejects an oversimplified dichotomy and recognizes the potential for humanitarian actors to have "translocal and transcultural entanglements."[56] Our volume recognizes this complexity by engaging with not only the range of actors that are involved but also the many levels on which they operate.

Barbour, for example, takes a localization approach in arguing that advocacy for effective refugee protection need not begin around accession to the Refugee Convention, but rather with existing laws, policies, and

52 Amitav Acharya, 'How Ideas Spread: Whose Norms Matter? Norm Localization and Institutional Change in Asian Regionalism' 58(2) *International Organization* 239, 241.

53 ibid 245.

54 ibid 249.

55 Leiza Brumat, Andrew Geddes and Andrea Pettrachin, 'Making Sense of the Global: A Systematic Review of Globalizing and Localizing Dynamics in Refugee Governance' (2022) 35(2) *Journal of Refugee Studies* 827, 845.

56 Kristina Roepstorff, 'A Call for Critical Reflection on the Localisation Agenda in Humanitarian Action' (2020) 41(2) *Third World Quarterly* 284.

coordination mechanisms (see chapter 4). This "engages with the local context on its own terms." But his eye is not only on the local; he also emphasizes the role of *regional* dialogue and consensus. This approach complements insights previously made by scholars such as Nah, whose research on the Asia Pacific Refugee Rights Network, for example, showed how working through a formalized regional network changed the ways and the conditions under which local civil society actors engage in norm entrepreneurship.[57]

Speaking of civil society, several of the contributions highlight their central role as "brokers"[58] in how norms get adapted and translated into local contexts, while at the same time recognizing how civil society can work through policy networks to influence regional and global norms and institutions, feeding globalization processes.[59] A case in point is Thailand, where the government has long displayed hostility toward transnational alliances drawing on the language of international human rights. Previous studies have drawn attention to how local and transnational actors worked in tandem to successfully lobby the government.[60] Chotinukul's chapter on Thailand extends this research by demonstrating the significance also of international forums organized by UNHCR (see chapter 8). She argues, however, that fulfillment of pledges at the global level does not necessarily mean better protection for refugees at the local level.

Finally, of special importance to our interest in norm diffusion is the role of domestic courts. In non-signatory states, courts may – quite surprisingly, some would say – engage directly with specific provisions of the Refugee Convention. The work of Özlem Gürakar Skribeland is illustrative in this regard.[61] Examining the case law of the Turkish Council of State, she

57 Nah (n 48) 223.

58 Jana Hönke and Markus-Michael Müller, 'Brokerage, Intermediation, Translation' in Anke Draude, Tanja A Börzel and Thomas Risse (eds) *The Oxford Handbook of Governance and Limited Statehood* (OUP 2018).

59 Stefan Rother, 'Multi-Level Migrant Civil Society Activism in Southeast Asia' in Eva Hansson and Meredith L Weiss (eds) *Routledge Handbook of Civil and Uncivil Society in Southeast Asia* (Routledge 2023).

60 Naiyana Thanawattho, Waritsara Rungthong and Emily Arnold-Fernández, 'Advancing Refugee Rights in Non-Signatory States: The Role of Civil Society in Thailand' (2021) 67 *Forced Migration Review*.

61 Özlem Gürakar Skribeland, 'The Turkish Council of State's Engagement with International Refugee Law in Cases Involving "Non-European" Refugees' (2025) *International Journal of Refugee Law* <https://doi.org/10.1093/ijrl/eeae041> accessed February 2, 2025. On the context of Bangladesh, see also M Sanjeeb Hossain, 'Bangladesh's Judicial Encounter with the 1951 Refugee Convention' (2021) 67 *Forced Migration Review*.

demonstrates how that court has also been engaging with the Refugee Convention in cases involving non-European refugees. Her analysis suggests that the Turkish Council of State regards the Convention as a benchmark or standard to be followed, beyond what is required by Türkiye's treaty obligations and domestic law.

Drawing on case law from multiple jurisdictions, Gamze Ovacık and Aneesha Johny's contribution to this volume takes the discussions on the role of domestic courts further (see chapter 3). They identify both cases where domestic courts apply the 1951 Convention to resolve the disputes before them, as well as those where the judges merely cite the relevant provisions of the Refugee Convention without further discussion. Framing these as an active and passive engagement with the Refugee Convention, respectively, Ovacık and Johny argue that both types of engagement are significant in a context where the assumption would be that domestic courts do not engage with instruments by which the country is not formally bound.

Norm advancement in the judiciary can also be brought about through the above-mentioned translocal entanglement. In her chapter on the Republic of China, Song demonstrates how for decades lawyers advanced arguments based on the Refugee Convention in nearly a dozen cases before domestic courts, and how gradually and increasingly the judiciary came to value international refugee law norms (see chapter 7). Her findings are not wholly dissimilar from the Pakistani context, where Kazmi has recently examined the case law at different tiers of the judiciary, mapping local courts' engagement with international refugee law as well as the role of local lawyers in these processes.[62] As Kazmi shows, UNHCR can also be involved in such judicial processes. We will come back to this in the next section as part of our discussion on the role of UNHCR in non-signatory states.

5 Centering UNHCR

This section will spotlight some of the key issues concerning UNHCR's work in and with non-signatory states. As the UN's refugee agency, UNHCR's mandate is to provide international protection and seek permanent solutions for

62 Arjumand Bano Kazmi, 'Pakistan's Judicial Engagement with International Refugee Law' (2025) *International Journal of Refugee Law* <https://doi.org/10.1093/ijrl/eeaf001> accessed February 2, 2025.

the problem of refugees worldwide. The contributions to this volume demonstrate that the agency plays important roles in relation to non-signatory states, and as Behrman and Stevens aptly observe in their contribution, its unique standing in these states presents both opportunities and challenges for researchers (see chapter 2). Researchers must study UNHCR's provision of on-the-ground assistance and international protection, as well as its promotion of accession to the Refugee Convention and its role as an influential norm entrepreneur. These activities by UNHCR may, among other things and as observed by Guy Goodwin-Gill, lead to the emergence of *opinio juris*.[63]

UNHCR's competence with respect to refugees is described in its Statute in universal terms, ie without any geographical or time limitation.[64] Still, in its early days, UNHCR had Europe as its principal area of concern, and the organization only expanded its operations to the "the new problems" of refugees outside Europe in the late 1950s and 1960s.[65] This expansion also brought about a more active role; originally, its creators had not wanted an operational refugee agency, and they had limited its functions to international protection.[66] We know little about UNHCR's evolution, especially when it comes to its past operations in non-signatory states, including its role as a "colonial era institution."[67] It remains the case that, as for scholarship on the UN more generally, research based on the archives of UNHCR has largely centered on Western issues.[68]

Today, UNHCR provides both international protection and direct assistance in many non-signatory states, and some of its biggest operations are

63 Guy S Goodwin-Gill, 'The Office of the United Nations High Commissioner for Refugees and the Sources of International Refugee Law' (2020) 69(1) *International & Comparative Law Quarterly* 1, 40.

64 UN General Assembly, Statute of the Office of the United Nations High Commissioner for Refugees, A/RES/428(V), December 14, 1950, arts 1, 6, 8.

65 Gill Loescher, 'UNHCR's Origins and Early History: Agency, Influence, and Power in Global Refugee Policy' (2017) 33(1) *Refuge: Canada's Journal on Refugees* 77, 78.

66 Alexander Betts, Gil Loescher and James Milner, *UNHCR: The Politics and Practice of Refugee Protection* (2nd edn, Routledge 2012) 22–26.

67 Glen Peterson, 'The Uneven Development of the International Refugee Regime in Postwar Asia: Evidence from China, Hong Kong and Indonesia' 25(3) *Journal of Refugee Studies* 326. See also Loescher (n 65) 77; Lauren Banko, Katarzyna Nowak and Peter Gatrell, 'What Is Refugee History, Now?' (2022) 17(1) *Journal of Global History* 1.

68 Jordi Tejel and Ramazan Hakkı Öztan, 'The Special Issue "Forced Migration and Refugeedom in the Modern Middle East" Towards Connected Histories of Refugeedom in the Middle East' (2020) 6(1) *Journal of Migration History* 1. See also Alanna O'Malley and Lydia Walker, 'A Revisionist History of the United Nations' (2024) *Past & Present* <https://doi.org/10.1093/pastj/gtae008> accessed December 8, 2024.

or have been in such countries.[69] In some contexts, its role has become so encompassing that scholars even speak of UNHCR as a "surrogate state."[70] In 2019, more than one third of UNHCR's budget was for non-signatory states.[71] With a budget of 520 million USD in 2025, UNHCR's operation in Lebanon was the organization's second largest overall, only following Ukraine at 550 million USD.[72] Syria and Jordan were also on UNHCR's top 10 list of largest budgets for 2025.[73]

Non-signatory states are not only at the receiving end of UNHCR funds. While UNHCR depends heavily on the funding of just a few Western states, as Cole has highlighted, the organization has in recent years targeted new "growth markets," including in wealthy non-signatory states.[74] As she notes, this not only has implications for how UNHCR operates within these countries, but also where those funds are spent globally. More research is certainly needed to better understand the financial links between UNHCR and non-signatory states – both as beneficiaries and as donors – and the implications these have on protection.

Under the Refugee Convention, states parties have an express obligation to cooperate with UNHCR "in the exercise of its functions."[75] That does

69 Maja Janmyr, 'UNHCR and the Syrian Refugee Response: Negotiating Status and Registration in Lebanon' (2017) 22(3) *The International Journal of Human Rights* 393; and Gerald Walzer, 'UNHCR Operations in Pakistan in the Early 1980s' (2008) 27(1) *Refugee Survey Quarterly* 40. On Türkiye, see also <www.unhcr.org/tr/turkiyede-unhcr> accessed December 8, 2024.

70 Alice M Nah, 'The Ambiguous Authority of a "Surrogate State": UNHCR's Negotiation of Asylum in the Complexities of Migration in Southeast Asia' (2019) 35 *Revue européenne des migrations internationales* 63; and Michael Kagan, 'The UN "Surrogate State" and the Foundation of Refugee Policy in the Middle East' (2012) 18 *UC Davis Journal of International Law and Policy* 307.

71 In 2024, on the other hand, the ratio was less than one fourth, which can be explained, among other things, by the Ukrainian and Venezuelan refugee situations. Calculated based on a review of UNHCR's annual Global Appeal for 2019 and 2024, outlining the organization's budgeted activities for those years.

72 UNHCR Global Appeal 2025 <https://reporting.unhcr.org/global-appeal-2025/funding-unhcrs-programmes> accessed December 8, 2024. As of mid-2024, UNHCR's operation in Lebanon was also allocated the second highest amount of UNHCR flexible funds; only Ukraine received slightly more. See Florian Zandt, 'Where the UN's Refugee Agency Allocates Its Funds' (*Statista*, June 19, 2024) <www.statista.com/chart/32466/unhcr-operations-receiving-the-highest-amound-of-flexible-funds/> accessed December 8, 2024.

73 UNHCR Global Appeal (n 72).

74 Georgia Cole, 'Non-Signatory Donor States and UNHCR: Questions of Funding and Influence' (2021) 67 *Forced Migration Review*.

75 1951 Convention art 35(1).

not mean that non-signatory states can ignore UNHCR; they also have cooperation obligations stemming from the UNHCR Statute and the UN Charter itself.[76] In addition, and drawing on its Statute, UNHCR negotiates specific cooperation and special agreements with host-state governments, as critically explored by Janmyr, Hossain, and Turner (see chapter 10). These agreements, they argue, can constitute "alternative protection regimes" that offer meaningful protection to refugees in non-signatory states. By covering substantive elements in addition to addressing institutional legal questions, the agreements may as such also be seen to form part of international refugee law.[77]

UNHCR is required to provide for the protection of refugees, among other things, by "[p]romoting the conclusion and ratification of international conventions for the protection of refugees, supervising their application and proposing amendments thereto."[78] Among these, promoting ratification (ie accession) is key when it comes to non-signatory states. In connection with the 73rd anniversary of the Refugee Convention in July 2024, "UNHCR – as the guardian of the Refugee Convention" once again, "[urged] the remaining 46 UN Member and Observer States to accede to it."[79] According to the agency, accession "not only evidences a State's willingness to protect refugees in accordance with international legal obligations, it can also help avoid friction between States over refugee issues."[80]

Better understanding how UNHCR promotes accession, what kind of promotional activities work well, how non-signatory states react to these efforts, and, importantly, the reasons underlying continual unwillingness to accede are crucial for UNHCR's effective fulfillment of this responsibility. In the case of Indonesia, for example, Dewansyah discusses how UNHCR's varied promotional activities over several decades were influential in getting

---

76 See Report of the United Nations High Commissioner for Refugees (covering the period April 1, 1979 to March 31, 1980) A/35/12, para 58 <www.unhcr.org/excom/unhcrannual/4cc039db9/report-united-nations-high-commissioner-refugees-covering-period-1-april.html> accessed December 8, 2024; and Walter Kalin, 'Supervising the 1951 Convention relating to the Status of Refugees: Article 35 and Beyond' in Erika Feller, Volker Turk and Frances Nicholson (eds) *Refugee Protection in International Law: UNHCR's Global Consultations on International Protection* (UNHCR Geneva 2003) 618–19.

77 Marjoleine Zieck, *UNHCR's Worldwide Presence in the Field* (Wolf Legal Publishers 2006) 4–7, 321.

78 UNHCR Statute art 8(a).

79 <www.unhcr.org/news/briefing-notes/un-refugee-agency-marks-73-years-refugee-convention-urging-universal-accession> accessed December 8, 2024.

80 ibid.

accession onto Indonesia's formal action plans relating to human rights reform, even if these did not in the end succeed due to the country's overarching "non-accession stance" (see chapter 5).

UNHCR carries out refugee status determination (RSD) in about 50 countries, many of which are non-signatories to the Refugee Convention.[81] With the goal that each state will eventually develop the capacity to carry out its own RSD, UNHCR also supports various exercises to that effect. Research shows, however, that handovers of RSD from UNHCR to domestic authorities can sometimes occur prematurely, and at the expense of refugees, leading, for example, to lower-quality decision making.[82] Chotinukul's critical assessment of Thailand's new National Screening Mechanism (NSM) in this volume is therefore particularly welcome at this juncture, ie before an actual handover has occurred and as the Thai government continues to work on NSM's implementation, with UNHCR support – especially considering that other Southeast Asian states may be considering following in Thailand's footsteps (see chapter 8).

UNHCR functions as an important norm entrepreneur in many non-signatory states and its promotion of international refugee law takes various forms.[83] Cole examines the multitude of approaches employed by UNHCR to encourage increased state engagement with the Refugee Convention and the broader international refugee regime (see chapter 9). Applying a framework derived from Science and Technology Studies that emphasizes the explanation of *how* networks grow, she explores how UNHCR assembles various entities into the international refugee regime. Her contribution contains a warning, however: not only are understandings of key principles of the international refugee regime not necessarily aligned within UNHCR, but its strategies also often entail short-term compromises and pragmatic alliances to ensure a combination of protection, relevance, and growth. Her critical observations on UNHCR's norm entrepreneurship are echoed elsewhere.[84] The notion of "protection space" as applied in non-signatory states has, for

81 <www.unhcr.org/media/unhcr-refugee-status-determination-map-august-2021> accessed December 8, 2024.

82 Caroline Nalule and Derya Özkul, 'Exploring RSD Handover from UNHCR to States' (2020) 65 *Forced Migration Review*; and Derya Özkul and Natalie Welfens, 'UNHCR–State Relations: Transfer of Authority over Refugee Status Determination (2024) *Journal of Refugee Studies* <https://doi.org/10.1093/jrs/feae080> accessed December 8, 2024.

83 Janmyr, 'The 1951 Refugee Convention' (n 6).

84 Stevens (n 48). See also Lewis Turner, 'Who Is a Refugee in Jordan? Hierarchies and Exclusions in the Refugee Recognition Regime' (2023) 36(4) *Journal of Refugee Studies* 877; and Maja Janmyr, 'Sudanese Refugees and the "Syrian Refugee Response" in

example, drawn criticism for its potential to devalue the normative strength of obligations toward refugees.[85]

UNHCR's role in norm diffusion often includes involvement in domestic legal reform and collaboration with universities in non-signatory states.[86] This, in turn, arguably plays an important role in influencing the ways in which national and local actors reason and converse within the international refugee law paradigm.[87] An important example of the former is the case of Türkiye: Kemal Kirişçi has explored how UNHCR's "long-standing relationship" with the Turkish government and Turkish civil society "contributed to a slow but sure process of socialization of Turkey into the norms and rules" of the international refugee regime.[88] The agency was particularly active in the drafting of Türkiye's first primary legislation on asylum, and as part of this process, UNHCR consultants were seconded to the Turkish Ministry of Interior.[89]

As previously discussed by Geoff Gilbert, UNHCR's supervisory role allows it to engage in court cases through *amicus curiae* briefs but, strategically speaking, such engagement is not without its risks.[90] Of course, not all jurisdictions procedurally allow such interventions, but formal engagement in domestic court proceedings is not the only way UNHCR can be instrumental in furthering refugee protection. Kirişci describes, for example, how UNHCR encouraged and supported asylum seekers to approach domestic Turkish courts and try the appeal process in the late 1990s where previously there was no such practice in the country.[91] As part of their contribution on the

Lebanon: Racialised Hierarchies, Processes of *Invisibilisation*, and Resistance' (2022) 41 (1) *Refugee Survey Quarterly* 131.

85 Martin Jones, 'Moving Beyond Protection Space: Developing a Law of Asylum in South-East Asia' in Susan Kneebone, Dallal Stevens and Loretta Baldassar (eds) *Refugee Protection and the Role of Law: Conflicting Identities* (Routledge 2014); and Eveliina Lyytinen, 'Refugees' Conceptualizations of "Protection Space": Geographical Scales of Urban Protection and Host–Refugee Relations' (2015) 34(2) *Refugee Survey Quarterly* 45.

86 Janmyr (n 44) 205.

87 Janmyr, 'The 1951 Refugee Convention' (n 6).

88 Kemal Kirişçi, 'Turkey's New Draft Law on Asylum: What to Make of It?' in Seçil Paçacı Elitok and Thomas Straubhaar (eds) *Turkey, Migration and the EU* (Hamburg University Press 2012) 64. See also Stephan Scheel and Philipp Ratfisch, 'Refugee Protection Meets Migration Management: UNHCR as a Global Police of Populations' (2014) 40(6) *Journal of Ethnic and Migration Studies* 924, 928–29.

89 Özkul and Welfens (n 82).

90 Geoff Gilbert, 'UNHCR and Courts: Amicus curiae … sed curia amica est?' (2016) 28(4) *International Journal of Refugee Law* 623.

91 Kirişçi (n 88) 68.

role of courts in non-signatory states, Ovacık and Johny also explore UNHCR's role in domestic judicial processes, pointing to interesting examples of this influence (see chapter 3).

Finally, a striking example of UNHCR's collaboration with universities in non-signatory states can be seen in the case of Pakistan. Here the agency has entered into memoranda of understanding with individual universities setting out in detail how the parties will cooperate in setting up and maintaining course modules on international refugee law. As Kazmi and Shah show in their contribution, UNHCR thus plays a crucial role in the promotion and inclusion of international refugee law in Pakistani higher education. Such cooperation comes with many promises as well as some unique challenges (see chapter 11). It is therefore critical that further research examines in greater detail UNHCR's collaboration with universities in a broad range of non-signatory states, perhaps through a systematic study.

6 Conclusion

The present volume thus brings to the fore non-signatory states which host much of the global refugee population. It allows us to re-examine both the often-assumed centrality of the Refugee Convention for global refugee protection, as well as the concerns raised about its continued relevance. It further enables us to integrate jurisprudence and practice from "non-Western" refugee-hosting countries into international refugee law scholarship. These exercises are crucial for understanding the development of international refugee law across time and space. And by better understanding how international refugee law functions, we think that we can also gain valuable insights into the workings of international law more generally.

As noted at the outset, this book project was guided by diverse questions, and undoubtedly, there are numerous other discussions that would have been relevant to include in this volume. What "non-signatoryness" means for the protection of Palestinian refugees is one of these.[92] Exploring refugee-led initiatives in non-signatory states; historically unpacking UNHCR's past operations in non-signatory states; analyzing non-signatory states as members of the Executive Committee of the High Commissioner's Programme (ExCom); a systematic mapping of these states' contributions to the development of

92 For an interesting discussion, see Hasan Basri Bülbül, 'Recognising Palestinian Refugees: Applicability of Article 1D of the 1951 Refugee Convention in Turkey' (2024) 43(3) *Refugee Survey Quarterly* 280.

international refugee law via the UN General Assembly or other key global fora; further research into UNHCR's collaboration with universities in non-signatory states; a closer study of the financial linkages between UNHCR and non-signatory states and the implications for protection; further research into different aspects of spread of norms; and a systematic examination of the processes of state succession are just a few of the other obvious ones. There are also many non-signatory states that deserve "their own chapter," including, for example, Guyana, Libya, and Eritrea.

With this volume, we did not attempt to even touch upon all the important issues that relate to non-signatory states in international refugee law; that is simply not feasible. We intended the volume rather as a modest yet pioneering contribution towards fulfillment of an ambitious agenda. Our volume demonstrates that the Refugee Convention plays an important role in shaping responses to refugees in many non-signatory states. International refugee law more broadly conceived manifests itself in myriad ways in these states, and these states in turn contribute to its further development. In other words, regardless of their formal standing, international refugee law norms become internalized at different levels in non-signatory states, whose engagement with them in turn feeds back into international legal governance. Our hope is that *Non-signatory States in International Refugee Law* will further increase the burgeoning scholarly interest in non-signatory states and lead to much-needed further research in this area.

Acknowledgements

This work was supported by the European Union's Horizon 2020 research and innovation program under grant agreement No 851121 (ERC Starting Grant 2019). We wish to thank Hanna Gjelsvik Berg for her research assistance and Arjumand Bano Kazmi for insightful discussions during the writing of this chapter. Author contributions for this chapter were equal and names appear in alphabetical order.

CHAPTER 2

Reflections on Conducting Empirical Research in Non-signatory States

Simon Behrman and Dallal Stevens

1 Introduction

This chapter focuses on some experiences and challenges of conducting empirical research in and on non-signatory states, as scholars of the Global North. While all research is challenging and many aspects of conducting empirical research in non-signatory states compare with those relating to signatory states, there are some issues that are arguably of particular relevance to non-signatory states. It is also worth pointing out at the outset that there can be many similarities between non-signatory states from different regions, as well as many disparities. Comparison can be helpful, and we highlight here where this is the case, but we suggest that it is advisable to focus on the specific contexts of individual countries rather than reach for generic points of wide application.

That said, researchers in the field in both signatory and non-signatory states will always need to reflect on the following: the ethics of conducting fieldwork with potentially vulnerable participants; negotiating any ethical requirements of the researcher's own institution or organization and obtaining ethical approval; careful consideration of data collection and data security; the challenges of gaining access to asylum claimants and refugees, and stakeholders; navigating language barriers; identifying reliable interpreters; reflection on the identity and positionality of the researcher and any implications for the conduct of fieldwork;[1] carrying out accurate transcription; and understanding and applying appropriate coding software. In the case of non-signatory countries, there is of course one common factor shared by all: they are not party to the 1951 Convention relating to the Status of Refugees and its 1967 Protocol (together and individually "the Refugee Con-

1 Dila Bice Kurtoglu, Yasemin Karadag Avci, Irem Sengul and Dallal Stevens, 'Conducting Fieldwork on Forced Migration: Personal, Structural and Contextual Challenges' in Steve Meili and Dallal Stevens (eds), *A Research Agenda for Refugee Law* (Edward Elgar forthcoming).

DOI:10.1163/9789004710306_003

vention").[2] Nor do many of these states have domestic law governing refugee status. This lack of a codified set of standards and criteria for asylum presents some specific challenges, on which this chapter focuses.

In the 1990s and early 2000s, refugee law scholarship tended to be doctrinally oriented – that is, focused on treaty and case law and with a strong bias toward countries of the Global North with developed refugee status determination (RSD) frameworks. Whereas empirical studies of the refugee law of states parties to the Refugee Convention were relatively unusual,[3] focus by refugee lawyers on the treatment and protection of refugees in non-signatory states was almost non-existent.[4] In the main, any studies undertaken were by non-lawyers,[5] and where there was some coverage of applicable law,[6] this frequently lacked detail and was one issue of many discussed. A further limitation concerned the "myth of difference," as described by Chimni, between the classic refugee – white, European, and anti-Communist – whose contours are set within the Refugee Convention, and refugees from the Global South.[7] While law framed discussions of the former, the latter were often discussed in the context of anthropology or sociology.[8] For non-signatory states, all of whom are in the Global South, there has been limited attention paid to legal frameworks. There is an assumption that, without adherence to the Refugee Convention, there is *ipso facto* a lack of effective protection. This lacuna is the driver behind our focus on the question of refugee protection and law in, respectively, Bangladesh and Jordan.

2 Convention relating to the Status of Refugees (adopted July 28, 1951, entered into force April 22, 1954) 189 UNTS 137; Protocol Relating to the Status of Refugees (adopted January 31, 1967, entered into force October 4, 1967) 606 UNTS 267.

3 See, for example, Dallal Stevens, UK Asylum Law and Policy: Historical and Contemporary Perspectives (Sweet & Maxwell 2004); Robert Thomas, Administrative Justice and Asylum Appeals: A Study of Tribunal Adjudication (Hart Publishing 2011).

4 Perhaps, with the exception of Palestinian refugees on which there was considerable scholarship: eg Lex Takkenberg, *The Status of Palestinian Refugees in International Law* (OUP 1998); Susan Akram, 'Palestinian Refugees and Their Legal Status: Rights, Politics, and Implications for a Just Solution' (2002) 31(3) *Journal of Palestine Studies* 36.

5 See, for example, D Chatty and B Finlayson (eds), *Dispossession and Displacement: Forced Migration in the Middle East and North Africa* (The British Academy 2010); Géraldine Chatelard, 'Migration from Iraq Between the Gulf and Iraq Wars (1990–2003): Historical and Socio-Spatial Dimensions' (2009) COMPAS Working Paper 68.

6 For example, Leila Hilal and Dr. Shahira Samy, 'Asylum And Migration in the Mashrek, Asylum and Migration Country Fact Sheet: JORDAN' (2008) Euro-Mediterranean Human Rights Network.

7 BS Chimni, 'The Geopolitics of Refugee Studies: A View From the South' (1998) 11(4) *Journal of Refugee Studies* 350.

8 Chatty and Finlayson (n 5); Chatelard (n 5).

To inform the reader – and potential researcher – of some of the challenges and revelations of empirical work in non-signatory states, we draw upon our own experiences in these two countries. In summary, we found that, in the absence of a clear refugee law framework outlined in treaty, statute, or regulations, our research focused on the complex and – at times – ambiguous administrative and political aspects of refugee protection. On the one hand, such research can produce a richer account of the sociopolitical reality of asylum than the standard doctrinal approach of refugee law scholars writing about signatory states. On the other hand, the greater reliance on empirical research in non-signatory states presents a series of specific challenges, or more acute versions of those faced by researchers in signatory states. The lack of justiciable domestic refugee law led us to explore in greater detail historical contexts, political issues, and administrative decisions relating to refugee protection. Such exploration entailed a greater focus on the experiences of all stakeholders: refugees, the Non-Governmental Organizations (NGOs) and lawyers who work with them, as well as officials from government and organizations such as the United Nations High Commissioner for Refugees (UNHCR). Research undertaken in non-signatory states often requires a wide-ranging analysis to understand fully the refugee reception and protection landscape, and to probe more deeply into the rationales underlying policy.

The discussion opens with some background on Bangladesh and Jordan, and the research focus adopted, in order to situate three key themes of the chapter. Although these are not specific to empirical research in non-signatory states, as distinct from signatory states, they posed some significant challenges, due, in part, to the absence of a refugee law framework. These themes are: (i) access as researchers to large organizations, such as UNHCR, that tend to play an outsized role in non-signatory states; (ii) the phenomenon of both under- and over-researched interview subjects and places; and (iii) the additional ethical challenges faced when conducting empirical work specifically in non-signatory states.

2 Country-Specific Contexts

2.1 *Bangladesh*

Bangladesh is not a signatory to the Refugee Convention, nor does it have any domestic legal framework codifying access to asylum for refugees.[9] Decisions

9 See, for example, Navine Murshid, The Politics of Refugees in South Asia: Identity, Resistance, Manipulation (Routledge 2013); Antara Datta, Refugees and Borders in South Asia:

on entry, stay, or deportation tend to be ad hoc, administrative, and unreported as generally distinct from states with refugee law. While administrative decision making takes place in many signatory states, these tend to have some form of judicial oversight. In Bangladesh, there are no rules on the procedures for claiming asylum, for appealing against denial of asylum, nor are there consequent case reports.[10] The key legal provision concerning the status of refugees is the colonial-era Foreigners Act of 1946. Section 3 of that instrument gives a high degree of discretion to the central government on decisions regarding the entry, stay, and deportation of all non-citizens. As such, refugees are not distinguished from any other immigrant or visitor to the country in terms of their right of entry and stay. However, in 2017, the Supreme Court ruled that Bangladesh was bound under the customary principle of *non-refoulement*.[11] In the absence of a specific law on asylum, refugees are forced to find other means to establish status and access to basic rights, such as education and healthcare. Bangladesh is party to several human rights treaties such as the International Covenant on Civil and Political Rights, the Convention Against Torture, and the Convention on the Rights of the Child,[12] which taken together offer some basic protections for refugees within the country.[13]

The Great Exodus of 1971 (Routledge 2013); Ranabir Samaddar, 'Power and Care: Building the New Indian State' in R Samaddar (ed) Refugees and the State: Practices of Asylum and Care in India, 1947–2000 (Sage 2003).

10 In this volume Ovacık and Johny (chapter 3) and Song (chapter 7) describe how case law in Türkiye, India, and Taiwan advances protections for refugees. These cases tend to deal with piecemeal aspects of protection, mainly related to human rights treaties eg right of *non-refoulement*, or prohibition of arbitrary detention. Obviously, in non-signatory states, questions of legal status qua refugees and the ensuing scope of civil and political rights, are not judiciable. One outlier is the case of *Refugee and Migratory Movements Research Unit* (RMMRU) *v Government of Bangladesh* (2016) Writ petition No 10504, Bangladesh: Supreme Court, May 31, 2017, where the court asserted that the whole of the Refugee Convention was part of customary international law. This is not a position endorsed by any other authority that we are aware of, and, more to the point, the Bangladesh Supreme Court's ruling in this case only applied to the principle of *non-refoulement* as far as the Refugee Convention is concerned.

11 RMMRU v Bangladesh (2017).

12 International Covenant on Civil and Political Rights (adopted December 16, 1966, entered into force March 23, 1976) 999 UNTS 171; Convention Against Torture and Other Cruel, Inhuman or Degrading Treatment or Punishment (adopted December 10, 1984, entered into force June 26, 1987) 1465 UNTS 85; Convention on the Rights of the Child (adopted November 20, 1989, entered into force September 2, 1990) 1577 UNTS 3.

13 See chapter 4 for a more detailed account of how the absence of refugee law in many Asian states, including Bangladesh, does not mean that they have rejected legal protections for refugees.

An example of the ad hoc and administrative nature of asylum typical in non-signatory states, Bangladesh, in partnership with UNHCR, has granted a form of refugee status to the Rohingya fleeing persecution and generalized violence in Myanmar, although the government's preferred term is "Forcibly Displaced Myanmar Nationals." However, unlike refugee status under the Refugee Convention, this does not come with substantive rights to education, work, and welfare on the same terms as nationals. Rohingya refugees in Bangladesh merely have the right to basic amenities and rations within the UNHCR-administered camps located close to the border with Myanmar.[14]

The role of UNHCR is especially important in Bangladesh. In the absence of refugee law, either domestic or international, the management of Rohingya refugees in the country is governed by a succession of memoranda of understanding (MoUs). The first of these dates from 1993 and was drawn up in response to the arrival in Bangladesh of large numbers of Rohingya from Myanmar over the preceding two years. Again, in response to the even larger numbers who arrived after the genocidal attacks of 2017, a further set of MoUs was signed, detailing arrangements over data-sharing, voluntary repatriation, and the management of Rohingya relocated to the island of Bashan Char in the Indian Ocean. As stated by Hossain, despite the importance of these MoUs in delineating the scope of protection for Rohingya refugees, these agreements are treated as confidential and not publicly available.[15] This level of obscurity, a function of refugee protection without refugee law, further impels the researcher to rely heavily on empirical methods. It requires access to UNHCR and/or host-country officials to glean information, either on or off the record, and garner a clear picture of the nature and extent of refugee policy. The vagaries of obtaining such access are discussed below.

The research project in Bangladesh, on which the reflections in this chapter are based, focused on the barriers to citizenship among children of mixed marriages between Rohingya refugees and Bangladeshi citizens. Citizenship rights are not a function of the existence – or absence – of a refugee law framework. However, our interest arose partly out of curiosity as to how

14 The resources available to the refugees have diminished significantly over time. See, for example, the recent report by the World Food Programme and the European Commission, 'Food Ration Cuts in Bangladesh: A Year of Struggles and Hope for Rohingya Refugees', May 1, 2024 <https://civil-protection-humanitarian-aid.ec.europa.eu/news-stories/stories/food-ration-cuts-bangladesh-year-struggles-and-hope-rohingya-refugees_en> accessed 3 December 3, 2024.

15 M Sanjeeb Hossain, *ASILE Country Report: Bangladesh* (ASILE 2022), 19. For a discussion of MoUs, see also chapter 10.

refugees integrate with host societies in non-signatory states. More specifically, the complex overlapping of ethnic, religious, and cultural identities in South Asia has played a major role in the reception of refugees. The people of Bangladesh have experienced this as both refugees and hosts. During the liberation war of 1971, some nine million Bangladeshis sought sanctuary in the Indian state of West Bengal, where the host population shared a common Bangla cultural and linguistic identity.[16] Decades of Rohingya arrivals in Bangladesh have facilitated their assimilation into local communities through a common religion (Islam) and a language that is intelligible to people of the Chittagong region of Bangladesh that borders Myanmar. One historical feature of forced migrations in South Asia, and the closely intertwined identities of the region, is that, at least in the initial stages of migration, many refugees found themselves welcomed across borders in a much more generous fashion than elsewhere in the world.[17]

Ostensibly, the legal issues are clear: according to Bangladeshi law, children of just one Bangladeshi citizen are entitled to citizenship, which would consequently entitle them to all the usual rights to live, be educated, and work in the country. Under Section 5 of the 1951 Citizenship Act, a person "shall be a citizen of Bangladesh by descent if his [father or mother] is a citizen of Bangladesh at the time of his birth." Originally the reference was only to persons born to a father who was a Bangladeshi citizen. However, this was amended to include children of Bangladeshi mothers under Section 2 of The Citizenship (Amendment) Act 2009. This is important in the current context as many of the Rohingya children are born to Bangladeshi mothers and Rohingya fathers. And yet, in apparent contradiction with these statutory instruments, the government has issued a series of circulars, beginning in 2014, prohibiting the registration of marriages between Bangladeshi and Myanmar (ie all Rohingya) nationals.[18] This is critical as the marriage certificate is a key document required by parents to establish citizenship rights for their children. It is therefore unsurprising that in 2018, UNHCR reported that these children had been routinely denied citizenship.[19]

16 For example, Datta (n 9), chapter 9.

17 Simon Behrman, 'Laws of Asylum and Protection: The Indian Experience in a South Asian Context' (2019) 54 *Refugee Watch* 15.

18 UNHCR, Rohingya Refugee Crisis: Registration of the Marriages and Divorces of Refugees (April 2018).

19 UNHCR, Universal Periodic Review: 3rd Cycle, 30th Session (May 2018).

2.2 *Jordan*

Following the invasion of Iraq by the United States in 2003 and the consequent flight of many Iraqis across the border to neighboring states, the lacuna in research on non-Palestinian refugees in the region became increasingly apparent and concerning. The world witnessed Arab and Turkish neighbors hosting large numbers of refugees,[20] but the role of law – if any – remained opaque. This provided an opportunity to research the situation of Iraqi refugees in Jordan. Jordan is a vital non-signatory state in the Middle East: since the 2000s, and the Iraqi flight across the border, it has provided a key site of investigation for researchers from across the world. While the legal position of refugees in Jordan remained under-analyzed, there was also much to explore beyond law in relation to social policy and service provision to Iraqi refugees. In 2009, funding was obtained to explore the effect of legal status on human rights and access to services of Iraqi "refugees"[21] in Jordan.[22]

At the time, Jordan claimed to be hosting 500,000 Iraqi "refugees," representing about eight percent of the total population. Yet, as a non-signatory state, many Iraqis had no formal legal status as refugees recognized by the government of Jordan. Entry into Jordan by asylum seekers and refugees is controlled by Law No 24 of 1973 on Residence and Foreigners Affairs. Refugees are then subject to various directives and regulations that change frequently; and different nationalities are treated differently.[23] The aim of the study, with its multidisciplinary team, was to identify and analyze the connection between legal status and the economic, social, and cultural experiences of this vulnerable group. Although some studies at the time had examined the situation of Iraqi "refugees" in Jordan, few had focused on the issue of migration status and its connection to social well-being.

It was apparent from the outset that there were several challenges confronting the researcher in Jordan. Some of these might be generic to any empirical (legal) research, including, for example and as mentioned in the

20 Dallal Stevens, 'Legal Status, Labelling, and Protection: The Case of Iraqi "refugees" in Jordan' (2013) 25(1) *International Journal of Refugee Law* 1; Lamis Abdelaaty, 'Refugees and Guesthood in Turkey' (2019) 34(3) *Journal of Refugee Studies* 2827.

21 See below for discussion of the term "refugees" in the Jordanian context.

22 The project was carried out in collaboration with Professor Gillian Lewando Hundt (University of Warwick), Dr. Mahasen Aljaghoub (University of Jordan), and Dr. Sahar Almakhamreh (AlBalqa Applied University).

23 Lewis Turner 'Who Is a Refugee in Jordan? Hierarchies and Exclusions in the Refugee Recognition Regime' (2023) 36(4) *Journal of Refugee Studies* 877.

introduction: language barriers; need for interpreters; lack of familiarity with the country and its history; lack of a network; access issues; and ethical considerations; but there were others that could be attributed to the non-signatory status of Jordan. These included: the significance of UNHCR on account of the cooperation agreements with Jordan and its handling of asylum and resettlement;[24] the role of partner organizations in the delivery of services to refugees; the complex interplay between state, UN, (I)NGOs, law firms, and local civil society; limited focus on refugee law and (at the time) human rights law relating to refugees; and the developing concepts of "protection space" and "temporary protection" in the Middle East.[25]

On this last point, in 2009–2011, there was much discussion of the concept of "protection space" in relation to the hosting of Iraqi refugees in the countries of the Levant.[26] This was due to the fact that Jordan (and other states in the region) was not party to the Refugee Convention, and was heavily reliant on UNHCR and partner organizations to help address the rights and needs of displaced Iraqis in Jordan. Specifically, the Agreements between UNHCR and Jordan – in 1997[27] and 1998[28] – established the basis for UNHCR's presence in Jordan (1997); and, inter alia, the definition of a refugee, the respect for *non-refoulement*, the determination of refugees by UNHCR, the duties of asylum seekers and refugees to Jordan, the treatment of refugees, access to courts, and right to work, and the repatriation or resettlement obligations of UNHCR (1998). However, the expectation of the 1998 MoU – that the UNHCR office would work to ensure that temporary stay in Jordan did not exceed six months (by finding a permanent solution for the recognized refugee, either through voluntary repatriation to their home country or resettlement in a third coun-

24 1997 Agreement (Agreement Between the Government of the Hashemite Kingdom of Jordan and the United Nations High Commissioner for Refugees (July 30, 1997) and 1998 MoU (Memorandum of Understanding Between the Government of the Hashemite Kingdom of Jordan and The United Nations High Commissioner for Refugees, Jordanian Official Gazette, No 4277 (May 3, 1998) 1463; and see chapter 10.

25 Stevens (n 20).

26 Anne Evans Barnes, 'Realizing Protection Space for Iraqi Refugees: UNHCR in Syria, Jordan and Lebanon' (2009) UNHCR Research Paper 167.

27 The 1997 Agreement set out "the basic conditions under which UNHCR shall within its mandate, cooperate with the Government, open office in the country, and carry out its international protection and humanitarian assistance functions in favor of refugees and other persons of its concern in the host country" (art III (1)).

28 The aim of the 1998 MoU is to establish a mechanism for addressing matters related to refugees and other persons under the care of UNHCR in Jordan. An additional noteworthy point is that this MoU can be difficult to find (see chapter 10). The formal translated version is available in the Jordanian Official Gazette but is not online.

try) – soon proved to be impossible. The notion of temporary stay was swiftly stretched to several months and, ultimately, years. Consequently, UNHCR promoted the idea of "protection space" for the thousands of Iraqi "refugees" who were hosted for lengthy periods on Jordanian soil. Despite an admission that the term was undefined, it encompassed a practical approach to the status quo in countries such as Jordan, which found themselves hosting large numbers of displaced people but without international refugee law obligations as provided by the Refugee Convention.[29]

The research on Iraqi refugees was followed by a study of Syrians who moved to Jordan from 2012 onwards. The focus of the work was the access to protection of Syrian refugees in Jordan and in 2019, fieldwork was conducted in Amman, the capital. This provided updated information on Jordan's approach to hosting refugees generally, and to Syrians specifically. It was soon clear that lessons had been learned from the Iraqi migration to Jordan. In many senses, the architecture of protection and service provision shifted smoothly across from the Iraqi crisis to the Syrian crisis. Yet, there was change, and even the seemingly minor can prove influential in a country such as Jordan. For example, one of the earlier peculiarities of the country, the refusal to use the term "refugee," no longer pertained; after initial reluctance, the government started to refer to "Syrian refugees," a concession to the wide international usage of the term and also, one suspects, for domestic advantage.[30] As Turner notes, "While Syrians were initially sometimes referred to as 'guests,' the language of refugeehood appears to have quickly become more politically and financially expedient for the government, in particular in conjunction with its efforts to use Za'atari Refugee Camp to raise the profile of, and funding for, Syrians living in Jordan."[31] Thus, for the researcher, such shifts open up new questions and areas for investigation and analysis.

29 "While the notion of protection space does not have a legal definition, it is a concept employed by the Office to denote the extent to which a conducive environment exists for the internationally recognized rights of refugees to be respected and their needs to be met," UNHCR, 'UNHCR Policy on Refugee Protection and Solutions in Urban Areas', September 2009, para 20 <www.unhcr.org/media/unhcr-policy-refugee-protection-and-solutions-urban-areas> accessed November 14, 2024.

30 For example, Ayman Safadi, Jordan's Deputy Prime Minister and Foreign Affairs Minister, addressing the Seventh Brussels Conference on the Future of Syria and the Region: 'Jordan Calls for Global Fund for Voluntary, Safe Return of Syrian Refugees', *Jordan Times* (Amman, June 16, 2023).

31 Turner (n 23).

2.3 *Context Shaping Research*

The fact that both Bangladesh and Jordan were non-signatory states shaped our research and necessitated a broader, interdisciplinary analysis that examined law and policy in context, as well as empirical research into the experiences of those implementing and at the receiving end of administrative decisions. Of course, interdisciplinary approaches to research on refugee protection are not limited to non-signatory states but, in the absence of a state-run refugee determination system that includes domestic refugee law, first-instance decision makers, and an appellate process, context and policy assume much greater significance.

In the absence of such a system, asylum seekers are forced to fall back on ad hoc administrative arrangements. These typically involve a bureaucratic process, which tends to be opaque and open to abuse. Administrative measures also tend to involve greater discretion in decision making by government officials and a lack of assertable rights by those seeking asylum. In these circumstances, processes will be less consistent and more hidden. Painting an accurate picture will require first-hand empirical research, drawing on lived experiences of refugees and the various officials involved in decision making or support services. Of particular importance in this regard is the enormous role of UNHCR, which takes on much of the administration and management of refugees in non-signatory states (and in some signatory states). The somewhat indeterminate details of the MoUs that guide UNHCR's work necessitate researchers gaining access to key officials to understand the processes they follow, and the rights, if any, of refugees within those processes. Access is thus the first substantive challenge to which we now turn.

3 Obtaining Access

Often, the first problem in carrying out empirical research, in any context, is obtaining access to interview subjects. How does one find the appropriate interview participant in large international organizations working with refugees such as UNHCR or the International Organization for Migration? How does one identify refugees to interview who are living in camps with limited access?

In the research project on the Rohingya, local knowledge proved vital. A Bangladeshi co-researcher had studied law in the country and worked as a consultant for a legal NGO. His relationships with the NGO, fellow alumni who had since become legal practitioners in Bangladesh, as well as former professors, enabled us to find judges and lawyers willing to be interviewed.

When access to refugee camps in Cox's Bazar proved impossible, due to a Covid-19 outbreak and a series of security issues,[32] his connections in Bangladeshi academia proved crucial to finding a reputable local researcher to conduct interviews on our behalf.

It was more difficult to gain access to people working in major NGOs and Intergovernmental Organizations (IGOs) involved in running the refugee camps. Initially, we sent an email to the UNHCR regional office in Dhaka, explaining our project and asking if there was anyone available to speak to us, either in person or remotely via internet or telephone, but we received no response. In our experience these types of organizations are so large, but also overstretched, that such requests from academics are ignored. Again, it was through a personal link that we were able to make contact: a family connection with close friendships with two UNHCR officers working elsewhere helped us obtain the email addresses of key personnel working in Bangladesh. Through this chain of personal connections and introductions, we were eventually able to secure an interview with the senior legal official at the UNHCR office in Cox's Bazar. As a result of that interview, we were then introduced to one of the official's colleagues working more closely with the Rohingya refugees and local NGOs, and were able to interview them the next day. Thus, it was only through fortuitous personal relationships that the project gained access to key figures, at least with relative ease.

Once the interviews started, it was apparent that our participants were nervous about sharing certain information due to the climate of political repression, and sensitivities over the issue of Rohingya refugees. One judge asked us to switch off our recording device when we came to the issue of political influence on the judiciary in cases of Rohingya rights claims, although all interviewees were offered complete anonymity from the outset. The diplomats to whom we spoke would only speak off the record, with no recording and no specific quotes permitted. As they explained, questions about Rohingya refugees in the context of inter-state negotiations over aid and resettlement were highly sensitive, with any perceived criticisms of the Bangladesh government creating serious problems for these discussions.

Similar issues arose in the projects on Jordan. At the time of the research on Iraqi displacement, we lacked research experience in the Middle East and were not accustomed to the context of Jordan, where personal or familial in-

32 Ruma Paul, 'Sixth Fire at Bangladesh Rohingya Camp This Year Makes About 2,000 Homeless', *Reuters* (March 8, 2022); Anbarasan Ethirajan, 'Rohingya: Gang Violence Stalks World's Largest Refugee Camp, *BBC News* (August 24, 2023).

troductions often proved essential. Once in the field, the absolute necessity of local knowledge and collaboration became evident. Without the Jordanian co-investigators, access to interview subjects would have been very difficult. They provided names of potential participants in UNHCR, law firms, legal aid providers, a human rights body, and local as well as international non-governmental organizations and charities supporting Iraqi refugees. There were underlying sensitivities in the political environment of Jordan's hosting of large numbers of Iraqi people (one such revolved around Jordan's refusal to refer to displaced Iraqis as "refugees," preferring either "guests" or "Arab brethren"), and the potential for this to constrain the researcher; some participants were willing to discuss human rights, but others were clearly nervous and preferred not to. As in Bangladesh, key figures – in this case in the Ministry of Interior – were only willing to talk without any record made, digital or written.

When the later research on Syrian refugees was conducted, it was still necessary to utilize local collaborators, contacts, and networks. Foreign residents working in NGOs often accepted requests for interviews, even at a senior level, whereas Jordanians based in the ministries, law firms, local NGOs, and UNHCR/United Nations Relief and Works Agency for Palestine Refugees (UNRWA) were less responsive. This is unsurprising. Jordan is a small country and nationals working on refugee-related matters are in high demand – in their work and by researchers (see below for further discussion). In addition, following the arrival of large numbers of Syrians, a new challenge emerged for the researcher: the introduction of camps, such as Za'atari, which was first opened in July 2012. Once more, access was an issue. Obtaining admission to refugee camps can be problematic in any country – signatory or non-signatory – but, in the early days of Za'atari's existence, there was governmental nervousness about enabling research on site. Over time, this changed somewhat, and researchers were able to access the camp, but this was not always straightforward: special permission from the Jordanian government was required to enter Za'atari camp.

In summary, access to subjects in large bureaucratic organizations or refugees in camps, where movement is often strictly controlled, is a challenge in any context. However, in the absence of refugee law, the political sensitivities around the roles played by UNHCR, NGOs, and others in relation to the host state, meant that not only was access a challenge in itself, but so too was gaining the trust of interview participants. As shown, personal relationships and local knowledge were vital to the success of our projects, and they also assisted us when faced with the phenomena of over-/under-researched subjects.

4 Over-/Under-Researched Participants and Places

A feature of large and protracted refugee situations is their tendency to attract academic scholars, due in part to the high profile, topicality, and opportunities such situations offer the researcher. Where non-signatory states are concerned, as discussed, key questions often cannot be answered using desk-based research alone; consequently, fieldwork is vital due to the lack of archival material, creating a greater demand for interviews with numerous actors *in situ*. Arguably, this leads to research fatigue, both among refugees and those working for relevant organizations, and to the possibility of over-researched people and places.[33]

An illustration of such fatigue and its potential impact is provided by our research in Bangladesh. Notwithstanding the personal introductions that gave us access to interviewees, the research team had to overcome interview exhaustion. A senior official at UNHCR's field office in Cox's Bazar appeared at first to be both weary and suspicious. However, over the course of the interview, as we demonstrated our expertise on the topic, they relaxed visibly and engaged more seriously with us. For example, following a question that probed the sensitivities of providing legal advice to refugees in challenging government-sanctioned discrimination, our interviewee was much more forthcoming. Indeed, we felt that we connected specifically over a key problem inherent in navigating refugee protection in non-signatory states, namely the extent to which IGOs and NGOs can challenge political or administrative decisions in the absence of a codified set of refugee rights. It was also at that point that they suggested we follow up on some of our more detailed enquiries the following day with one of their colleagues who had more field experience.

Like Bangladesh, Jordan, too, has generated a research industry, with the resultant weariness or refusal if the researcher is at the end of a long line of interview requests. A prime example of the over-researched in Jordan is Za'atari camp. Notwithstanding the early restrictions on access, it soon became a focal point for investigation and, consequently, another victim of excessive research interest. This increase in interest proved problematic. Dalal, in his own research, comments:

---

33 See, for example, Mayssoun Sukarieh and Stuart Tannock, 'On the Problem of Over-Researched Communities: The Case of the Shatila Palestinian Refugee Camp in Lebanon' (2013) 47(3) *Sociology* 494; Naohiko Omata, '"Over-Researched" and "Under-Researched" Refugee Groups: Exploring the Phenomena, Causes and Consequences' (2020) 12(3) *Journal of Human Rights Practice* 681.

> In 2015, I visited Zaatari camp as the main protagonist for one of Al Jazeera's documentaries. While this gave me the opportunity to follow up on the spatial transitions occurring in the camp, and to conduct interviews and collect data for my PhD research, it was also obvious that refugees and relief workers were becoming worn out by the pressure of external visitors to the camp. The camp was turning into a field of "innovative" operations, inviting projects from all over the world. This was exhausting for the camp management, and the refugees there were turning into another "over-researched community."[34]

Yet, as highlighted above, despite Jordan being over-researched, we were able to conduct several elite interviews with stakeholders in the country. Some of these proved particularly insightful, especially when unique questions were asked of the interview participant and a novel discussion ensued. This was the case in relation to our research on access to protection of Syrians in Jordan, when discussions on protection proved illuminating and astonishing. Except for the Senior Legal Officer at UNHCR, none could define clearly what protection meant. A range of views were offered, but few talked about legal rights. When asked what they understood refugee protection to be in the Jordanian context, some went so far as to say: "That is a very interesting question; I haven't really thought about it!" The Senior Legal Officer, by contrast, was clearly gratified to be asked questions by a legal academic that explored their views about protection, law, and process.

This distinction between legal and non-legal research and participants was also evident in our research in Bangladesh, where the lawyers and judges whom we interviewed were much more enthusiastic and engaged from the start. They were eager to share their experiences and opinions. None of them had been interviewed by academic researchers in this way before, and from extensive research on the topic of Rohingya we could not find any other academic publications based on interviews with Bangladeshi judges or lawyers. Indeed, our interviewees were often sharing information – at least on this topic – for the first time and thus it was fresh.

This group was asked questions on two important topics: the applicability of relevant international law and norms regarding refugees; and the administrative/legal barriers to citizenship claims by the children of mixed marriages. The responses to the first illustrated that while knowledge of general human rights norms was substantial, there was a gap when it came to refugee

34 Ayman Dalal, From Shelters to Dwellings: The Zaatari Refugee Camp (Transcript Verlag 2022), 36.

law. For example, one of the lawyers who pleaded the seminal case of RMMRU *v Government of Bangladesh* (2017) told us that the judges before him, among the most senior in the country, lacked any detailed knowledge of the principle of *non-refoulement*.[35] This was a result of a lack of courses on the fundamentals of international refugee law in Bangladeshi law schools. Until the recent arrivals of Rohingya, the necessity for legal expertise relevant to those seeking asylum in Bangladesh was comparatively low, and thus generations of legal professionals have remained unaware of key legal principles on these questions. Several lawyers and judges with whom we spoke felt that rectifying this gap in college law courses was a matter of urgency.[36] On the second topic we covered with this group, two themes emerged. The first is that the Rohingya question had become so politically sensitive in the context of both the huge numbers of arrivals in 2017 and an increasingly authoritarian government, that even the most senior judiciary was nervous about addressing any legal claims made by the Rohingya.[37] Several interviewees noted that the RMMRU case was decided a few months before the crisis of summer 2017, and that the outcome could have been different had it come to a conclusion post-2017.

Arguably, what our research reveals is that when a non-signatory country hosts large numbers of refugees over a long period, the *raison d'être* of the international refugee regime – protection – can be lost amid the day-to-day practicalities of supporting displaced people in need. There was a lack of knowledge about the role of law in protecting refugees – largely because there is an absence of data on this or issues of access to justice are left to others to consider. Researchers are often from non-legal backgrounds and consequently engage with non-legal issues and research, resulting in over-research of non-legal aspects of refugee hosting, but under-research of law and legal processes.

These issues of over- and under-researched communities in Bangladesh and Jordan, and of non-legal versus legal research, are reflected in published outputs. At the time of writing, a leading interdisciplinary journal on refugees, the *Journal of Refugee Studies*, had, over a 13-year period, published 14 articles on the Rohingya in Bangladesh and India and 15 on non-Palestinian refugees in Jordan. By contrast, the *International Journal of Refugee Law* had only published two on non-Palestinians in Jordan, and none on the Rohingya or Ban-

35 In *RMMRU v Bangladesh* (n 10) aspects of the judgment exposed the gaps in knowledge.

36 See chapter 11 in on key aspects that should be considered when developing legal education on refugee law in non-signatory states.

37 It must be noted that our interviews were carried out in late 2022, almost two years before the sudden collapse of the government of Sheikh Hasina in summer 2024.

gladesh. In short, though some of the largest groups of refugees have been the subject of widespread non-legal research, they have been significantly under-researched by legal scholars. Many of the published studies are empirical in nature and have drawn upon interviews with refugees and with those working in UNHCR, the International Committee of the Red Cross, or various NGOs. Interestingly, though, none of the many pieces we consulted reflect on the issue of research fatigue of interview participants from such organizations.

5 Ethical Challenges

There are ethical challenges in researching any situation involving vulnerable interview participants. Vulnerability is particularly heightened among refugees, who are often existing in a state of extreme precarity. We argue that these vulnerabilities can be more pronounced in non-signatory states, where there are few legal avenues for refugees to plead their case as refugees per se, with the accompanying protections and rights. To begin, we reflect on examples that we found in our work in Bangladesh.

Rohingya in Cox's Bazar were interviewed in Kutupalong camp at a time (summer 2022) when movement in or out was highly restricted. As a result, the interviews had to be conducted by a research assistant (RA) we employed, who was himself a Rohingya refugee in Bangladesh. There was, therefore, less of a gap between interviewer and interviewee than is normally the case. However, some of the tensions inherent in carrying out research on vulnerable research subjects still came to the fore in several interviews.

Interviews had a semi-structured format, with the final question being open-ended: "Is there anything else that you wish to share about your experiences seeking citizenship in Bangladesh?" Numerous times the interviewees asked whether the information they had provided could be used to resolve their legal status or to access education and other services, by our making representations to the authorities on their behalf. On occasion, they hoped that our research would help resolve their situation. In some cases, there was justified cynicism: "It will be no use sharing my problems with you. If you were from the government, it would be useful for me."[38] This echoes Naohiko Omata's experiences researching Somali refugees in camps in Kenya. He reports their disillusionment and anger, after being told that their testimonies

38 Rohingya interview #4, Kutupalong Refugee Camp, July 23, 2022.

would not help inform better policies in the camps.[39] He identifies this as closely linked to the issues of over-researched subjects, as discussed above, where refugees can experience being used by researchers without any benefit to themselves – that is, extractive research.

These responses, of course, raised difficult issues for the research team. On the one hand, we were clear at the outset about who we were and the purpose of our study. We also gave each of the refugees we interviewed a gift in the form of food packages as a token of our gratitude and respect for their time in speaking with us and sharing often traumatic details of their personal histories.[40] On the other hand, some people expected us to be able to provide practical assistance to them. Given that they were living in effective confinement, without clear legal status, legal advice, or representation, it was understandable that they grasped at any opportunity for help. In a signatory state, where legal status as a refugee and the concomitant substantive rights are codified, there is the potential for relying on legal processes as a guarantor of certain rights, even if the system is skewed, as is often the case. A common feature of non-signatory states, such as Bangladesh, is that the grant of status is in the hands of government officials and is highly discretionary. This distinction between signatory and non-signatory states is critical as it can increase the vulnerability of refugees in non-signatory states, which in turn exacerbates the ethical challenges faced by researchers.

It is important to acknowledge that researchers from the Global North are often reliant on collaborators, interpreters, and research assistants from the region or countries concerned. Few researchers from the United Kingdom, for example, speak Rohingya or Arabic and many do not understand the history and local context of countries such as Bangladesh or Jordan. The identification of collaborators and interpreters is difficult, and the use of local research assistants can be exploitative. Sukarieh and Tannock report on a case study of the experiences of local research assistants employed on UK-directed research projects on Syrian refugees in Lebanon. They reveal how assistants experience alienation, exploitation, and disillusionment with the research on which they work.[41] They argue that these "problems and inequities" are

39 Omata (n 33) 684–85.

40 See Maja Janmyr on some of the complexities of ethnographic research with refugees, including the right not to participate: 'Ethnographic Approaches and International Refugee Law' (2022) *Journal of Refugee Studies* feac042 <https://doi.org/10.1093/jrs/feac042> accessed November 14, 2024.

41 Mayssoun Sukarieh and Stuart Tannock, 'Subcontracting Academia: Alienation, Exploitation and Disillusionment in the UK Overseas Syrian Refugee Research Industry' (2019) 51(2) *Antipode* 664.

common where researchers from the Global North conduct fieldwork in the Global South.[42]

In the case of our work in Bangladesh, the Rohingya research assistant was paid the appropriate rate for any RA in Bangladesh, and we took care to involve him in discussions around the design of the questionnaire, on how to carry out the interviews, as well as the results. This, we hope, ensured that he felt part of the project rather than simply an instrument of it. It also, of course, ensured our work was better prepared and informed. In Jordan, one research assistant, who came from the West Bank, was paid the UK rate, as outlined in the research grant, and local interpreters were paid the appropriate Jordanian rate. A second researcher of Iraqi origin, who was based in the UK, was paid UK research assistant rates. Both RAs were fully involved in the design of the projects, in workshops, and in drafting interview schedules. In addition, in planned or published publications, the RA contributions are – or will be – fully acknowledged. In summary, the researcher must ensure that research assistants are paid fairly, have secure contracts, are acknowledged appropriately by primary investigators, and share authorship and intellectual property rights.

6 Conclusion

Arguably then, empirical research in a non-signatory state that is hosting large numbers of displaced peoples is often much more complex than in a signatory state with a well-established refugee determination system and reception, and with support structures that are provided by government. In countries such as Bangladesh and Jordan, the availability of citizenship rights, "protection space", or a "conducive environment" acquire much greater significance than international refugee law, with implications for research. From the researcher's perspective, the study of such issues is crucial and requires a multidimensional approach and a need for a multidisciplinary skill set, to overcome a lack of knowledge of the legal issues in the countries concerned.

Limited understanding of the legal environment in non-signatory states among Global North scholars is understandable to a certain extent. In the absence of domestic asylum or refugee law, the role of administrative law and bureaucratic discretion takes precedence. The doctrinal bent of most refugee law scholarship will therefore avoid the complex interplay of politics

42 ibid 677.

and often unclear administrative processes, which key actors – refugees; UNHCR, NGO, and government officials; lawyers and judges – are forced to negotiate. Empirical research is therefore a key tool in developing a more nuanced understanding of asylum in non-signatory states. In the non-signatory state, where the extra-refugee law framework is extremely important, and where it is often difficult to obtain legal material from outside the country, it can be challenging to gain an understanding of the domestic legal regime governing asylum seekers and refugees without conducting fieldwork, as described in this chapter.

The involvement of UNHCR, non-governmental organizations, and state administrations in receiving and supporting refugees, which is far more determinative in non-signatory states than those with refugee law, presented many opportunities as well as challenges for the researcher. The first significant challenge in Jordan was to understand the complexities of protection and service delivery in a multi-stakeholder setting; and the second was to gain access to both interview participants and to partnership meetings where specific issues were discussed (for example, health-related matters and education). The importance for the researcher of attending meetings between partner organizations, which also, at times, included government representatives, cannot be overstated. These provide a much clearer picture of stakeholders on the ground and of the issues they consider crucial. Again, the involvement of Jordanian collaborators who worked in non-legal fields, such as social work, helped facilitate access to such meetings.

Access issues were also a major hurdle at the outset of our research with a reliance on personal connections, which proved key to overcoming obstacles. For both authors, once access had been achieved, there were further difficulties regarding research fatigue and managing the many ethical dilemmas of working with refugees where their legal status was highly ambiguous and the means for asserting rights often obscure and/or obstructed.

What we learn from our experiences in both Bangladesh and Jordan is that in non-signatory states, where the context and the communities affected may be over-researched, the legal questions and personnel are often under-researched. Arguably, this is symptomatic of the largely neglected study of legal frameworks in non-signatory states by scholars, as discussed. The presumption appears to be that without refugee law, there is an absence of legal protections for refugees and, consequently, a lack of interest in examining law in those states.[43] Instead, the focus tends to be on international agencies and

---

43 Maja Janmyr, 'The 1951 Refugee Convention and Non-Signatory States: Charting a Research Agenda' (2019) 33(2) *International Journal of Refugee Law* 188, 195.

charities that provide direct services to refugees. And, yet, in our research, we required a deeper understanding of the specific political landscape of the country to navigate the critical gaps in legal knowledge of the rights of refugees, the reasons for these gaps, and the context of rights assertion; without speaking to legal personnel, answers to these important questions would have eluded us.

There are many underexplored issues that are ripe for research among legal professionals in non-signatory states. In signatory states, interviewing legal professionals generally revolves around the extent to which adherence to the Refugee Convention, regional treaties, or domestic law is being observed. Indeed, this might account for the relatively conservative or doctrinal approach to studies of asylum in signatory states, especially by refugee law academics. Analysis of the refugee phenomenon in signatory states often starts from questions on whether RSD procedures are being followed appropriately, or whether those seeking protection fall within the legal definition of a refugee. In non-signatory states, our questions involved a more nuanced and complex set of enquiries around social, political, and administrative issues.

The point is not to deny the relevance of law in non-signatory states, but quite the opposite. Our research addressed questions of legal status in Bangladesh and Jordan, and the extent to which authorities in both countries adhered to relevant legal instruments. This reinforces an argument that is central to this volume and to the BEYOND project overall: that there is much that we can and must learn about legal aspects of asylum from non-signatory states. However, the absence of a doctrinal delineation of asylum meant that the conversations we had with legal professionals and others necessarily involved wider sociopolitical issues, whereas in a signatory state such issues, though illuminating, are not as essential to understanding the workings of the asylum system.

All fieldwork is challenging but there are many challenges that are peculiar to – or exacerbated in – non-signatory states. As we have discussed, these include: a politically sensitive environment; lack of legal rights for refugees and a lack of transparency or clarity on access to justice; the significance of "protection space" and alternative routes to legal status; access issues; the importance of multidisciplinary teams and interdisciplinary approaches; over-researched communities; specific ethical issues that result from the enhanced vulnerabilities; and the role of the research assistant. While it must be emphasized that many of the issues we have identified in this chapter are specific to the circumstances in Bangladesh and Jordan, there are commonalities between them that are rooted in the fact of being non-signatory states, which we hope can help inform other researchers working in this area.

CHAPTER 3

Judicial Engagement with International Refugee Law: An Exploratory Study on Domestic Courts in Non-signatory States

Gamze Ovacık and Aneesha Johny

1 Introduction

This chapter studies how domestic courts in states that are non-signatory to the 1951 Convention[1] and/or the 1967 Protocol[2] engage with international refugee law. 71 percent of the world's refugees are hosted in low- and middle-income countries,[3] an important portion of which are non-signatory states. These states play a crucial role in global refugee protection but their function in shaping international refugee law has not been fully studied in the literature. Non-signatory states have considerable influence in shaping international refugee law and vice versa, and in this regard, the key institutions and actors in this interaction need further study.[4] Throughout the chapter, we use the term international refugee law with an inclusive scope to refer to all international legal instruments that together build the international regime of refugee law, including foremost the 1951 Convention and its 1967 Protocol, relevant provisions of global and regional international human rights treaties, as well as non-binding instruments, such as the Global Compact for Refugees, General Comments by UN bodies, and UNHCR Executive Committee Conclusions.

The potential role of the judiciary in non-signatory states in creatively injecting international refugee law into domestic law is significant, especially

1 Convention relating to the Status of Refugees (adopted July 28, 1951, entered into force April 22, 1954) 189 UNTS 137.

2 Protocol relating to the Status of Refugees (adopted January 31, 1967, entered into force October 4, 1967) 606 UNTS 267.

3 'UNHCR Refugee Data Finder Key Indicators' <www.unhcr.org/refugee-statistics> accessed November 29, 2024.

4 Maja Janmyr, 'The 1951 Refugee Convention and Non-Signatory States: Charting a Research Agenda' (2021) 33(2) *International Journal of Refugee Law* 188, 189–92.

DOI:10.1163/9789004710306_004

in the absence of a domestic legal framework.[5] This grants "a back-door entry" to international refugee law in non-signatory states.[6] Initiatives such as the International Association of Refugee and Migration Judges attempt to advance the role of judges globally for harmonizing case law on refugee protection across countries.[7] In this respect, the judiciary can be presented as a legal apparatus to fill in the legislative gaps and offer rights protection to refugees.[8] Independence of judiciary from other state functions makes courts significant for balancing the interests of states and refugees.[9] Considering this potential role of the judiciary in non-signatory states, further research on domestic case law is needed. In this context, this research is crucial for identifying how the judiciary links national and international law, and influences the advancement of international refugee law.[10]

This chapter highlights the impact of domestic courts in bringing non-signatory states in the broad ambit of international refugee law through judicial engagement. In so doing, the analysis focuses on patterns of how domestic courts engage with international refugee law through legal interpretation and direct reference to sources of international refugee law. This is a study on how international refugee law is reflected in local court decisions. In that respect, the study differs from an analysis of the content of refugee protection and the application of substantial refugee rights by domestic courts. Based on the common patterns observed in case law across jurisdictions, the analysis here focuses on the engagement of domestic courts with the 1951 Convention and the 1967 Protocol, with other international instruments, and with the principle of *non-refoulement*. The

---

5 Srinivas Burra, 'India's Refugee Protection Obligations Beyond the 1951 Refugee Convention and the 1967 Protocol' in S Irudaya Rajan (ed), *The Routledge Handbook of Refugees in India* (Routledge India 2022) 184.

6 Fazal Abdali, 'Discourse Around the Refugee Protection Paradigm in India' in S Irudaya Rajan (ed), *The Routledge Handbook of Refugees in India* (Routledge India 2022) 161.

7 International Association of Refugee and Migration Judges, 'Constitution of the International Association of Refugee and Migration Judges (IARMJ)' <www.refworld.org/legal/resolution/iarlj/2018/en/122585> accessed November 29, 2024.

8 Stellina Jolly and Nafees Ahmad, 'Climate Refugees: The Role of South Asian Judiciaries in Protecting the Climate Refugees', *Climate Refugees in South Asia: Protection under International Legal Standards and State Practices in South Asia* (Springer 2019) 212.

9 Samuel Berhanu Woldemariam and Muhizi Pacifique, 'Securitisation of Refugee Protection: The Judiciary's Role in the Protection of the Rights of Refugees: Attorney General v Kituo Cha Sheria & 7 Others' (2024) 43(2) *Refugee Survey Quarterly* 169, 186.

10 Geoffrey Case, 'The Judiciary, the State, and the Refugee: The Evolution of Judicial Protection in Asylum: A UK Perspective' (2004) 28 *Fordham International Law Journal* 1421, 1427.

analysis also focuses on the role of UNHCR in judicial practices in these states.

Methodologically, this chapter relies on an empirical study of domestic court decisions and secondary literature on domestic case law of non-signatory states. In gathering our empirical data, we were faced with constraints in accessing court decisions in different jurisdictions, including language barriers and limited numbers of publicly available court decisions, meaning that our sample is not exhaustive. Another methodological challenge is that the domestic application of international refugee law is influenced by the effects of the monist and dualist theories of incorporation governing the relationship between international and domestic legal orders. For instance, while Mauritius requires specific incorporation of international treaties into domestic law, India follows direct incorporation of international law when it is not contrary to domestic law.[11]

With these constraints in mind, our sample includes judgments from India, Pakistan, Bangladesh, Hong Kong, and Malaysia from Asia; Türkiye, Jordan, and Lebanon from the Middle East; and Mauritius from Africa.[12] We were able to review the court decisions in their original language version in English in the cases of India, Pakistan, Bangladesh, Hong Kong, and Malaysia, and in Turkish in the case of Türkiye. Across jurisdictions, we also relied on official English translations of judgments and secondary sources composed of case law reports and scholarly literature. For these reasons, we see our chapter as a pilot study that allows us to observe certain judicial patterns and thus paves the way for further research on the role of domestic courts in non-signatory states.

Following this introduction, Part 2 looks at the engagement of domestic courts in non-signatory states with the 1951 Convention. This is followed in Part 3 by a discussion of judicial engagement with other international and human rights obligations of non-signatory states. Part 4 addresses the engagement of domestic courts with the principle of *non-refoulement*. In Part 5, the role of UNHCR in the judicial processes in non-signatory states

11 Aparna Chandra, 'India and International Law: Formal Dualism, Functional Monism' (2017) 57(1–2) *Indian Journal of International Law* 25, 26–30.

12 For the purposes of this study, Türkiye is framed as a non-signatory state due to maintaining its geographical limitation to the 1951 Convention leaving refugees arriving from non-European countries – almost the whole refugee population in Türkiye – outside the scope of the Convention. Mauritius is included in the non-signatory category because it is a non-signatory to the 1967 Protocol maintaining its temporal limitation to the 1951 Convention.

is discussed. Finally, Part 6 offers some concluding observations and outlines possible directions for future research.

2 Engagement with the Refugee Convention

This section examines the engagement of domestic courts with the 1951 Convention and the 1967 Protocol. It may appear counterintuitive to expect courts to engage with instruments the country is not bound by. Our findings, however, complicate the assumption that courts in non-signatory states do not at all engage with the 1951 Convention and the 1967 Protocol.

We have identified many judgments where courts engage with the 1951 Convention actively or passively. Active engagement refers to cases where the courts apply the 1951 Convention to resolve the dispute before them. In the sample we reviewed, this happens inconsistently on a case-by-case basis. Passive engagement, on the other hand, indicates cases where the judges merely cite the relevant provisions of the 1951 Convention without further legal reasoning. This is still significant because it indicates an acceptance that the 1951 Convention is considered within the body of law applicable in the domestic setting even though the state in question is not formally bound by it.

Beginning with the active, more substantial, engagement of the judiciary in non-signatory states, we find key examples in countries like Hong Kong, Pakistan, India, and Bangladesh. The Hong Kong Court of Final Appeal, for instance, categorically held that the country's Immigration Department must independently determine whether the claim of the person subject to removal is well founded and fulfills the criteria of the refugee definition set out in the 1951 Convention.[13] Similarly, in Pakistan, the High Court of Islamabad discussed the applicability of the 1951 Convention in a recent case concerning an Afghani police officer who had fled to Pakistan without a visa. In its landmark judgment, the Court noted that it does not matter whether the 1951 Convention has been signed by Pakistan or not,[14] before going on – for

13 *C, KMF and BF v Director of Immigration and Secretary for Security* [2013] The Hong Kong Court of Final Appeal FACV Nos 18, 19, and 20 of 2011.

14 *Rahil Azizi v State of Pakistan* [2023] High Court of Islamabad, Pakistan Writ Petition 1666.

the first time in Pakistan's judicial history – to rely on the Convention's article 31.[15]

Courts in India have also relied on the 1951 Convention in their judgments – with one local court even arguing that the country's non-accession stance is no longer a valid reason for not engaging with the Convention considering the large number of refugees hosted by India.[16] The court then went on to affirm the existence of a well-founded fear of persecution as per the 1951 Convention and the 1967 Protocol.[17] And in Bangladesh the Supreme Court relied on the 1951 Convention to uphold the rights of a refugee who was detained in prison for five years.[18] The Court reasoned in this judgment that the 1951 Convention had become customary international law, a perspective that is contested by legal scholars.[19]

The judiciary in non-signatory states also passively engages with the 1951 Convention. Lebanese courts, for example, have made inconsistent and passive references to the Convention without engaging substantially. In one case,[20] a Lebanese court relied on the Lebanese Constitution together with the prohibition of arbitrary arrest under the Universal Declaration of Human Rights (UDHR)[21] to order release of detained Iraqi refugees who were issued deportation orders after being convicted of illegal entry into Lebanon. In a similar case, the court ordered the release of a detained Iraqi refugee basing its reasoning on UDHR, the Convention

---

15 Arjumand Bano Kazmi, 'Pakistan's Judicial Engagement with International Refugee Law' (2025) *International Journal of Refugee Law* <https://doi.org/10.1093/ijrl/eeaf001> accessed February 2, 2025.

16 *State v Chandrakumar* [2011] Court of Metropolitan Magistrate (Dwarka), New Delhi FIR No 78/10.

17 Aishwarya Birla, 'Evaluating the Indian Refugee Law Regime: How Has the Judiciary Responded to Refugee Claims in Light of International Law Obligations, and How Can It Do Better?' (2023) 35(1) *International Journal of Refugee Law* 81, 87.

18 *Refugee and Migratory Movements Research Unit* (RMMRU) *v Government of Bangladesh* [2016] Supreme Court of Bangladesh Writ Petition No 10504.

19 M Sanjeeb Hossain, 'Country Report Bangladesh' (ASILE Project 2022) 10, 14 <www.asileproject.eu/wp-content/uploads/2022/05/D4.2-Bangladesh-Interim-Country-Report-Final.pdf> accessed November 29, 2024; Janmyr (n 4) 207.

20 Lebanese Court of First Instance (Civil) Urgent Matters Section, Judge Maalouf, Decision, June 20, 2014.

21 Universal Declaration of Human Rights (adopted December 10, 1948) UNGA res 217A (III).

Against Torture (CAT),[22] and the *non-refoulement* principle under the 1951 Convention.[23]

In some cases, like Türkiye, domestic courts engage with the 1951 Convention both actively and passively. As observed in the reviewed case law, Turkish judges displayed judicial inconsistency in their level of engagement with the 1951 Convention. Some judgments maintained passive engagement whereas others included active engagement with the Convention provisions. A recent study examined such court engagement in the era before and after the legal reform marked by the adoption of the Turkish legal framework on migration and asylum in 2013.[24] Before this reform, Turkish courts had an inconsistent practice of actively engaging with the provisions of the 1951 Convention, especially with article 31 on non-penalization for illegal entry or presence. This can be explained by the lack of a legal basis for refugee rights in domestic legislation. Following the reform, however, this gap was filled by domestic legislation and courts arguably shifted to a general trend of passive engagement.

Passive referencing of the 1951 Convention would typically take place when the Turkish Council of State cited Convention provisions in cases of international protection but rested its decisions in favor of public order and national security concerns under Turkish law. This would often be in the form of verbatim reproduction and non-engagement with substantial provisions related to non-discrimination, the personal status of refugees, refugees unlawfully in the country, expulsion, and *non-refoulement*. The study further showed, however, that both before and after the reform, Turkish courts consistently relied on the 1951 Convention and the domestic legal framework while deciding on *non-refoulement* cases.[25] Examples are cases concerning removals to Iraq[26] and Pakistan.[27] Other subjects of engagement were the obligations of refugees in the host state and cooperation with UNHCR, enshrined in articles 2 and 35 of the 1951 Convention.

---

22 Convention against Torture and Other Cruel, Inhuman or Degrading Treatment or Punishment (adopted December 10, 1984, entered into force June 26, 1987) 1465 UNTS 85.

23 Lebanese Court of First Instance (Criminal), Judge Mkanna, April 15, 2008.

24 Özlem Gürakar Skribeland, 'The Turkish Council of State's Engagement with International Refugee Law in Cases Involving "Non-European" Refugees' (2025) *International Journal of Refugee Law* <https://doi.org/10.1093/ijrl/eeae041> accessed February 2, 2025.

25 ibid.

26 *E 2015/453 K 2015/811* (Sakarya 1 Administrative Court), September 14, 2015.

27 *E 2018/970 K 2018/1592* (Izmir 1 Administrative Court), February 11, 2018.

The passive and active engagement by domestic courts with the 1951 Convention can be seen as a progressive way of bringing in the Convention to a domestic setting for ensuring refugee protection. While some domestic courts appear reluctant to rely on provisions of the 1951 Convention, in many decisions the courts attempt to fill the lacunae arising from non-accession by engaging with it. This is an example of the unique role that domestic courts play in shaping the development of refugee law in non-signatory states.

Finally, some courts ascribe their deliberate non-engagement with the Convention – or with refugee law obligations more generally – to the fact that the state in question is not formally bound by the Convention. We observed this in the cases of Mauritius and India. In Mauritius, the Supreme Court stated that the 1951 Convention was not applicable because the country had not acceded to the 1967 Protocol that removed the temporal limitation.[28] Considering that administrative practices are inconsistent in Mauritius,[29] the role of courts becomes even more important for an adequate refugee response. Therefore, this dismissal of judicial engagement with the 1951 Convention constitutes a missed opportunity for bringing international refugee law into the domestic legal realm. Also in India, in a few cases, the courts declined to apply the 1951 Convention on the grounds of India's being a non-signatory.[30] Other reasons for India's non-engagement with the 1951 Convention have been a lack of domestic asylum legislation, and the absence of a formal status granted to UNHCR. India's non-signatory status is a contributing factor to these reasons, if anything.[31]

---

28 *Mahmotaky MA v The Secretary for Home Affairs* [2003] Supreme Court of Mauritius SCJ 238; Jamil Ddamulira Mujuzi, 'Mauritian Courts and the Protection of the Rights of Asylum Seekers in the Absence of Dedicated Legislation' (2019) 31(2–3) International Journal of Refugee Law 321, 326–27.

29 Nora Milch Johnsen and Maja Janmyr, 'State Succession to the 1951 Refugee Convention: The Curious Case of Mauritius' (*Refugee History*, September 30, 2021) <https://refugeehistory.org/blog/2021/9/30/state-succession-to-the-1951-refugee-convention-the-curious-case-of-mauritius> accessed November 29, 2024.

30 *Mohammed Sadiq v Government of India* (Civil Rule Writ No 405/98); *Khadija v Union of India* (Writ Petition (Criminal) No 658 of 1997).

31 Birla (n 17) 81, 94.

3 Engagement with International Legal Instruments Other Than the 1951 Convention

Judges in signatory states have at their disposal a comprehensive legal toolbox assembled to resolve legal disputes involving refugees. This toolbox includes the 1951 Convention, as well as domestic legislation on refugee protection interlinked with it. In non-signatory states, in contrast, non-accession to the 1951 Convention is frequently coupled with a lack of corresponding domestic legislation. In filling this legal lacuna, courts in non-signatory states often engage with international legal instruments other than the 1951 Convention. This engagement appears in the form of references to human rights treaties these states may have ratified and to non-binding instruments of international refugee law. Courts also address the question of the status of international legal instruments in the national legal order.

3.1 *Judicial References to International Human Rights Treaties*

Several international human rights treaties contain provisions that overlap in substance with the 1951 Convention. Such treaties can be seen as integral parts of the broader framework of international refugee law. The most obvious example is the principle of *non-refoulement* developed within the frame of the 1951 Convention, the International Covenant on Civil and Political Rights (ICCPR),[32] and CAT. Courts bring international refugee law into a domestic setting by engaging with these instruments, in the absence of direct reference to the 1951 Convention. We see this as a testament to the complementary dynamic between the 1951 Convention and other international human rights instruments. The judgments we reviewed do not make any further analysis as to how these instruments apply to specific cases at hand, but the very existence of references to them is significant in terms of judicial engagement with international refugee law. Court decisions from Hong Kong, Bangladesh, Lebanon, Taiwan, Pakistan, India, Malaysia, and Türkiye included references often to multiple treaties.

To begin with, according to the landmark judgment from Hong Kong,[33] in deportation cases, high standards of fairness must be followed for the

32 International Covenant on Civil and Political Rights (adopted December 16, 1966, entered into force March 23, 1976) 999 UNTS 171.

33 *Secretary for Security v Sakthevel Prabakar Final Appeal Judgment* [2004] Hong Kong Court of Final Appeal FACV No 16 of 2003, 2004 7 HKCFAR 187, 2004 HKCFA 43, 2005 1 HKLRD 289. See chapter 4.

assessment of a well-founded risk of torture as per CAT. National authorities must make an independent assessment benefiting from the General Comments of the UN Committee Against Torture instead of merely following UNHCR decisions rejecting asylum applications. A new administrative procedure for CAT claims was created after this judgment. Another judgment found that blanket denial of access to a legal representative in interviews and to free legal advice breaches the high standards of fairness.[34] Other judgments refer to CAT as a basis for the principle of *non-refoulement* originating from the 1951 Convention.[35] However, courts also concluded that CAT does not ensure a particular immigration status in the host country[36] or allow illegal entry with false travel documents.[37] Other courts refer to CAT as a basis for *non-refoulement* obligations as well, to order the release of Rohingya refugees from detention in Bangladesh[38] and to prevent the deportation of an Iraqi refugee in Lebanon.[39]

Judgments from Taiwan, Pakistan, India, and Malaysia contain multiple references to relevant international treaties. In Taiwan, numerous court decisions acknowledge the applicant's right to seek asylum and include references to ICCPR, CAT, and in general terms to international human rights law. These judgments reason that Taiwan should comply with these instruments as a member of the international community (see chapter 7). In a recent case from Pakistan, the court used the ICCPR and the CAT as a hinge to consider the relevance of the 1951 Convention within domestic law, in consideration of the doctrine of incorporation.[40] In India, a court referred to the ICCPR in a case related to detained Iraqi asylum seekers facing expulsion. The referenced provisions were on the right to life, liberty, and security of person, and on the prohibitions of torture and arbitrary detention. As a point of analysis, the court underlined that the ICCPR

34 *FB and others v Director of Immigration and Secretary for Security First Instance Judicial Review* [2008] Court of First Instance 2009 1 HKC 133.

35 *C v Director of Immigration First instance* [2008] Hong Kong High Court as Court of First Instance HCAL 132/2006, 2008 2 HKC 165, 2008 HKCFI 109; *C, KMF and BF v Director of Immigration and Secretary for Security* (n 13).

36 *CH v Director of Immigration Appeal Judgment* [2011] Hong Kong High Court as Court of Appeal CACV 59/2010.

37 *RV v Director of Immigration and Secretary for Justice First Instance Decision* [2008] Hong Kong High Court as Court of First Instance HCAL 2/2008.

38 *Refugee and Migratory Movements Research Unit* (*RMMRU*) *v Government of Bangladesh* (n 18).

39 [2008] Lebanese Court of First Instance (Criminal) Judge Mkanna (n 23).

40 *Rahil Azizi v State of Pakistan* (n 14) paras 22–24.

provision against arbitrary detention is enforceable in domestic law.[41] Another judgment from India referred to the ICCPR in connection with asylum seekers from Myanmar, and highlighted that the country's legal obligations under other international instruments required respecting the rights of asylum seekers to seek protection from persecution despite India's not being a signatory to the 1951 Convention.[42] The Convention on the Rights of the Child (CRC)[43] was also cited by an Indian court in its conclusion that the best interest of the child required the release of Rohingya child asylum seekers from detention.[44] Malaysian courts also sought the support of the CRC when it argued that the detention of Rohingya children would prevent their access to assistance and protection.[45]

Finally, as Türkiye is a party to the European Convention on Human Rights (ECHR),[46] local court decisions there typically cite ECHR provisions on the right to life and prohibition of torture in explaining the *non-refoulement* principle, but engagement is often superficial and does not go beyond a standard text referencing the relevant articles.[47] Courts refer to ECHR articles together with the 1951 Convention but this does not necessarily translate into improved refugee protection, and sometimes these references are to the detriment of refugees.[48] For instance, Turkish courts often refer to the "real risk" standard developed in the European Court of Human Rights case law when finding that claims of asylum seekers do not satisfy this benchmark.[49]

---

41 *Ktaer Abbas Habib Al Qutaifi and Taer Al Mansoori v Union of India* [1998] Gujarat High Court 2 GLH 1005.

42 *Nandita Haksar v State of Manipur* Manipur High Court Writ Petition (Criminal) No 6 of 2021.

43 Convention on the Rights of the Child (adopted November 20, 1989, entered into force September 2, 1990) 1577 UNTS 3.

44 *State v Sd 'CCL'* [2021] Juvenile Justice Board in India FIR No 13/21.

45 *Ruwaida Royeda Binti Muhammad Siddiq and Six Other Children v Commandant Immigration Depot Belantik, Kedah* [2018] High Court of Malaya KA-44-81-09/2018.

46 European Convention on Human Rights (Convention for the Protection of Human Rights and Fundamental Freedoms, as amended) (November 4, 1950).

47 *E 2021/621 K 2022/236* (Uşak Administrative Court); *E 2022/1794 K 2022/1600* (İzmir Regional Administrative Court); *E 2021/524 K 2021/1574* (İzmir 1 Administrative Court); *E 2019/428 K 2019/1700* (Bolu Administrative Court); *E 2014/2068 K 2015/849* (Ankara 1 Administrative Court); *E 2018/94 K 2018/1401* (Ankara 1 Administrative Court).

48 Gürakar Skribeland (n 24).

49 *E 2021/2384 K 2022/677* (Council of State Administrative General Chamber); *E 2021/1998 K 2022/676* (Council of State Administrative General Chamber); *E 2021/6561 K 2021/5561* (Council of State 10th Chamber); *E 2016/2787 K 2016/3852* (Council of State 10th Chamber); *E 2016/2062 K 2018/1822* (Council of State 10th Chamber); *E 2016/1829 K 2018/1823*

3.2 *Judicial References to the Non-binding Instruments of International Refugee Law*

Of significance are also the cases where courts refer to non-binding instruments of international law, such as the UDHR and the Global Compact for Refugees (GCR).[50] This may be significant in demonstrating that domestic courts sometimes accept these instruments as sources of international law applicable in the domestic setting.

In several instances, Lebanese courts have made important references to the UDHR. These judgments show an increasing trend of relying on international human rights law in the Lebanese judiciary.[51] In deciding against sanctions for irregular entry by Syrian refugees, for example, one court referred to the UDHR's article 14 on the right to seek asylum. Similarly, in another case, the court relied on the right to seek asylum in UDHR to prevent the deportation of an Iraqi refugee.[52] In yet another case, the court made use of the UDHR's prohibition of arbitrary arrest, detention, and exile to release an Iraqi refugee who was facing conviction and deportation on the basis of having entered the country illegally.[53] This shows the potential of international human rights obligations for providing a basis to local courts against asylum detention and deportation.[54]

Indian courts have also explicitly referenced the UDHR. One court case stressed that the right to seek asylum under the UDHR implies that persons who are granted asylum cannot be sent back to their countries.[55] Courts in this context have also – quite remarkably – employed the GCR to frame India's obligations concerning refugees.[56]

(Council of State 10th Chamber); *E 2016/1476 K 2018/1824* (Council of State 10th Chamber).

50 Global Compact on Refugees (2018) UN doc A/73/12 (Part II).

51 Martin Clutterbuck and others, 'Alternative Protection in Jordan and Lebanon: The Role of Legal Aid' (2021) 67 *Forced Migration Review* 52, 54.

52 [2008] Lebanese Court of First Instance (Criminal) Judge Mkanna (n 23).

53 [2014] Lebanese Court of First Instance (Civil) Urgent Matters Section Judge Maalouf (n 20).

54 Maja Janmyr and Dallal Stevens, 'Regional Refugee Regimes: Middle East' in Cathryn Costello, Michelle Foster and Jane McAdam (eds), *The Oxford Handbook of International Refugee Law* (OUP 2021) 350–51.

55 *State of Arunachal Pradesh v Khudiram Chakma* [1993] Supreme Court of India Civil Appeal No 2181 of 1993, 1994 SCC Supp (1) 615.

56 *Nandita Haksar v State of Manipur* (n 42).

4 Engagement with the Principle of *Non-refoulement*

The principle of *non-refoulement* is at the heart of international refugee law and is generally seen to have become part of customary international law.[57] The principle finds its expression in article 33 of the 1951 Convention. A similar legal obligation emanates from the prohibition of torture, enshrined in human rights treaties such as ICCPR, CAT, and ECHR. The parallel provisions reflect the complementary nature of international refugee law and human rights law.[58] Thus, the principle of *non-refoulement* has a multilayered character in international law ranging from being a customary norm to a legal obligation within international refugee law and human rights law. Development of the principle in the case law of regional courts and international bodies such as the European Court of Human Rights, Inter-American Court of Human Rights, and the Human Rights Committee paves the way for expanded judicial dialogue.[59] Its recognition beyond the scope of the 1951 Convention enables the judiciary in non-signatory states to develop a powerful strategy for shaping the protection space for refugees.[60] Three ways of engagement with the principle of *non-refoulement* emerge from the reviewed case law: acceptance of the principle of *non-refoulement* as a customary law principle; direct reliance on article 33 of the 1951 Convention to recognize the principle; and recognition of the principle through the interpretation of constitutional and domestic law. The case analysis also reveals instances where courts reject the application of the principle of *non-refoulement* and demonstrate a lack of consistency in their engagement with it.

---

57 Cathryn Costello and Michelle Foster, '*Non-Refoulement* as Custom and Jus Cogens? Putting the Prohibition to the Test' in Maarten den Heijer and Harmen van der Wilt (eds), *Netherlands Yearbook of International Law 2015: Jus Cogens: Quo Vadis?* (TMC Asser Press 2016) 282.

58 Gamze Ovacık, *Turkish Judicial Practices on International Protection, Removal and Administrative Detention in Connection with the Safe Third Country Concept* (On Iki Levha Publications 2021) 83.

59 Penelope Mathew, '*Non-Refoulement*' in Cathryn Costello, Michelle Foster and Jane McAdam (eds), *The Oxford Handbook of International Refugee Law* (OUP 2021) 902.

60 Special Rapporteur Dire Tladi, 'Fourth Report on Peremptory Norms of General International Law (Jus Cogens)' International Law Commission) A/CN.4/727; Abdali (n 6) 157.

4.1 *Principle of Non-refoulement as a Customary Law Principle*

Courts in Bangladesh, Taiwan, and India have acknowledged the customary nature of the principle of *non-refoulement*. In Bangladesh, the Supreme Court's *RMMRU* decision referred to *non-refoulement* as a customary law principle applicable to judicial decision making on asylum. The landmark judgment allowed other courts to follow suit in making such an assessment.[61] In Taiwan, the Taipei High Administrative Court similarly recognized the customary law status of the principle of *non-refoulement* but limited its applicability to recognized refugees. Two judgments by the Supreme Administrative Court of Taiwan nonetheless held that the principle of *non-refoulement* is applicable not only to refugees but also to asylum seekers (see chapter 7).

In a case concerning Chakma refugees having fled to India from Bangladesh, the Indian Supreme Court found that the principle of *non-refoulement* is applicable to India as part of customary international law and cannot be violated except for reasons of national security or public order.[62] Based on this principle, the court ruled that the national authorities are obliged to ensure the safety of these refugees. Similarly, a lower court decision stated that India is bound by the principle of *non-refoulement* and also highlighted the urgent need to develop a refugee law framework based on the principle. Interestingly, the court emphasized the need to train judges on international refugee law in order to ensure a human rights-based approach in refugee matters.[63] That said, judicial practices in India are not consistent, and in some cases the Supreme Court has not made any reference to the principle of *non-refoulement*, applying only domestic law. This approach arguably opens the way for lower courts to deny the application of the principle of *non-refoulement*.[64]

4.2 *Direct Reference to Article 33 of the 1951 Convention*

In several jurisdictions, the courts engaged with the principle of *non-refoulement* by directly referencing article 33 of the 1951 Convention. This was notably done by a court in Hong Kong and, only one year later, a mechanism based on that principle and the court decision was established with a

61 M Sanjeeb Hossain, '"Doing" Legal History in Refugee Law: A Snapshot of Bangladesh's Engagement with *Non-Refoulement*' (2023) 36(4) *Journal of Refugee Studies* 2; *Refugee and Migratory Movements Research Unit* (*RMMRU*) *v Government of Bangladesh* (n 18).

62 *NHRC v State of Arunachal Pradesh* Supreme Court of India AIR 1996 SC 1234.

63 *State v Chandrakumar* (n 16).

64 Birla (n 17) 92, 100.

view to determining refugee status. Thus, judicial interpretation enabled recognition of the principle as a binding legal obligation in the domestic setting, by triggering the establishment of the Unified Screening Mechanism (see chapter 4).[65] In Türkiye, courts – including the Council of State – relied on article 33 as the legal basis of Türkiye's *non-refoulement* obligation. This practice is followed by lower courts as well. This is significant because the cases almost always concern applicants coming from non-European countries who are not within the ambit of the 1951 Convention due to Türkiye's geographical limitation.[66] Likewise in Pakistan, the High Court of Islamabad defined the principle of *non-refoulement* under article 33 of the 1951 Convention as the cornerstone of international refugee law.[67]

4.3 *Recognition of the Principle through Constitutional and Other Domestic Law Interpretation*

In some instances, judicial engagement with the principle of *non-refoulement* takes place through constitutional and other domestic law interpretation. It is significant that the application of the principle of *non-refoulement* is based on domestic law, without any reference to international law. However, given the central role of the principle of *non-refoulement* in the 1951 Convention, we consider this to be an indirect engagement with international refugee law by non-signatory states.

Mauritius courts rely on Extradition and Immigration Acts and on the Constitutional provision on the prohibition of torture as a basis for the principle of *non-refoulement*.[68] This is how the courts prevented the extradition of asylum seekers due to risk of *refoulement* in cases where extradition was requested on the basis of violation of conditions of admission[69] and use of forged documents.[70]

Similarly, there are multiple examples where Indian courts have engaged with the principle of *non-refoulement* through constitutional interpretation. In one judgment, the Manipur High Court quoted a dictionary definition of *non-refoulement* and underlined that it has great significance under the

65 Rachel Li, Isaac Shaffer and Lynette Nam, 'Hong Kong's Unified Screening Mechanism: Form Over Substance' (2021) 67 *Forced Migration Review* 48, 49.

66 Gürakar Skribeland (n 24).

67 *Rahil Azizi v State of Pakistan* (n 14).

68 Mujuzi (n 28) 335.

69 *Green v Prime Minister and Minister of Home Affairs* Supreme Court of Mauritius 1993 MR 209 1993 SCJ 389; *Ramankhan MF v The Commissioner of Prisons* Supreme Court of Mauritius 2002 SCJ 140 2002 MR 73.

70 *Police v Toma Nasem Jabrail* [2009] Mauritius Court MBG 64; Mujuzi (n 28) 327.

Indian Constitution within the scope of the right to life, an inalienable right guaranteed to all human beings irrespective of their citizenship status.[71] The Court considered the imminent threat to the lives of refugees and declared *non-refoulement* to be fundamental to their protection. In another decision, the Gujarat High Court similarly relied on the principle of *non-refoulement* in granting interim relief to two applicants facing deportation to Yemen where a civil war was ongoing.[72] The court again recognized the principle of *non-refoulement* as part of the constitutional right to life.

Also in Lebanon and Jordan, domestic law provisions were utilized to uphold the principle of *non-refoulement*, to protect refugees from deportation and detention, and to provide them with the right to stay. In Lebanon, the judiciary used its discretion to uphold the principle of *non-refoulement* by reading human rights obligations into national legislation.[73] However, this is not a settled judicial practice and is observed in an inconsistent fashion. In Jordan, inconsistency is observed in this area due to the differential treatment of Syrian and non-Syrian refugees. Jordanian courts give a domestic character to the principle of *non-refoulement* by deciding on the legality of deportation orders mainly based on procedural aspects, adequacy of reasons for deportation, and compliance with Jordanian law.[74]

4.4 *Evading the Principle through Non-signatory Status*

There are also examples where domestic courts have declined to apply the principle of *non-refoulement* on the basis of the country's lack of formal commitment to the 1951 Convention. In India, three interim orders held that for this reason the principle was not binding, and in consequence the court allowed the deportation of Rohingya refugees. The court rejected the applicants' arguments that the principle of *non-refoulement* should be applied in line with India's human rights obligations.[75] Historically, Bangladesh courts have come to a similar conclusion.[76] Likewise, a detailed examination of Turkish case law[77] reveals that despite frequent references in court decisions to the principle of *non-refoulement* as enshrined in the 1951 Convention, non-signatory status was cited as a reason to deviate from the 1951

71 *Nandita Haksar v State of Manipur* (n 42).

72 *Ktaer Abbas Habib Al Qutaifi and Taer Al Mansoori v Union of India* (n 41).

73 [2008] Lebanese Court of First Instance (Criminal) Judge Mkanna (n 23).

74 Clutterbuck and others (n 51) 54–55.

75 *Mohammad Salimullah v Union of India* Supreme Court of India AIR 2021 SC (Civil) 1753.

76 Hossain (n 61) 16.

77 Ovacık (n 58).

Convention in some deportation cases.[78] Finally, in Lebanon, it is noteworthy that the majority of court decisions penalized and deported refugees due to unauthorized entry, with only very few judgments cancelling deportation orders by applying the principle of *non-refoulement*.[79]

5 UNHCR in Judicial Processes

UNHCR's role in refugee protection in non-signatory states is often extensive and significant. This is in no small part due to the lack of a domestic legal framework as well as to constraints in host states' institutional capacity. As this section will discuss, the key role of UNHCR in these settings manifests itself in judicial processes. We will show how judicial decision making takes into consideration UNHCR refugee status determination (RSD) as well as other functions carried out by UNHCR. Courts in non-signatory states also recognize UNHCR's role when it comes to standard setting and knowledge production. Domestic courts in non-signatory states acknowledge UNHCR as an authority in refugee law and protection, and attach importance to its functions in ways that exceed the 1951 Convention framework. Courts are as such platforms where standards of the international refugee law framework are reflected through UNHCR's activities.

5.1 *Impact of UNHCR's Assessment of Asylum Claims on Judicial Decision Making*

When UNHCR is involved in the RSD process as the principal responsible body or alongside national authorities, courts appear inclined to prioritize the outcome of the UNHCR assessment over contrary convictions of the government authorities and lower courts. Indian courts consider UNHCR's assessment of asylum claims in granting constitutional protection and requiring governmental authorities to comply with the principles of due process.[80] In one case brought by Iraqi applicants claiming risk of persecution upon deportation, the court called upon UNHCR to take a more active interest in the matter considering it recognized the applicants as refugees.[81] In

78 *E 2016/1644 K 2016/1776* (İzmir 1 Administrative Court); *E 2017/2832 K 2018/285* (Hatay Administrative Court).

79 Clutterbuck and others (n 51) 54.

80 Roshni Shanker and Hamsa Vijayaraghavan, 'Refugee Recognition Challenges in India' (2020) 65 *Forced Migration Review* 24, 25.

81 *Ktaer Abbas Habib Al Qutaifi and Taer Al Mansoori v Union of India* (n 41).

another case, the court relied on the refugee status granted by UNHCR and ordered the claimants not to be deported. The court also requested an assessment of their asylum claims by the national authority, and consultation with UNHCR on the option of their deportation to a third country.[82]

Refugee status granted by UNHCR is a factor considered by the courts in Pakistan as well. To that end, the landmark decision by the High Court of Islamabad in 2023, discussed in Section 2, signals a positive change especially for refugees from Afghanistan.[83] The court accepted that the claimant should not be subject to arrest and return due to illegal entry. Significantly, UNHCR intervened in the case confirming that it had issued an asylum-seeker certificate to the claimant and reminding the government of the established practice of refraining from *refoulement* and arbitrary detention for certificate holders.[84] In an earlier case concerning Somali applicants, the same court's recognition of the socio-economic rights of refugees, including access to medical services and education on the same basis as nationals, was based on their registered status with UNHCR.[85]

UNHCR refugee status also serves as a gateway to UNHCR's intervention in judicial processes through legal aid and representation, as well as a basis for the dismissal of criminal charges for lack of travel and identity documents.[86] In a case brought by Turkish citizens against the Pakistani government's deportation order, in granting them stay, the court took into account the asylum-seeker certificates issued by UNHCR. The judgment remarkably quoted UNHCR's website on its RSD mandate in Pakistan and stated that Pakistan's international position dictates compliance with UNHCR's final decision on asylum.[87] Overall Pakistan courts consistently give recognition to refugees parallel to UNHCR assessment, and respect UNHCR's mandate for protecting refugees.[88] It is significant that courts offered protection to asylum seekers with pending applications before UNHCR, in addition to those with refugee statuses granted by UNHCR. Similarly, in many instances, Turkish courts at different levels relied on the refugee status accorded by UNHCR

82 *Kham and Mang v India and Foreign Regional Registration Officer* [2016] Delhi High Court Writ Petition (Criminal) Number 1884/2015, 226 DLT 208.

83 Kazmi (n 15).

84 *Rahil Azizi v State of Pakistan* (n 14) paras 10–11.

85 *Saeed Abdi Mehmud v NADRA* [2018] Pakistan CLC 1588.

86 Kazmi (n 15).

87 *Aamir Aman v Federation of Pakistan* (PLD 2020 Sindh 533).

88 Kazmi (n 15).

when they overruled deportation[89] or refusal of asylum,[90] and when they granted interim measures against deportation.[91]

Despite the significant weight attached to UNHCR assessments, there are also instances where the local courts divert from UNHCR's opinion and rule in the contrary direction. In Türkiye, some courts approve the decisions of national authorities for the withdrawal of asylum applications,[92] deportation, or rejection of asylum applications,[93] diverging from UNHCR's recognition of need for asylum. In such cases, the courts typically refer to UNHCR's *advisory*, rather than *decisive*, role in determining asylum claims. These decisions emphasize that the principal authority rests with the Turkish government.[94] Judgments along these lines became more frequent after UNHCR's

89 *E 2014/1442 K 2015/44* (Kayseri 2 Administrative Court); *E 2015/1344 K 2015/2015* (İstanbul 1 Administrative Court); *E 2015/1412 K 2016/837* (İstanbul 1 Administrative Court); *E 2015/842 K 2015/1814* (Ordu Administrative Court); *E 2015/136 K 2015/159* (Aksaray Administrative Court); *E 2015/1447 K 2015/1362* (Aksaray Administrative Court); *E 2015/1449 K 2016/162* (Aksaray Administrative Court); *E 2015/1450 K 2016/163* (Aksaray Administrative Court); *E 2018/218 K 2018/635* (Kayseri 1 Administrative Court); *E 1999/154 K 2000/2756* (Council of State 10th Chamber); *E 1999/749 K 2000/2755* (Council of State 10th Chamber); *E 1999/746 K 2000/5403* (Council of State 10th Chamber); *E 1999/5050 K 2001/823* (Council of State 10th Chamber); *E 1999/5194 K 2001/821* (Council of State 10th Chamber); *E 1999/5498 K 2001/822* (Council of State 10th Chamber); *E 2004/8769 K 2007/2735* (Council of State 10th Chamber); *E 2004/3045 K 2007/3124* (Council of State 10th Chamber); *E 2010/2346 K 2010/5971* (Council of State 10th Chamber); *E 1998/6347 K 2000/2717* (Council of State 10th Chamber); *E 1998/1481 K 2000/131* (Council of State 10th Chamber).

90 *E 2015/581 K 2015/1519* (Ankara 1 Administrative Court); *E 2014/2068 K 2015/849* (Ankara 1 Administrative Court).

91 *2015–1832* [2015] Constitutional Court MAGJ; *2015–1834* [2015] Constitutional Court MAGJ.; *2015–6721* [2015] Constitutional Court Mohammad Abdul Khaliq; *2015–13854* [2015] Constitutional Court Farah Abdulhameed Mohammed Ali Al-Mudhafar; *2015–15277* [2015] Constitutional Court Majid Mahmood Ahmed Aljamal; *2015–17658* [2015] Constitutional Court Mohammad Esmaeilzadeh and Others; *2015–17761* [2015] Constitutional Court AAK; *2015–18582* [2015] Constitutional Court Azizjon Hikmatov; *2016–2894* [2016] Constitutional Court Mahmoud Maghmoumi; *2016–5126* [2016] Constitutional Court Haider Subhi Amenn Amenn.

92 *E 2016/1841 K 2016/3846* (Council of State 10th Chamber).

93 *E 2017/1182 K 2017/1133* (Ankara Regional Administrative Court 10 Chamber of Administrative Lawsuits); *E 2019/428 K 2019/700* (Bolu Administrative Court); *2016–5126* (n 91) paras 12–15.

94 *E 2016/3216 K 2017/911* (Council of State 10th Chamber); *E 2016/1841 K 2016/3846* (n 92); *E 2016/12530 K 2017/3488* (Council of State); *2016–4405* [2015] Constitutional Court FR [8–28]; *E 2016/1030 K 2018/1674* (Council of State 10th Chamber); *E 2008/6039 K 2012/1678* (Council of State 10th Chamber); *E 2021/2384 K 2022/677* (n 49).

RSD function in Türkiye ceased in 2018 which explains the shift in judicial approach.[95]

In one case in Hong Kong the situation was exactly the opposite. Despite UNHCR's rejection of the asylum claims of the applicants, the court, contrary to the usual domestic practice, decided that the government should carry out independent assessment subject to high standards of fairness considering the powerful humanitarian considerations involved.[96] This difference in the standards of assessment of torture claims by the government and assessment of asylum claims by UNHCR led to the creation of a national mechanism called the Unified Screening Mechanism which replaced the RSD conducted by UNHCR (see chapter 4).

5.2 *Judicial Engagement Based on UNHCR's Presence in the Host State*

Another aspect of UNHCR's role in host countries that draws the attention of the judiciary is UNHCR's functions as embodied in its agreements or memoranda of understanding with host states (see chapter 10). Whereas the judicial references to these agreements or memoranda of understanding are rather superficial and do not yield to legal analysis, they reflect the recognition of UNHCR's role within the asylum governance in the country. Courts in Pakistan attach weight to these agreements by calling on the government to respect their terms. They particularly refer to UNHCR's role in refugee protection as "a proxy to determine the refugee status."[97] Similarly, a court in Hong Kong also referred to a memorandum of understanding with UNHCR to define the scope and nature of RSD performed by UNHCR.[98] UNHCR's presence and role in the host state also sometimes directly influence case outcomes. In Bangladesh, for example, a court ordered the release of the Rohingya applicants from detention based on UNHCR's assurances to the court. Such assurances were submitted to the court through a petition and were then annexed to the judgment.[99]

5.3 *Judicial Reference to UNHCR's Standard-Setting Functions*

The final aspect of UNHCR's significance in the case law of non-signatory states relate to its authoritative role in refugee protection more generally –

---

95 Gürakar Skribeland (n 24).

96 *C, KMF and BF v Director of Immigration and Secretary for Security* (n 13).

97 *Aamir Aman v Federation of Pakistan* (n 87); *Rahil Azizi v State of Pakistan* (n 14).

98 *C, KMF and BF v Director of Immigration and Secretary for Security* (n 13).

99 *Refugee and Migratory Movements Research Unit (RMMRU) v Government of Bangladesh* (n 18).

that is, beyond whatever specific role UNHCR may have in the country concerned. For example, a court decision from India took into consideration that the Iraqi applicants' accounts were in line with UNHCR reports on Iraq.[100] In Türkiye, the Constitutional Court similarly refers to UNHCR Executive Committee Conclusions as part of the applicable legal framework without distinguishing them from other sources of law, despite being a repetitive reference to the same expressions on conditions of detention of asylum seekers.[101] Turkish courts also refer to UNHCR's country of origin reports in assessing applicants' appeals against asylum decisions or deportation orders. This reflects confidence in their perception of UNHCR's reliability. Several judgments referred to UNHCR's reports and criticized their lack of review by governmental authorities.[102]

6 Conclusion

Judicial engagement with international law relevant to refugee protection becomes crucial in non-signatory states due to the legal vacuum created by a lack of formal commitment to the 1951 Convention. In this chapter, we have argued that the engagement of domestic courts with the 1951 Convention, other relevant international instruments, and the principle of *non-refoulement* considerably shapes the national legal landscapes.

This research constitutes a pioneering study on the judicial engagement of non-signatory states with international refugee law. As such, it is an effort to decentralize refugee law studies with a shift from Global North to Global South. Our chapter contributes to methodological debates on judicial decision making in the asylum field by defining the notions of active and passive engagement with international refugee law. Active engagement signifies courts' reliance on the 1951 Convention as a legal basis when resolving a dispute before them whereas passive engagement indicates cases that

---

100 *Ktaer Abbas Habib Al Qutaifi and Taer Al Mansoori v Union of India* (n 41).

101 *2016–35009* [2019] Constitutional Court Abdulkadir Yapuquan; *2014–15824* [2016] Constitutional Court IS and Others; *2014–15876* [2016] Constitutional Court II; *2013–8735* [2016] Constitutional Court FK and Others; *2013–8810* [2016] Constitutional Court TT; *2014–2841* [2016] Constitutional Court AS; *2014–13044* [2015] Constitutional Court KA; *2013–655* [2016] Constitutional Court FA and MA; *2013–1649* [2016] Constitutional Court AV and Others; *2013–9673* [2013] Constitutional Court RB.

102 *2015–17762* [2015] Constitutional Court Abdolghafoor Rezaei [8–19]; *E 2018/94 K 2018/1401* (Ankara 1 Administrative Court); *E 2019/970 K 2020/357* (Bursa 1 Administrative Court); *E 2022/1626 K 2023/255* (Kastamonu Administrative Court).

reference the relevant provisions of the 1951 Convention in general terms. UNHCR also occupies an important space in judicial processes based on its duties in non-signatory states and its norm-setting function in international refugee law. Judicial engagement with international refugee law often supports the enhancement of refugee protection. However, judicial approaches in non-signatory states are often inconsistent and at times, courts refer to the lack of formal commitment to the 1951 Convention as a reason to avoid engagement.

This study entailed methodological challenges, especially in forming a representative sample of court decisions in a wide range of jurisdictions. However, the method of analysis developed herein bears the potential of being transferable to other studies on judicial practices. Inconsistencies in judicial interpretation within and across jurisdictions point to the importance of further research and sharing of best practices through platforms such as the International Association of Refugee and Migration Judges. Further efforts would bring us closer to a systematic understanding of judicial approaches to international refugee law across the globe.

CHAPTER 4

Asian Exceptionalism Revisited

Brian Barbour

1 Introduction

Countries in Asia are hosting millions of the world's refugees.[1] Despite the magnitude of need, only 21 of the 49 jurisdictions in UNHCR's Asia Pacific region are party to the 1951 Convention[2] and its 1967 Protocol[3] (together and individually "the Refugee Convention").[4] Furthermore, only 16 of those states parties have passed specific legislation.[5] Even where refugee law exists, it is often not implemented or is characterized by unfettered discretion and a lack of transparency. In this context, asylum seekers are frequently subject to human rights violations throughout the region, including forcible return to persecution (*refoulement*); arbitrary and prolonged detention; lack of access to healthcare, education, and livelihoods; trafficking; and torture or cruel, inhuman, or degrading treatment and punishment.

The lack of Asian state participation in international human rights and refugee law regimes is well covered in the literature, with many scholars attempting to understand and explain what is sometimes characterized as

1 This chapter makes no attempt to define the membership of an Asian region. Regions do not have the same kind of politically defined borders that states do, and some inconsistency between various actors' perceptions is tolerated. Statistics are sourced from the United Nations High Commissioner for Refugees ("UNHCR") within UNHCR's "Asia Pacific" region.

2 Convention relating to the Status of Refugees (adopted July 28, 1951, entered into force April 22, 1954) 189 UNTS 137.

3 Protocol relating to the Status of Refugees (adopted January 31, 1967, entered into force October 4, 1967) 606 UNTS 267.

4 See official list of states parties of the 1951 Convention at <https://treaties.un.org/Pages/ViewDetailsII.aspx?src=TREATY&mtdsg_no=V-2&chapter=5&Temp=mtdsg2&clang=_en> accessed October 14, 2024; and the 1967 Protocol at <https://treaties.un.org/Pages/ViewDetails.aspx?src=IND&mtdsg_no=V-5&chapter=5&clang=_en> accessed October 14, 2024.

5 Australia, Cambodia, Fiji, Iran (Islamic Republic of), Japan, Kazakhstan, Republic of Korea, Kyrgyzstan, Macau SAR, Nauru, New Zealand, Papua New Guinea, Philippines, Tajikistan, Timor-Leste, and Turkmenistan.

 | DOI:10.1163/9789004710306_005

"Asian exceptionalism."[6] Understanding the analysis put forward by this scholarship is a common starting point for research on regional refugee protection in Asia.[7] This chapter will revisit the premise and conclusions of the Asian exceptionalism literature. After considering the various reasons put forward to explain the "Asian rejection," the chapter concludes that these reasons are at best an oversimplification. With regard to any particular country in the region, there is no single overarching explanation for non-accession to the Refugee Convention. Dewansyah's analysis of Indonesia in chapter 5 is a case in point. This is even more true if we try to apply the explanation to the entire region. Furthermore, non-accession to the Refugee Convention should not be conflated with rejection of all legal obligations toward refugees.[8] Asian states do not reject refugee law.

The following section will provide an overview of the most common positions taken by scholars in the Asian exceptionalism debate. After rejecting both its premise and conclusions, the chapter considers critiques put forward by scholars of Third World Approaches to International Law (TWAIL) that generally emphasize the impact of history. The chapter adopts a TWAIL approach and concludes that the "resistance" perceived among Asian states is not a resistance to human rights or refugee law, but a resistance to Global North hegemony.

With this understanding, the chapter begins anew. Instead of starting with the Refugee Convention, Section 3 considers if custom or general principles can be identified among non-signatory states in the region.[9] Ascertaining what customary norms are accepted by these states is a matter of identifying both state practice and *opinio juris* (evidence that the practice is conformed with because it is understood to be a legal obligation).[10] The evidence provided below supports the view that all of the countries reviewed have generally provided temporary refuge to displaced persons and that they respect the *non-refoulement* obligation in practice. Much more could be said about each

---

6 See Ben Saul, Jacqueline Mowbray and Irene Baghoomians, 'The Last Frontier of Human Rights Protection: Interrogating Resistance to Regional Cooperation in the Asia-Pacific' (2011) 18 *Australian International Law Journal* 23.

7 Sébastien Moretti, The Protection of Refugees in Southeast Asia: A Legal Fiction? (Routledge 2022) 26.

8 ibid 236.

9 Statute of the International Court of Justice 1946, art 38.

10 International Law Commission, *Draft Conclusions on Identification of Customary International Law with Commentaries* (2018) Part Two, 'Basic Approach', Conclusion 2, 'Two constituent elements'.

state's juridical views on status and treatment, but this is not within the scope of the present chapter.[11]

2 Why Do Asian States Not Accede to the Refugee Convention? (the Wrong Question)

2.1 *Asian Exceptionalism*

Moretti writes that the question of why most states in Asia have not acceded to the Refugee Convention is "not only an 'important political puzzle', but it is also the point of departure for any reflection on international refugee law in Southeast Asia."[12] Indeed it is the focus of much of the scholarship looking at refugee protection in Asia. The accession by a small number of Asian states to the Refugee Convention and other human rights agreements has been characterized as a "rejection,"[13] a "resistance,"[14] and an "ambivalence."[15]

Davies's seminal work on "The Asian Rejection" identifies the Eurocentric development of international refugee law, and "the failure to construct an inclusive refugee law instrument that considered the plight of those outside of Europe" as the primary reason for rejection of the Refugee Convention among Asian states.[16] Muntarbhorn considered the reasons put forward to explain non-accession and suggested that they are complex, the simple answer being "political expediency," and that the question of refugee protection is always a matter of executive discretion.[17] He further notes that accession might surrender the leverage that Asian states have to bring others to the table to negotiate responsibility-sharing arrangements.[18] Other authors identify different considerations, from economic factors including views about the economic burdens that taking on refugee protection would en-

11 A more extensive analysis was conducted for my PhD thesis: Brian Barbour, 'A "Whole-of -Society Approach" to Refugee Protection in Asia' (PhD thesis, University of New South Wales 2024) <https://doi.org/10.26190/unsworks/30176> accessed October 15, 2024.

12 Moretti (n 7) 26.

13 Sara E Davies, *Legitimizing Rejection: International Refugee Law in South East Asia* (Martinus Nijhoff 2008); Sara E Davies, 'The Asian Rejection?: International Refugee Law in Asia' (2006) 52(4) *Australian Journal of Politics and History* 562.

14 Saul and others (n 6).

15 Simon Chesterman, 'Asia's Ambivalence about International Law and Institutions: Past, Present and Futures' (2017) 27(4) *European Journal of International Law* 945.

16 Davies, 'The Asian Rejection?' (n 13); Davies, *Legitimizing Rejection* (n 13).

17 Vitit Muntarbhorn, *The Status of Refugees in Asia* (Clarendon Press 1992) 11, 33.

18 ibid 53.

tail;[19] to state strategic policy choices;[20] and concerns about ethnic or cultural identity.[21] Asian exceptionalism is also sometimes tied to debates about "Asian values,"[22] and reference is sometimes made to Asia's insistence on the "non-interference" principle as an explanation for the resistance to refugee and human rights.[23]

Each of these explanations has some logic, but different scholars come to so many different conclusions that it is reasonable to wonder who is right. Perhaps they are all correct to some degree, in that they have each identified a *partial* reason for non-accession. Yet, to the extent that any of the above explanations is considered definitive, it is, at best, an oversimplification. In the end, most scholars recognize the fact of mixed motives and complexity, and that takes us back to the place from which we began. None of these explanations lead us very far to understanding the approaches actually taken in the region toward refugees.

It turns out that non-accession to the Refugee Convention was never the appropriate point of departure. If we return to the paragraph that started this chapter, we can see that it only provides a snapshot. It is ahistorical. A longer history should be considered if we hope to understand how we got here.[24] Furthermore, the same description of non-implementation and rights violations could be (and often is) used to describe many state party contexts, so accession is no guarantee of effective implementation.[25] The history takes us to a second school of thought, put forward by scholars of Third World Approaches to International Law ("TWAIL").

2.2 *A TWAIL Critique*

TWAIL scholars emphasize that "most [modern day forced displacements] occur within the Third World itself … [this] enables a dominant narrative to

19 Richard Towle, 'Processes and Critiques of the Indo-Chinese Comprehensive Plan of Action: An Instrument of International Burden-Sharing' (2006) 18(3–4) *International Journal of Refugee Law* 537; see also Davies, *Legitimizing Rejection* (n 13).

20 Saul and others (n 6); see also Muntarbhorn (n 17) 11, 33.

21 Myron Weiner, 'Rejected Peoples and Unwanted Migrants in South Asia' (1993) 28(34) *Economic and Political Weekly* 1737.

22 Martha Meijer, Dealing with Human Rights: Asian and Western Views on the Value of Human Rights (Worldview Publishing 2001); see also Saul and others (n 6).

23 Amitav Acharya, Constructing a Security Community in Southeast Asia: ASEAN and the Problem of Regional Order (Routledge 2001); Moretti (n 7) 26.

24 Natasha Yacoub, 'A New History of Refugee Protection in Post-World War Two Southeast Asia: Lessons from the Global South' (2023) 13(2) *Asian Journal of International Law* 220.

25 See, for example, Jane McAdam and Fiona Chong, *Why Seeking Asylum is Legal and Australia's Policies are Not* (UNSW Press 2014).

emerge that blames the Global South for being dysfunctional and erases the historical context … the reality is much more complex and structurally imposed."[26] TWAIL scholars ask us to consider history. Hundreds of years of colonialism by European empires, which subjugated non-European peoples and exploited their resources, is a common Asian experience.[27] Colonialism is responsible for population movements and transfers, partitions, privileging elites and generating ethnic divides, drawing borders around and through communities, and extensive plunder and exploitation. These actions have directly and subsequently generated political instability, further movement, and conflict.[28]

Colonialism is also recent, not ancient, history, with many Asian states (re)gaining independence through a decolonization process primarily following World War II. Perhaps most notorious in the decolonization era was the partition that led to the creation of India and Pakistan and displacing millions in the process.[29] Bangladesh (formerly East Pakistan) later gained independence from Pakistan in 1971 and saw a similar mass displacement. Malaysia became independent in 1957, with Sabah and Sarawak joining in 1963, and Singapore becoming independent from Malaysia in 1965. Hong Kong was returned by the British to China in 1997, and Macau by the Portuguese in 1999. Timor-Leste came under Indonesian authority from Portugal in 1975, and later gained independence from Indonesia in 2002.

Decolonization took place alongside the Cold War, with proxy wars that literally divided Korea and Vietnam in half also displacing large numbers of refugees across the region. Also, while freedom of movement and trade had been used to justify colonialism, decolonization saw the rise of strict border control and visa regimes when people from the Global South sought to move in the other direction toward the Global North.[30]

---

26 Samuel Berhanu Woldermariam, Amy Maquire, Jason von Meding, 'Forced Human Displacement, the Third World and International Law: A TWAIL Perspective' (2019) 20(1) *Melbourne Journal of International Law* 248.

27 For a look at the practice in the 16th, 17th, and 18th centuries, see CH Alexandrowicz, *An Introduction to the History of the Law of Nations in the East Indies: 16th, 17th, and 18th Centuries* (Clarendon Press 1967); For a look at the practice in the 19th century onwards, see Antony Anghie, 'Finding the Peripheries: Sovereignty and Colonialism in International Law' (1999) 40(1) *Harvard International Law Journal* 1.

28 Chaloka Beyani, 'Migration in Africa, an Enduring Phenomenon?' (September 15, 2011) *The Nansen Lecture* <https://saiia.org.za/wp-content/uploads/2011/09/spe_nansen_beyani_sept_2011.pdf> accessed October 14, 2024; Muntarbhorn (n 17) 7–9.

29 Sunil S Amrith, Migration and Diaspora in Modern Asia (CUP 2011) 90.

30 E Tendayi Achiume, 'Reimagining International Law for Global Migration: Migration as Decolonization?' (2017) 111 *AJIL Unbound* 142. Achiume argues that colonialism can be

Over the most recent decades, a "non-entrée" regime has been developed through which states in the Global North are introducing domestic restrictions and extraterritorial controls designed to keep refugees from ever reaching their borders and, through various policies, are furthermore seeking to contain refugees in the Global South.[31] Chimni has argued that "instead of accepting the principle of burden sharing the Northern States increasingly practice burden shifting."[32] He warns that there is an erosion of well-established norms of international refugee law that allows dominant states to implement containment policies, turn repatriation into the only solution, deny any responsibility, and securitize refugee protection.[33] With an understanding of this reality, is it still accurate to describe Asia as exceptional in its neglect of refugees?

It is a shared experience of colonial violence and domination that gives rise to a particular intellectual consciousness. This view perceives hypocrisy and selective application of norms among powerful states who don't seem to be held to account for their violations or the lengths that they go to avoid responsibility. If we listen and try to understand this historical and ongoing experience of marginalization, then how does this temper our incredulity about non-participation in legal regimes that were developed before these states had a seat at the table? Through a TWAIL analysis, we can see more clearly that the "resistance" that is perceived by the Asian exceptionalism literature is not a resistance to human rights or refugee protection obligations. It is a resistance to power politics, double-standards, and selectivity in the application of human rights standards.

With this understanding, the next section will turn to non-signatory states themselves comparing both state practice and the legal position (*opinio*

---

viewed as "migration from Europe to the rest of the world" with at least 62 million Europeans migrating to colonies around the world, and extracting human and natural resources in the other direction. She argues that now the Global North has established a double standard: it is antagonistic to migration, insisting on an almost entirely unfettered discretion at the border.

31 Thomas Gammeltoft-Hansen and James C Hathaway, 'Non-Refoulement in a World of Cooperative Deterrence' (2015) 53(2) *Columbia Journal of Transnational Law* 235; BS Chimni, 'The Geopolitics of Refugee Studies: A View from the South' (1998) 11(4) *Journal of Refugee Studies* 350.

32 BS Chimni, 'Reforming the International Refugee Regime: A Dialogic Model' (2001) 14(2) *Journal of Refugee Studies* 151, 164.

33 BS Chimni, 'Globalization, Humanitarianism and the Erosion of Refugee Protection' (2000) 13(3) *Journal of Refugee Studies* 243; see also BS Chimni, *The Law and Politics of Regional Solution of the Refugee Problem: The Case of South Asia* (Regional Centre for Strategic Studies 1998) 4.

juris) of these states. *Opinio juris* is expressed in domestic law, policy, and jurisprudence, and expressed regionally among states that are members of the Asian African Legal Consultative Organization (AALCO),[34] an intergovernmental body with juridical personality.[35] Through AALCO, states have given extensive consideration to the status and treatment of refugees and have decided by consensus to recognize certain general principles.[36] These include temporary refuge, *non-refoulement*, and some human and refugee-specific rights.

3 Does Asia Protect Refugees? A Review of State Practice and *Opinio Juris*

In the context of non-signatory states, questions about the existence of custom and general principles become more prominent, but identifying custom can be controversial. From a TWAIL perspective, state practice and *opinio juris* have largely been assigned meaning through the lens of Global North states.[37] TWAIL scholars insist on *greater legitimacy*. The members of AALCO have called for "further precision and more concrete criteria …"; "a rigorous and systematic approach"; and "representativeness … based on fitting criterion, rather than superficial or mechanical representations."[38] The important point is the diligence and care that should be taken, including to consider the representativeness of participation, and procedural legitimacy, and not settle for Global North jurisprudence and literature to conclude that a customary norm is binding on the Global South.

---

34 In 1958 the Statutes were amended to change the name from "Asian Legal Consultative Committee" (ALCC) to the "Asian-African Legal Consultative Committee" (AALCC), to include African states. In 2001, at the 40th Session, the name was changed to the "Asian-African Legal Consultative Organization" (AALCO). This chapter will generally refer to AALCO even when discussing its earlier work done under the name ALCC or AALCC.

35 Asian African Legal Consultative Committee (AALCO), *Immunities and Privileges of the Asian-African Legal Consultative Organization* (adopted at its Sixth Session, Cairo 1964) art II: Juridical Personality (AALCO Immunities and Privileges).

36 AALCO, *Bangkok Principles on the Status and Treatment of Refugees* (as amended and adopted at the 40th Session, New Delhi 2001) <www.refworld.org/docid/3de5f2d52.html> accessed October 14, 2024 ("2001 Bangkok Principles").

37 Yasuaki Onuma, *International Law in a Transcivilizational World* (CUP 2017) 158; see also BS Chimni, 'Customary International Law: A Third World Perspective' (2018) 112(1) *American Journal of International Law* 1, 6.

38 AALCO, *Report of the Chairman of the AALCO's Informal Expert Group on Customary International Law* (Beijing 2015).

Noting that a large number of refugees are physically present whether the jurisdiction is party to the Refugee Convention or not, the next section considers how these states respond in practice. It concludes that the non-signatory states in Asia consistently host large numbers of refugees, that they have done so for hundreds of years, that normative frameworks and systems exist wherever large numbers of refugees are found, and that these states have recognized certain general principles with regard to the status and treatment of refugees. These include obligations to provide temporary refuge and ensure the respect of *non-refoulement* among other rights as a matter of regional custom.

3.1 *A Comparative Analysis of National-Level Responses*

3.1.1 History

Every country in Asia has its own ancient and enduring experience of displacement and providing refuge. There are many early examples in China from the famous historical figure Liu Bei during the "Three Kingdoms" period (in refuge around 201–208),[39] and more recent examples during the Opium Wars, the Taiping Rebellion, Punti-Hakka Wars, the Boxer Rebellion, and the Chinese Civil War.[40] The history of Southeast Asia is also one of movement, conflict, and integration among diverse ethnic groups, kingdoms, and empires.[41] Examples also abound in South Asia. For example, at the time of the conquest of Persia (starting around the year 630), the Parsi sought and were granted refuge in India.[42] They remain in India today.

Non-signatory states in Asia also have decades of recent experience of large influxes and prolonged displacement. India's more recent examples include: the Tibetan government in exile; millions who fled East Pakistan during the war for Bangladesh independence; hundreds of thousands of Tamil refugees from Sri Lanka; and thousands from Afghanistan and Myanmar. Pakistan has

---

39 The actions of Liu Bei are recorded in the official history *Annals of the Three Kingdoms* by Ch'en Shou, including in particular his attempt to lead a group of refugees to safety. See Lo Kuan-Chung, *Romance of the Three Kingdoms* (CH Brewitt-Taylor tr, Charles E Tuttle Company 1959).

40 Ngai Yeung, 'Hidden Hong Kong: Hong Kong's colourful legacy of immigration', (*Localiiz*, September 16, 2020) <www.localiiz.com/post/culture-history-hong-kong-immigration-legacy> accessed October 14, 2024.

41 George Coedès, *The Making of South East Asia* (Routledge & Kegan Paul 1966).

42 Gyaneshwer Chaubey, Qasim Ayub, Niraj Rai and others, '"Like Sugar in Milk": Reconstructing the Genetic History of the Parsi Population' (2017) 18 *Genome Biology* 110.

hosted millions of refugees from Afghanistan for decades.[43] Over 100,000 Bhutanese refugees were hosted for decades in Nepal along with large numbers of Tibetans. Thailand has its own history of displacement and finding refuge, and it has hosted Vietnamese refugees for at least two centuries.[44] Thailand continues to host hundreds of thousands from Myanmar in nine camps along the border. Malaysia likewise has hosted hundreds of thousands of refugees consistently every year from the time of its independence, including hundreds of thousands of Filipino refugees fleeing from Mindanao and the Sulu islands, hundreds of thousands during the Indochinese refugee crisis, and now hundreds of thousands from Myanmar among others.[45]

The list goes on, and historical analysis makes clear that every context has its own experience with displacement and providing refuge. These are shared, ancient, and universal concepts that predate the Refugee Convention by millennia.

3.1.2 The Numbers

The number of refugees hosted in UNHCR's Asia and the Pacific region is consistently high. According to the most recent UNHCR Global Trends, 5.3 million refugees were hosted in Asia and the Pacific in 2023.[46] The countries hosting the largest numbers are Iran, Pakistan, and Bangladesh, each hosting nearly or more than 1 million.[47] India and Malaysia host hundreds of thousands, and Thailand hosts nearly 100,000.[48] Globally, statistics remain imprecise and in some cases are misleading because of the numbers of unregistered popula-

43 See, for example, Pakistan, 'Good Practices: Joint Government of Pakistan and UNHCR Comprehensive Documentation and Registration Process' <https://globalcompactrefugees.org/good-practices/how-pakistan-helps-afghans-get-back-their-feet> accessed October 14, 2024.

44 David K Wyatt, *Thailand: A Short History* (2nd edn, Yale University Press 2003); see also Yacoub (n 24); and Muntarbhorn (n 17) 125–26.

45 Ahmad Sharif Haron, Mohd Irwan Syazli Saidin, Zarina Othman, 'The Human (In)Security of Syrian Refugees in Malaysia' (2023) 12(6) *Social Sciences* 317; see also Chong Eng Leong, 'The Facts on Sabah IMM13, Burung Burung and Sijil Banci', *Borneo Today* (June 27, 2020); Tharani Loganathan, Zhie X Chan, Fikri Hassan, Zhen Ling Ong, Hazreen Abdul Majid, 'Undocumented: An Examination of Legal Identity and Education Provision for Children in Malaysia' (2 Feb 2022) 17(2) *PLOS One*.

46 UNHCR, *Global Trends: Forced Displacement in 2023* (June 2024) <www.unhcr.org/global-trends> ('Global Trends'). Full annexes available at <www.unhcr.org/refugee-statistics/insights/annexes/trends-annexes.html?situation=1> accessed October 14, 2024.

47 ibid.

48 ibid.

tions, people keeping under the radar without legal status, and questionable practices and reporting by states, among other issues.[49]

The numbers demonstrate that whether they are party to the Refugee Convention or not, many countries in Asia are in fact hosting large numbers of refugees. The global trends provide an annual snapshot, but put together with data from previous years and in the context of the longer history set out above, there has been a demonstrable, long, and consistent commitment to hosting large numbers of refugees.

3.1.3 Laws, Policies, and Systems

The legal framework that may be applicable to refugees in these countries is a patchwork of various provisions, from the Constitution to various pieces of legislation and national policies. The fact that these jurisdictions are not party to the Refugee Convention does not mean that there is a complete absence of legal obligation. Each context is unique, but in every jurisdiction, there are international and domestic legal obligations to which those states have consented and are therefore binding and impose duties. This section will compare the legal frameworks currently being applied in identified non-signatory contexts.

In Indonesia, the right to seek and obtain asylum are ensured by the Constitution and legislation. The Constitution states that "every person shall have the right to be free from torture or inhumane and degrading treatment, and shall have the right to obtain political asylum from another country."[50] Furthermore, legislation provides that "everyone has the right to seek and receive political asylum from another country."[51] In 1999, Indonesia's legislature directed the President to determine policy with respect to refugees, and although it took more than a decade, a policy was pronounced in 2016 as the Presidential Regulation on the Handling of Refugees.[52]

Likewise, in India, the primary source of protection for refugees has been the constitution, which guarantees some fundamental rights to all persons regardless of citizenship, including the protection of life, liberty, and equality

49 Jeff Crisp, '"Who has counted the refugees?" UNHCR and the politics of numbers' (1999) *New Issues in Refugee Research* Working Paper 12.

50 Constitution of the Republic of Indonesia 1945, art 28G.

51 Indonesia Law No 39 of 1999 on Human Rights 1999, art 28(1).

52 Indonesia Act No 37 of 1999 on Foreign Relations 1999, art 27; and Regulation of the President of the Republic of Indonesia No 125 Year 2016 Concerning the Handling of Foreign Refugees 2016; see also Regulation of Director General of Immigration No IMI-0352 gr 02 07 (2016) on the Handling of Illegal Migrant Claiming to be Asylum-Seeker or Refugee 2016.

before the law.[53] *Non-refoulement* has long been recognized by the courts as encompassed within article 21 of the constitution.[54] Executive regulation has also been important. Standard Operating Procedures were issued by the Ministry of Home Affairs in 2011, with reference to persons claiming to be refugees.[55] They identified categories of persons eligible for long-term visas, set out procedures, and identified a set of "benefits" for those with such a visa.[56]

As the Indian example brings out, judicial engagement is often an important source of legal protection.[57] The impact of the judiciary is well illustrated by developments in Hong Kong. A series of judicial review cases between 2003 and 2013 resulted in a "unified screening mechanism" (USM).[58] Through the USM, the Hong Kong government now assesses for *non-refoulement* under the Convention Against Torture (CAT);[59] *non-refoulement* under the International Covenant on Civil and Political Rights (ICCPR);[60] and *non-refoulement* under article 33 of the Refugee Convention, despite remaining a non-signatory to the latter.[61]

53 Constitution of India 1949.

54 Ktaer Abbas Al Qutafi and Another v Union of India and Others [1999] CRI L J 919 (Gujarat High Court); see also Nandita Haksar v State of Manipur [2021] WP (Crl) No 6 of 2021 (Manipur High Court); Dongh Lian Kham & Anr. V Union of India & Anr [2015] WP(CRL) No 1884/2015 (Delhi High Court); State v Sd "CCL" [2021] FIR No 13/ 21 (Juvenile Justice Board of India). A number of other published and unpublished decisions are referenced in BS Chimni, 'Status of Refugees in India: Strategic Ambiguity' in Ranabir Samaddar (ed), *Refugees and the State: Practices of Asylum and Care in India, 1947–2000* (Sage 2003).

55 *Internal guidelines to deal with the foreign nations in India, who claim to be 'refugees'* (India Ministry of Home Affairs) 2011 (on file with author); see also reference in India Ministry of Home Affairs, 'Long Term Visas' (2018) <https://mha.gov.in/PDF_Other/AnnexVI_01022018.pdf> accessed October 14, 2024.

56 These include some access to work and education, free movement including some access to re-entry documents, access to bank accounts and driving licenses.

57 See chapter 3 on the role of domestic courts.

58 Secretary for Security v Sakthevel Prabakar [2004] 7 HKCFAR 187 (Hong Kong Court of Final Appeal) (Prabakar); FB v Dir. Of Immigration [2009] 2 HKLRD 346 (Hong Kong Court of Appeal) ('FB'); and C & Ors v the Director of Immigration and Another [2013] HKCFA 21 (Hong Kong Court of Final Appeal) ('C').

59 Convention Against Torture and Other Cruel, Inhuman, and Degrading Treatment or Punishment (adopted December 10, 1984, entered into force on June 26, 1987) 1465 UNTS 85 (CAT).

60 International Covenant on Civil and Political Rights (adopted December 16, 1966, entered into force March 23, 1976) 999 UNTS 171 (ICCPR).

61 Hong Kong Immigration Department, 'Making a Claim for Non-Refoulement Protection in Hong Kong' <www.immd.gov.hk/eng/useful_information/non-refoulement-making-claim.html> accessed October 14, 2024. On how the USM relates to the Refugee Conven-

In Pakistan, a recent judgment of the Islamabad High Court[62] relied on its constitution,[63] and noted that submissions from the Ministries of Interior and Law and Justice relied on a 1993 Cooperation Agreement between the government of Pakistan and UNHCR.[64] The Court also considered the ICCPR, CAT, and *non-refoulement* as set out in the Refugee Convention (though Pakistan is not party to the latter), noting that comity among nations requires respect for international law where it is not in conflict with domestic acts of parliament, and using these Conventions to interpret the Foreigners Act.

As the Pakistan and Hong Kong examples show, among countries not party to the Refugee Convention, most are nevertheless party to a number of other human rights treaties. These include the CAT and the ICCPR, both of which contain *non-refoulement* obligations.[65] These other human rights conventions often serve as a source of protection. There is also a UNHCR office in each of these jurisdictions, and each of these states cooperate with UNHCR as it conducts operations under its mandate including reception, registration, documentation, various protection and assistance programs, refugee status determination (RSD), and resettlement.[66]

Taiwan is an exception in that it has no access to UNHCR because it is no longer a member of the UN.[67] Still, it has a number of provisions in its laws including a delegated responsibility to the National Immigration Agency in its Organizing Act for "determining the status of potential refugees and handling

62 *Azizi v The State & Others* (2023) Writ Petition No 1666 of 2023 (Islamabad High Court); see also Arjumand Bano Kazmi, 'Pakistan's Judicial Engagement with International Refugee Law' (2025) *International Journal of Refugee Law* <https://doi.org/10.1093/ijrl/eeaf001> accessed February 2, 2025.

63 Constitution of the Islamic Republic of Pakistan (1973). The Court referred to art 4 which requires treatment in accordance with law and protection of the law, art 9 which requires that a person not be deprived of life or liberty save in accordance with law, art 10A right to a fair trial and due process, and art 14 on the inviolability of dignity and freedom from torture.

64 See chapter 10.

65 Bangladesh, Hong Kong, Indonesia, Pakistan, and Thailand are all party to both CAT and the ICCPR. India is also party to the ICCPR and has signed, but not ratified, CAT. Given that Taiwan has not been permitted to become a formal party at the UN level, it has given effect to the ICCPR through its domestic legislation.

66 See chapter 10.

67 Restoration of the Lawful Rights of the People's Republic of China in the United Nations, UNGA Res 2758 (1971) GAOR 26th Session Supp 29. See chapter 7.

matters relating to refugee asylum and sheltering."[68] Taiwan also protects refugees in the context of *non-refoulement* obligations under the ICCPR.[69]

Like Hong Kong and Taiwan, Thailand appears to be developing an alternative protection regime outside the Refugee Convention.[70] Refugee protection is managed under discretionary authority granted by legislation.[71] This discretion has been exercised repeatedly. For example, it has been used to permit Myanmar refugees to reside in nine camps along the Thai–Myanmar border. Furthermore, Thailand has recently developed a new National Screening Mechanism, along with new institutions to operationalize it including a new inter-Ministerial Screening Committee and Sub-Division 4 within the Immigration Bureau.[72] It launched on September 25, 2023.[73]

Bangladesh has something in common with all of the other jurisdictions. Protection for refugees in Bangladesh has been found through jurisprudence,[74] human rights obligations,[75] national-level policy,[76] efforts of UNHCR,[77] and efforts of the local legal community.[78]

---

68 Organization Act of the National Immigration Agency 2005 (as amended in 2013) art 2. There are specific provisions for persons from mainland China, persons from Hong Kong or Macau, and stateless persons from India or Nepal (Tibetans) in: Act Governing Relations between the People of the Taiwan Area and the Mainland Area 1992 (as amended in 2022); Laws and Regulations Regarding Hong Kong & Macao Affairs 1997 (as amended in 2022); and Immigration Act 1999 (as amended in 2022).

69 See chapter 7.

70 See chapter 8.

71 State Administration Act (BE 2534) 1991, Section 11 (8); Immigration Act (BE 2522) 1979, Section 17; see also UNHCR, Camp Profiles (2011) <www.cas.go.jp/jp/seisaku/nanmin/yusikishakaigi/dai6/siryou4.pdf> accessed October 14, 2024. Vitit Muntarbhorn, 'Refugee Law and Practice in the Asia and Pacific Region: Thailand as a Case Study' (2004) *Refugee Law Reader*.

72 Regulation of the Office of the Prime Minister on the Screening of Aliens who Enter into the Kingdom and are Unable to Return to the Country of Origin (BE 2562) 2019.

73 For details, see chapter 8.

74 *Refugee and Migratory Movements Research Unit* (RMMRU) *v Government of Bangladesh* [2019] Writ Petition No 10504 of 2016 (RMMRU); Case summary provided in 'Case Law Summaries' (2019) 31(4) *International Journal of Refugee Law* 597, 598; M Sanjeeb Hossain, 'Bangladesh's Judicial Encounter with the 1951 Refugee Convention' (2021) 67 *Forced Migration Review*.

75 Bangladesh is party to ICCPR, ICESCR, CAT, CRC, ICERD, and CEDAW.

76 In 2013, Bangladesh adopted a National Strategy on Myanmar Refugees and Undocumented Myanmar Nationals (copy on file with the author).

77 A Joint Response Plan and Joint Multi-Sector Needs Assessments are conducted annually to inform the massive humanitarian response, <https://reliefweb.int/report/bangladesh/2024-joint-response-plan-rohingya-humanitarian-crisis-january-december-2024> accessed October 14, 2024.

The Indonesian government interviewees in Dewansyah's research in chapter 5, seem to sit with an internal contradiction. On the one hand they use the lack of accession to the Refugee Convention to deny any legal obligations towards refugees at all, while on the other hand, they acknowledge that 'the Refugee Convention and Protocol have become customary international law and part of our national law, especially [the principle of] non-refoulement'. The former position is understandable rhetoric coming from government officials, but the Constitution, legislation, policies/regulations, many human rights treaties that Indonesia is party to, and custom all demonstrate a recognition of specific legal obligations towards refugees that are accepted by Indonesia.

3.1.4 Conclusions on Comparative National-Level Responses

On the basis of the comparative analysis provided above, we can conclude that states receive and host large numbers of refugees consistently and have done so throughout their history. In practice, they are providing temporary refuge and respecting *non-refoulement* obligations in every case. If this is correct, then we could conclude that effective refugee protection in these contexts need not begin with advocacy around accession to the Convention. Instead, it requires engagement with existing laws, policies, and coordination mechanisms. We can start with refugees themselves and try to understand their needs, and then engage collaboratively to consider how existing needs can more effectively be addressed. This makes refugee protection a practical question and engages with the local context on its own terms.[79]

With each of the jurisdictions described above we could identify at least two major trends: (1) those that are developing policies and practices designed to manage large and often protracted displacement (these include Bangladesh, Indonesia, Malaysia, and Pakistan); and (2) those that, although they are not party to the Refugee Convention, are developing alternative protection regimes (these include Hong Kong, India, Taiwan, and Thailand).[80] This is not

---

78 Mediation guidelines have been developed to facilitate informal justice mechanisms in the camps (copy on file with the author).

79 The longer-term goal can still remain, ultimately, accession with a view to improving responsibility-sharing arrangements and expanding the network of harmonized protection systems regionally and globally. However, the approach advocated by the analysis here will promote improvements to protection outcomes for persons in need of protection along the way.

80 It is also worth emphasizing that there are states parties to the Refugee Convention in Asia: Afghanistan, Cambodia, China (PRC), Iran, Japan, South Korea, Macau, the Philippines, and Papua New Guinea.

to suggest that existing systems are adequate, or that the trajectory is always a progressive one. Negative trends include restrictive encampment, border closures, boat pushbacks, indefinite detention, and growing xenophobia. Yet existing systems must be utilized even as negative trends and breaches of the law are persistently challenged.

What if we now zoom out from the national level? Some trends have already been suggested among states in the region. However, a number of scholars compare Asia with Africa, Latin America, and Europe, noting the absence of a regional human rights regime. Does this mean that there is no regional consensus on the status and treatment of refugees?

3.2 *Regional Dialogue and Consensus*

Moretti has suggested that Asian states tend to prefer formal and informal spaces for dialogue and practical cooperation, and that this has resulted in what he has described as a "migration regime complex."[81] The complex includes regional bodies like the Association of Southeast Asian Nations (ASEAN) or the South Asian Association for Regional Cooperation (SAARC), regional consultative processes like the Bali Process on People Smuggling Trafficking in Persons and Related Transnational Crime, and periodic meetings such as those that resulted in the Jakarta Declaration.[82] Within these fora very little law has been created, and that is often an explicit choice. For example, Bali Process members have expressed a preference for "practical cooperation," insisting that it is a "non-binding forum for policy dialogue."[83] This does not mean that there is no normative value to such dialogue and cooperation. These fora may inform both state practice and *opinio juris*.[84] However, to understand the juridical position of states, it is necessary to consider the positions that they take on legal matters at the national level (described above), and in bodies like AALCO (described below).

81 Sébastien Moretti, 'UNHCR and the Migration Regime Complex in Asia-Pacific: Between Responsibility Shifting and Responsibility Sharing' (2016) 283 *New Issues in Refugee Research Paper* 2 <www.refworld.org/docid/5857e4554.html> accessed October 14, 2024.

82 ibid 20–21.

83 See *Bali Declaration on People Smuggling, Trafficking in Persons, and Related Transnational Crime*, (March 23, 2016). <www.refworld.org/legal/resolution/radr/2016/en/111333> accessed October 14, 2024.

84 See, for example, ASEAN, *Phnom Penh Statement on the Adoption of the ASEAN Human Rights Declaration* (November 19, 2012) <https://asean.org/wp-content/uploads/2021/01/6_AHRD_Booklet.pdf> accessed October 14, 2024.

AALCO is an intergovernmental body with "juridical personality."[85] It was established in 1956 and is considered to be an important outcome of the Bandung Conference.[86] Member states appoint legal experts to serve as official "delegations," and these representatives are required to "consult their respective Governments before taking a decision."[87] AALCO conducts extensive and detailed legal analysis of comparative state practice, and states actively participate and provide official legal views. All substantive decisions must be made by consensus.

In sum, this means that member governments are giving their official legal views on matters of international law, in a juridical forum, and deciding by consensus to recognize certain general principles. The decisions of AALCO can, therefore, appropriately be characterized as *opinio juris*. Along with other sources, including state practice discussed above, conclusions can be drawn about recognized custom and general principles to which AALCO members have consented.

In 1966, AALCO adopted the Bangkok Principles on the Status and Treatment of Refugees.[88] The Bangkok Principles assure access to temporary refuge, protect refugees from *refoulement*, and enumerate a number of specific rights.[89] Following adoption of the Bangkok Principles in 1966, refugees remained on the agenda of AALCO. Addenda were adopted in 1970 and 1987, and a model law was adopted in 1995. Finally, revised and consolidated Bangkok Principles were adopted in 2001.[90]

---

85 The most appropriate analogy would be with the International Law Commission. See AALCO (n 35).

86 AALCO, Putrajaya Declaration on Revitalizing and Strengthening the Asian-African Legal Consultative Organization (adopted at the 48th Session, Putrajaya 2009) art 1.

87 See AALCO, *Statutory Rules* (adopted in 1957, as amended at the 28th Session, Nairobi 1989) arts 2, 6, 12, and 22.

88 AALCO, *Bangkok Principles on the Status and Treatment of Refugees* (adopted at the Eighth Session, Bangkok 1966) 207–27 ("1966 Bangkok Principles") <www.aalco.int/report8thAS> accessed October 14, 2024. AALCO considered the status and treatment of refugees from its 5th–8th Sessions, receiving detailed comments from member governments, expert views, and submissions. The numerous submissions considered are well documented in appendices of the 8th Session Report comprising 409 pages.

89 1966 Bangkok Principles (n 88) arts III(3), III(4), and VIII; and 2001 Bangkok Principles (n 36) art III(1–2). Identified rights include: freedom from arbitrary arrest; freedom to profess and practice his own religion; protection by the executive and police authorities of the state; access to the courts of law; access to legal assistance. Art IX also includes a savings clause that "nothing in these articles shall be deemed to impair any higher rights and benefits granted or which may hereafter be granted by a State to refugees."

90 2001 Bangkok Principles (n 36).

Throughout the drafting and negotiation process, states were openly stating and developing their positions. For example, Pakistan stated that, although not a party to the Refugee Convention, it had been extending facilities to Afghan refugees, and "continued to maintain the generous approach to refugees provided by Islam, over 1400 years ago ..."[91] Indonesia stated at the 46th Session in 2007 that:

> Indonesia applies standards of treatment, which highly respect human rights in dealing with asylum, and status of refugees, [and] although Indonesia has not ratified the Convention, it applies article 31 of the Convention, that is, no immigration action taken in relation to asylum-seekers and refugees; and article 33 ... "*non-refoulement*" ... which means refugees and asylum seekers, cannot be forced to be return to their homeland.[92]

Most Asian states are now members of AALCO and were members at the time of the 2001 revision of the Bangkok Principles.[93] Yet, despite its relevance as an articulation of Asian state positions on questions of refugee law, the Bangkok Principles are given little attention in the literature.[94] Too often they are disregarded as "declaratory and non-binding in character."[95] The underappreciation of AALCO and its work may be the result of an overly positivist view of international law that ignores any source not expressly binding, even despite the fact that it may serve as evidence of custom or general principles, as is the case here. It may also be the result of a Global North bias, failing to seriously consider the voices and authority of juridical decisions of the Global South. AALCO has put extensive work into determining and declaring the applicable general principles of international refugee law. Custom and general principles are binding sources of international law, but the Bangkok Principles are not a treaty, and AALCO leaves it to member states to determine "how it should give

91 AALCO, *Selected Documents of the 39th Session of AALCC – Status and Treatment of Refugees* (2000) 39th Session: Discussions <www.aalco.int/39thsession/strcairoIV.pdf> accessed October 15, 2024.

92 AALCO, *Verbatim Record of the Fourth General Meeting of AALCO's 46th Session* (Cape Town 2007) 184–85 <www.aalco.int/verbatim46thAS> accessed October 14, 2024.

93 See <www.aalco.int/Members> accessed October 14, 2024.

94 But see Yacoub (n 24); and Pia Oberoi, Exile and Belonging: Refugees and State Policy in South Asia (OUP 2006).

95 See Moretti (n 81) 5.

effect" to these principles.[96] As regional custom, the Bangkok Principles serve as a minimum standard against which state practice can be measured. Among others, the Bangkok Principles recognize an obligation to provide temporary refuge and respect *non-refoulement*.

3.2.1 Temporary Refuge

Temporary refuge ensures admission to a state temporarily, providing refugees with protection while solutions are pursued.[97] Temporary refuge generally protects any person in danger as a result of armed conflict, massive violations of human rights, disasters, indiscriminate violence, or other situations which put their life and security in danger. It does not require an individual assessment next to the refugee definition.[98] Work has been undertaken by states and UNHCR in the refugee law context to further understand and develop the concept of temporary refuge.[99] Moreover, temporary refuge is also a norm of humanitarian and human rights law.[100]

---

96 AALCO, Report of the 8th Session in Bangkok (1966) 10, 33 ("... having regard to the functions of the Committee, which were purely of an advisory nature, the appropriate manner in which it could deal with the subject was to define the term 'Refugee' and then proceed to formulate principles regarding the right of asylum, the rights and obligations of refugees, and the minimum standard of treatment in the State of asylum ... it was up to the government of each participating country to decide as to how it should give effect to the recommendations of the Committee on this subject, whether by entering into multilateral or bilateral arrangements or by embodying these principles in their national laws. In view of this position, the Committee formulated the general principles governing the subject in a Final Report which it adopted unanimously ...")

97 Deborah Perluss and Joan F Hartman, 'Temporary Refuge: Emergence of a Customary Norm' (1986) 26 *Virginia Journal of International Law* 551; see also 2001 Bangkok Principles (n 36).

98 Perluss and Hartman (n 97).

99 In 1966, the original version of the Bangkok Principles (n 88) had already articulated the concept of temporary refuge in art III(4), and this principle remains in the 2001 revision (n 36) art III(1)–(2). See also *Declaration on Territorial Asylum*, UNGA Res 2312(XXII) (1967) GAOR 22nd Session Supp 16, art 3 <www.refworld.org/docid/3b00f05a2c.html> accessed November 14, 2024; Executive Committee of the Programme of the United Nations High Commissioner for Refugees ('ExCom'), *Conclusion Nos. 15, 19, and 22;* and UNHCR, *Guidelines on Temporary Protection or Stay Arrangements* (2014). Regional human rights regimes in Africa, the Americas, and Europe all also recognize an obligation to provide temporary refuge.

100 Perluss and Hartman (n 97) 553–54. Common art 3 of the Geneva Conventions requires that the wounded, sick, and shipwrecked shall be collected and cared for; and that humanitarian access by impartial humanitarian bodies such as the ICRC be guaranteed. Temporary refuge under human rights law is based on the right to life, freedom from

The practice of granting temporary refuge has been described as one of the main contributions of Asia to the development of the international refugee regime.[101] A number of authors recognize the particular role that Asian states have played in the development of this principle, particularly through the era of the Indochinese Refugee Crisis and the Comprehensive Plan of Action, finding that Asian states have a long tradition of offering temporary refuge to people in need of international protection.[102]

Much of the state practice described above already provides ample evidence of respect for temporary refuge obligations. Temporary refuge does not rule out any possible solution and expects efforts to be made to achieve more equitable responsibility-sharing while temporary refuge is provided. Goodwin-Gill has examined the relationship between *non-refoulement*, temporary refuge, and asylum, and argues that temporary refuge provides the nexus between admission of refugees and the attainment of solutions, calling this "*non-refoulement* through time."[103] The Bangkok Principles recognize "burden-sharing" obligations and include an expectation of international cooperation on comprehensive solutions.[104] Asian states recognize and respect a temporary refuge obligation, but this is directly linked with burden-and responsibility-sharing internationally. The state of refuge can be seen as acting on behalf of the international community, and temporary refuge emphasizes the obligation of states at large to find solutions.

3.2.2 *Non-refoulement*

Non-refoulement protects non-nationals from forced return to "any country where he or she is likely to face persecution, torture, or other serious ill treatment."[105] Much of the state practice described above already illustrates the widespread respect shown by states for *non-refoulement* obligations. Incidents of *refoulement* occur (as they do in state party jurisdictions), but they are con-

---

torture and cruel, inhuman, and degrading treatment or punishment, and the right to seek asylum.

101 ibid 562.

102 Guy S Goodwin-Gill, 'Non-Refoulement, Temporary Refuge, and the 'New' Asylum Seekers', in David James Cantor and Jean-François Durieux (eds) *Refuge from Inhumanity? War Refugees and International Humanitarian Law* (Brill NIjhoff, 2014) 434; see also Perluss and Hartman (n 97) 561–64, 575.

103 Guy S Goodwin-Gill, 'Non-Refoulement and the New Asylum Seekers' (1986) 26 *Virginia Journal of International Law* 897, 913–14.

104 2001 Bangkok Principles (n 36) arts VIII and X.

105 Guy S Goodwin-Gill and Jane McAdam, *The Refugee in International Law* (4th edn, OUP 2021) 241.

spicuous when placed next to the number of people consistently protected from *refoulement* as they arrive each year and remain in protracted displacement. Furthermore, violations are consistently criticized as legal breaches when they occur.[106]

Many states in the region, even if they are not party to the Refugee Convention, are nevertheless party to CAT or the ICCPR, both of which also impose *non-refoulement* obligations.[107] There have been a number of court decisions recognizing *non-refoulement* obligations.[108] *Non-refoulement* has also been repeatedly recognized and accepted by AALCO every time it has been considered since the Bangkok Principles were first adopted in 1966.[109]

4 Conclusion

After rejecting the premise and conclusions of the Asian exceptionalism literature, this chapter engaged in an empirical analysis of state practice and *opinio juris* comparing national approaches in 3.1 and regional consensus in 3.2. The countries in Asia are hosting millions of the world's refugees, and they

106 Less than a month after the 2021 coup in Myanmar, Malaysia returned over 1,000 Myanmar nationals. The return was in defiance of a domestic court order, and was criticized domestically as a violation of the *non-refoulement* obligation (Ida Lim, 'Malaysia Must Immediately Stop Deporting Asylum Seekers to Myanmar, Advisory Group Tells Govt' *Malay Mail* (Selangor, October 21, 2022) <www.malaymail.com/news/malaysia/2022/10/21/malaysia-must-immediately-stop-deporting-asylum-seekers-to-myanmar-advisory-group-tells-govt/34908> accessed October 14, 2024. A joint communication to the Malaysian government was made by special rapporteurs under OHCHR Special Procedures. The Malaysian government response suggested that it had "taken internal measures to ensure that none of the detainees were refugees/asylum-seekers and that all of them have given their voluntary consent to return to Myanmar." Its response asserts that its actions were consistent with the *non-refoulement* obligation, not that no obligation exists. See Office of the High Commission for Human Rights, *The Government of Malaysia's Response to the Joint Urgent Appeal from Special Procedures*, JUA MYS 2/2021 (March 31, 2022) <https://spcommreports.ohchr.org/TMResultsBase/DownLoadFile?gId=36871> accessed November 14, 2024.

107 Bangladesh, Hong Kong, Indonesia, Pakistan, and Thailand are all party to both CAT and the ICCPR. India is also party to the ICCPR and has signed, but not ratified, CAT. Taiwan has not been permitted to become a formal party at the UN level, but it has given effect to the ICCPR through its domestic legislation.

108 See, for example, Prabakar (n 58), 'FB' (n 58), 'C' (n 58); RMMRU (n 74); Mohamad Huson v Public Prosecutor [2020] Criminal Revision No KA-44-23-07/2020 (Alor Setar High Court), summary provided in 'Case Law Summaries' (2021) 33(1) International Journal of Refugee Law 137, 141; Azizi (n 62).

109 1966 Bangkok Principles (n 88).

have been doing so consistently for decades. Laws, policies, and systems do exist to manage protracted displacement. The evidence supports the position that Asian states do not reject refugee law. These countries all generally grant temporary refuge and recognize and respect *non-refoulement* obligations among other rights.

It is appropriate to question the relevance and utility of existing laws and policies when we consider breaches, the conditions for refugees in protracted displacement, and the dearth of solutions. Furthermore, we can lament the lack of political will or how much the system depends on executive policy and discretion. Yet, it is equally important to utilize existing laws and policies to protect refugees who are present and have legal needs whether the state is party to the Refugee Convention or not. This chapter argues that instead of starting with accession to the Refugee Convention, focusing on the local context including its history and existing normative frameworks can prove more productive. This book and its chapters engage in this important work. Such an approach will take us further toward understanding the region and contribute to improving conditions for refugees, as well as developing a more harmonized approach. An approach that improves responsibility-sharing globally, and ultimately may even move through more incremental steps, toward accession of the Refugee Convention.

CHAPTER 5

Acceding to the Refugee Convention: Indonesia's Persistent Reluctance

Bilal Dewansyah

1 Introduction

Why do non-signatory states choose not to accede to the 1951 Convention[1] and/or its 1967 Protocol[2] (together and individually "the Refugee Convention")? This question has dominated the work of many scholars of refugee studies. From a Southeast Asian perspective, the Eurocentrism that influenced the drafting of the Refugee Convention is a frequently used justification for non-accession.[3] Other common interpretations relate to the perception of refugees as a threat to national security, the fear of increased social and economic burdens, and the primacy of the principle of non-interference among countries in the region.[4] However, much of the research on this topic globally has generalized the creation of international refugee law and observations of narratives on a regional level.[5] Yet, as Barbour shows in chapter 4 of this volume, research specifically on non-signatory states in Asia offers very different explanations and therefore lacks a clear understanding of non-accession at the regional level. Only a few research studies have examined the relationship between individual states' internal dynamics and actors' engagement in domestic politics on the one hand, and the international refugee regime on the other.[6]

1 Convention relating to the Status of Refugees (adopted July 28, 1951, entered into force April 22, 1954) 189 UNTS 137.

2 Protocol relating to the Status of Refugees (adopted January 31, 1967, entered into force October 4, 1967) 606 UNTS 267.

3 Sara E Davies, Legitimising Rejection: International Refugee Law in Southeast Asia (Martinus Nijhoff 2008) 18, 225.

4 ibid 10; Sébastien Moretti, The Protection of Refugees in Southeast Asia: A Legal Fiction? (Routledge 2022) 26–36.

5 Maja Janmyr, 'The 1951 Refugee Convention and Non-Signatory States: Charting a Research Agenda' 33(2) *International Journal of Refugee Law* 188.

6 See especially Pia Oberoi, 'South Asia and the Creation of the International Refugee Regime' (2001) 19(5) *Refuge* <https://refuge.journals.yorku.ca/index.php/refuge/article/view/21228> accessed July 20, 2024; Maja Janmyr, 'No Country of Asylum: "Legitimizing" Lebanon's

This chapter addresses this gap by drawing on original, empirical research on Indonesia.

As Indonesia is a non-signatory state, refugees are mainly treated under immigration laws (currently Law 6/2011) that consider them as illegal immigrants, especially due to lack of documentation.[7] Permission to stay in Indonesia is based on humanitarian grounds.[8] However, their circumstances are generally described as lacking effective legal protection.[9] Even though Indonesia has ratified some international human rights treaties and adopted international human rights law into its national laws, the implementation of human rights instruments toward refugees varies and is inconsistent.[10] At the end of 2016, the government enacted Presidential Regulation (PR) 125/2016 on the Treatment of Refugees to provide clear guidance for the many government agencies involved in dealing with refugees in the field, which included a responsibility to rescue refugees in emergencies. Although the Regulation illustrates the active role that Indonesia is playing in dealing with refugee issues, it does not mean that the government intends to follow the Refugee Convention.[11] Indeed, Indonesia's official policy has persistently been not to accede to the Convention and not to fully adopt norms embedded in the Convention within national law and policy.

Previous research on Indonesia has identified some factors that influence such a policy: the fear that being a party to the Refugee Convention would be a "pull factor" for more refugees coming to Indonesia; the perception of refugees as an economic burden; a concern about potential conflict with locals;

Rejection of the 1951 Refugee Convention' (2017) 29(3) *International Journal of Refugee Law* 438.

7 Bilal Dewansyah and Irawati Handayani, 'Reconciling Refugee Protection and Sovereignty in ASEAN Member States: Law and Policy Related to Refugee in Indonesia, Malaysia and Thailand' (2018) 12(4) *Central European Journal of* International and Security Studies 477.

8 Susan Kneebone, Antje Missbach and Balawyn Jones, 'The False Promise of Presidential Regulation No 125 of 2016?' (2021) 8(3) *Asian Journal of Law and Society* 431, 441–42.

9 Nikolas Feith Tan, 'The Status of Asylum Seekers and Refugees in Indonesia' (2016) 28(3) *International Journal of Refugee Law* 365.

10 For example, regarding refugee reception, *refoulement* practices occasionally happen even in emergencies like maritime arrivals. Moreover, refugees also have limited access to formal education and healthcare, and do not have the right to work. Tan (n 9) 375–76; Azadeh Dastyari and Asher Hirsch, 'The Ring of Steel: Extraterritorial Migration Controls in Indonesia and Libya and the Complicity of Australia and Italy' (2019) 19(3) *Human Rights Law Review* 435, 443.

11 Interview with Achsanul Habib, Director of Human Rights and Humanitarian Affairs, Ministry of Foreign Affairs 2019–2024 (Jakarta, Indonesia, February 11, 2022).

and consideration of national security.[12] Another explanation relates to Indonesia's relationship with Australia: it is believed that a policy of non-accession has the effect that Australia – a signatory country – ends up taking greater responsibility for refugees who continue their journey there.[13] These earlier studies take a largely state-centric approach and thus disregard how the discourse on accession and non-accession also takes place in a multi-actor setting within Indonesian government agencies and in their interactions with non-state actors.[14] Moving away from a purely state-centric stance in the discussion of accession, this chapter will explore the roles and views of various actors, including in government and civil society, and within the United Nations High Commissioner for Refugees (UNHCR).

The research for this chapter took the form of document analysis and 13 interviews, conducted between July 2021 and March 2022, with officials from the Indonesian government, members or former members of the Indonesian House of Representatives, UNHCR staff, and civil society organizations.[15] Based on this research, which focuses on the making of PR 125/2016 and the 2011 Immigration Law, the chapter puts forward three additional factors contributing to Indonesia's reluctance to accede to the instruments of international refugee law. First is the narrative of Indonesia being a transit country for refugees seeking sanctuary in a country other than Indonesia. Second, a "silo mentality" among government agencies impedes decision making and implementation concerning potential accession. Third, the "selective policy

---

12 Penelope Mathew and Tristan Harley, 'Refugee Protection and Regional Cooperation in Southeast Asia: A Fieldwork Report' (The Australian National University, March 2014), 15 <https://openresearch-repository.anu.edu.au/server/api/core/bitstreams/468e096a-3cc1-4522-8b96-c2df944de19e/content> accessed July 8, 2024; Carly Gordyn, 'Pancasila and Pragmatism: Protection or Pencitraan for Refugees in Indonesia?' (2018) 2(2) *Journal of Southeast Asian Human Rights* 336, 344, 350; Fitria Fitria, 'Perlindungan Hukum Bagi Pengungsi di Negara Ketiga: Praktik Indonesia' (2015) 2(1) *Padjadjaran Jurnal Ilmu Hukum* [Journal of Law] 113–14.

13 Gordyn (n 12) 349–50.

14 ibid 350 and Fitria (n 12) 113 have identified different views about the Refugee Convention among government officials in the different ministries/agencies. However, they did not elaborate further on why or how these different views contributed to the non-accession policy.

15 Empirical data used in this chapter are mainly from my PhD project at Leiden University concerning the law making and discretionary implementation of Indonesian asylum and refugee laws. See Bilal Dewansyah, 'Asylum and Refugee Law in Indonesia' (2023) 14(6/7) *Asiel & Migrantenrecht* 358. For the document analysis, I also used some UNHCR archive records. I thank Maja Janmyr for providing me with these documents.

principle" in immigration law echoes an anti-foreigner sentiment that is inherently linked to Indonesia's colonial history.

The examination shows that although Indonesia is persistently reluctant to accede to the Refugee Convention, its non-accession policy is not unanimously supported by policy actors. In fact, various government actors, along with civil society organizations and UNHCR, have actively advocated for Indonesia's accession. More importantly, as I argue in this chapter, while a reluctance to accede to the Convention persists, the influence of these different actors has led to the gradual adoption and integration of the basic principles of international refugee law into state policy and practice.

In the following section, I discuss the efforts of government actors supported by civil society organizations and UNHCR to promote accession. I examine how the "accession agenda" was included in two consecutive periods of the National Human Rights Action Plan (NHRAP) without ever being implemented. In this section, I also discuss how the failure to execute this agenda led to another approach – the adoption of a more practical refugee policy, namely Presidential Regulation 125/2016 on the Treatment of Foreign Refugees. In Sections 3 to 5, I present and analyze my findings on factors influencing Indonesia's non-accession attitude, and how and why these factors emerged. In view of the link between one of the three factors (the selective policy principle) and Indonesia's colonial history, I engage in Section 5 with postcolonial studies literature on migration. Finally, in Section 6, I summarize my main findings and reflect on how Indonesia's case can contribute to explaining non-accession behavior in general, especially for states with colonial experiences.

2 Indonesia's Efforts to Adopt International Refugee Norms

After the initiation of political reforms in Indonesia in 1998, there was a growing move by politicians to incorporate international human rights norms comprehensively into the national legal system. This started with the adoption of the first generation of the NHRAP in August 1998, which included plans to accede to international human rights conventions,[16] but not the Refugee Con-

16 Before this period, Indonesia had ratified only two main international human rights instruments: the Convention on the Elimination of All Forms of Discrimination Against Women (adopted December 18, 1979, entered into force September 3, 1981) 1249 UNTS 13, signed by Indonesia on July 29, 1980, ratified September 13, 1984 and the Convention on

vention.[17] This was followed by the ratification of two important international human rights instruments, the Convention Against Torture in 1998 and the Convention on the Elimination of All Forms of Racial Discrimination in 1999.[18] This period also saw the adoption of national human rights instruments, such as the 1998 Human Rights Charter and the Human Rights Chapter in the Constitutional Amendment (2000) which also guaranteed some important rights for asylum seekers and refugees, such as freedom from torture and the right to asylum.[19]

A commitment to accede to the Refugee Convention became more explicit when the NHRAP 2004–2009 was adopted, with plans for the accession of the instrument by 2009.[20] This development was undeniably influenced by UNHCR's efforts to promote international refugee law in the country since 1981, which, according to Soeprapto, intensified following the 1998 fall of Suharto's New Order, a repressive authoritarian regime known for various human rights atrocities.[21] UNHCR attempted to influence Indonesian actors through various activities, ranging from seminars, workshops, expert meetings, and training for various groups including government officials and members of the House of Representatives (the Indonesian parliament), to the establishment of an inter-ministry working group at the initiative of the Department of Justice and Human Rights.[22] In November 2000, the working group completed its study and recommended that Indonesia accede to the

the Rights of the Child (adopted November 20, 1989, entered into force September 2, 1990), 1577 UNTS 3, signed by Indonesia on January 26, 1990, ratified September 5, 1990.

17 Majda El Muhtaj, 'A Critical Analysis of The Indonesian Human Rights Action Plan 1998–2020' (2022) 13(3) *Jurnal HAM* 519, 523–34.

18 Convention against Torture and Other Cruel, Inhuman or Degrading Treatment or Punishment (adopted December 10, 1984, entered into force June 26, 1987) 1465 UNTS 85, signed by Indonesia on October 23, 1985, ratified October 28, 1998, and the International Convention on the Elimination of All Forms of Racial Discrimination (adopted March 7, 1966, entered into force January 4, 1969) 660 UNTS 195; Indonesia acceded on June 25, 1999.

19 Bhatara Ibnu Reza, 'Challenges and Opportunities in Respecting International Refugee Law in Indonesia' in Angus Francis and Rowena Maguire (eds), *Protection of Refugees and Displaced Persons in the Asia Pacific Region* (Ashgate 2013) 121–22.

20 Annex of Presidential Decree 40/2004 on the 2004–2009 NHRAP.

21 Enny Soeprapto, 'Promotion of Refugee Law in Indonesia' (2004) 2(1) *Indonesian Journal of International Law* 57, 62. For more information on human rights abuses during the New Order, see Amnesty International, 'Indonesia: Power and Impunity: Human Rights under the New Order' (ASA 21/017/1994, September 1, 1994) <www.refworld.org/reference/countryrep/amnesty/1994/en/91506> accessed October 1, 2024.

22 ibid 63–64.

Refugee Convention with reservations on some articles.[23] Although it is unclear which government actors were involved in this working group, this recommendation is likely to have influenced the inclusion of the Refugee Convention accession agenda in the human rights action plan, which was administered by the same government department under a new name: the Department of Law and Human Rights.

Mohammad Anshor, the former Director of Human Rights and Humanitarian Affairs of the Ministry of Foreign Affairs (MoFA) who was involved in drafting the NHRAPs in the 2004–2009 and 2011–2014 periods, has explained that the key ministries agreed upon the plan to ratify/accede to all international human rights instruments, including the Refugee Convention although this latter was not a priority.[24] This can be seen primarily in the 2004–2009 NHRAP, in which the Refugee Convention is at the bottom of the ratification list scheduled for 2009.[25] In the end, the plan was never executed during this period, and the government only acceded to two out of 12 international human rights instruments.[26]

In the next period of the NHRAP (2011–2014), the plan to accede to the Refugee Convention was once again included, along with the other outstanding human rights instruments.[27] In this period, refugee issues became more prominent in public discourse: with the increased number of refugees in Indonesia, the government, especially the Directorate General of Immigration, was being criticized for treating them mainly as illegal immigrants and placing them in immigration detention centers in accordance with the 2011 Immigration Law.[28] Criticism mainly came from members of Komnas-HAM, the Indonesian National Human Rights Commission, as they pushed the government to adopt a more active approach to refugee protection by acceding to the Refugee Convention.[29]

The demand to accede to the Refugee Convention was also made by civil society organizations within the Human Rights Working Group, a coalition of

23 The reservation was suggested for arts 8, 14, and 26 of the Convention; ibid 64.

24 Interview with Mohammad Anshor, Director of Human Rights and Humanitarian Affairs of MoFA 2010–15 (online, August 2, 2021).

25 See Soeprapto (n 21) 65.

26 Abdul Muthalib and others, 'Evaluasi Pelaksanaan RANHAM 2004–2009 dan Rencana Ratifikasi Optional Protocol to the Convention against Torture (CAT) dalam, RANHAM 2004–2009 dan Perencanaan RANHAM 2010–2014' (Task Force Pemantauan RANHAM, 2010) 44 <www.neliti.com/publications/424/evaluasi-pelaksanaan-ranham-2004-2009-dan-rencana-ratifikasi-optional-protocol-t> accessed July 15, 2024.

27 Presidential Regulation 23/2011 on the 2011–2014 NHRAP.

28 Banu Abdillah, 'Urgensi Ratifikasi Konvensi Pengungsi' (2012) 1(X) *Wacana HAM* 8.

29 ibid.

Indonesian non-governmental organizations promoting human rights.[30] Yet despite repeated pressure, the government did not fulfill this plan. Instead, it proposed a regulation on refugees initiated by the Directorate of Human Rights and Humanitarian Affairs of MoFA. Soemantri, a former sub-director in the directorate who was involved in the initial stage of drafting the regulation explained:

> [I]n 2010 there was increasingly strong pressure [to carry out] the ratification process (of the Refugee Convention). Komnas-HAM repeatedly called on the government to ratify [it], but we also heard strong arguments [to the contrary] … and this was therefore an alternative … to draft a PR (presidential regulation).[31]

Soemantri further referred to reasons for non-accession related to the perception of refugees as an economic burden while the country still had its own issues of poverty, and the concern of the possible social impact identified by previous studies, as explained at the beginning of this chapter.[32] Thus, the demand for accession from Komnas-HAM and civil society to implement the NHRAP was answered instead by a presidential regulation on refugees. In other words, this regulation (which later became PR 125/2016) was seen as a middle way to respond to the pressure of acceding to the international refugee instruments on the one hand, and the need to tackle refugee issues in the field on the other, thus adapting global norms to domestic regulation.[33]

However, drafting the regulation itself was quite a complex and contentious process, from its beginnings in 2010 until its final adoption in late 2016. As the initiator of this regulation, MoFA at first proposed an integrated Standard Operating Procedure or manual as common guidance for the relevant government agencies to deal with refugees, rather than a presidential regulation as mandated by the 1999 Foreign Relations Law.[34] As a manual, the earlier drafts of the regulation contained all aspects of refugee handling, from general

---

30 Interview with Muhammad Hafiz, former Program Manager of Human Rights Working Group (online, July 6, 2021).

31 Interview with Acep Soemantri, former Sub-Director for Economic, Social and Cultural Rights of MoFA (online, August 5, 2021). Author's translation of this and all subsequent quoted interviews.

32 ibid.

33 Qatrunnada Daysa Fitri and Dwi Ardhanariswari Sundrijo, 'The Adaptation of Global Norms: The 1951 Refugee Convention in Indonesia' (2024) 4(2) *Journal Eduvest* 570.

34 Interview with Masni Eriza, former Sub-Director for Humanitarian Affairs of MoFA (online, August 11, 2021); Interview Soemantri (n 31); Interview with Febi Yonesta, former

principles to technical details on the tasks and responsibilities of every key agency, including coordination between them.[35] It also explicitly included some basic principles of refugee protection taken directly from the Refugee Convention, especially *non-refoulement*, non-discrimination, and non-penalization, as well as the best interests of the child in the case of refugee children and some fundamental rights suggested by civil society such as access to education and healthcare, as well as rights for refugees with disabilities.[36] This shows that MoFA, with the involvement of civil society, tried to adopt the core substance of the Refugee Convention in the manual as a compromise to its policy of non-accession and in the context of the actual problems faced by government agencies at the time – namely a lack of coordination between them in the treatment of refugees.[37] However, when the draft was discussed at the ministerial level, it not only shifted in form, from manual to presidential regulation, but also had almost all human rights provisions removed, including principles derived from the Refugee Convention, amid delays, deadlocks, and compromises among the agencies involved. Why is Indonesia reluctant to accede to the Refugee Convention and engage with its key norms? I will explore three different factors in the following sections.

3 Transit Country Narrative

In this section, I argue that the narrative of Indonesia as a transit country justifies a non-accession stance in two interconnected contexts. First, it relates to the common motive of refugees who perceive Indonesia as a transit point to Australia. In this state of transit, it is argued, Convention protection would not be needed. Second, Indonesia perceives itself as inherently a transit country, for which accession to the Refugee Convention would have significant unintended consequences.

In the first context, the transit country narrative generally stems from Indonesia's geographical position in refugee migration routes: "Indonesia's geographical position near Australia and New Zealand has resulted in Indonesia

---

Founding Coordinator of SUAKA, an Indonesian association for the protection of refugee rights (online, July 9, 2021).

35 (Draft) Prosedur Tetap Terpadu tentang Penanganan Orang Asing Pencari Suaka dan Pengungsi (nd) 15, 22.

36 ibid 19; Draft Prosedur Tetap Penanganan Pencari Suaka dan Pengungsi Di Wilayah Indonesia, November 8, 2011, Part III (5), (7).

37 Interview with Hafiz (n 30); Interview with Soemantri (n 31); Interview with an official at MoFA (online, August 27, 2021).

becoming a transit country for asylum seekers and refugees to Australia and New Zealand as destination countries."[38] Asylum seekers, mainly from the Middle East, arrive at irregular intervals by boat, with Australia as their most common ultimate destination. As we already know, Indonesia hosted more than 100,000 Indochinese refugees between 1975 and 1995.[39] Then, around 1996, asylum seekers from Middle Eastern countries began arriving in Indonesia en route to Australia. Until 2000, numbers were still modest with fewer than 1,000 arrivals.[40]

In 2001, the number of asylum seekers and refugees increased significantly, and those leaving Indonesia for Australia peaked at 5,516.[41] This prompted an Indonesia–Australia partnership to intercept them in Indonesia under the 2001 Regional Cooperation Agreement, which also involved the International Organization for Migration (IOM) who provided financial assistance and accommodation for those affected. In 2007, another bilateral agreement – the Irregular Immigrant Management and Care Project – was concluded, leading to more intensive use of the immigration detention centers financed by IOM, also from Australian funds.[42] UNHCR was also informally involved in this cooperation, conducting refugee status determination (RSD) in the absence of a national asylum mechanism.[43] This development illustrates the Indonesian authorities' perception of accession to the Refugee Convention as being superfluous for a country that is merely a transit point. A former immigration high official suggests that Indonesia's accession to the Refugee Convention is probably more in the interests of Western countries, especially Australia, rather than in Indonesia's.[44]

However, government actors' narrative on Indonesia's transit status neglects refugees' own motives. Although resettlement in Australia was a common desire for refugees in Indonesia, research has shown that what pushed

38 The Explanatory Notes of Draft of Presidential Regulation concerning The Treatment of Asylum Seekers and Refugees, 17 September 2014, para 1.

39 Antje Missbach, *Troubled Transit: Asylum Seekers Stuck in Indonesia* (ISEAS-Yusof Ishak Institute 2015) 36.

40 ibid 44.

41 ibid 45.

42 Susan Kneebone, 'Australia as a Powerbroker on Refugee Protection in Southeast Asia: The Relationship with Indonesia' (2017) 33(1) *Refuge* 29, 32; Amy Nethery, Brynna Rafferty-Brown and Savitri Taylor, 'Exporting Detention: Australia-Funded Immigration Detention in Indonesia' (2013) 26(1) *Journal of Refugee Studies* 88, 95–96.

43 Savitri Taylor and Brynna Rafferty-Brown, 'Difficult Journeys: Accessing Refugee Protection in Indonesia' (2010) 36(3) *Monash University Law Review* 138.

44 Interview with Muhammad Indra, Acting Director General of Immigration 2009–11 (online, September 19, 2021).

them to take dangerous maritime journeys was much more varied. Besides the fact that Indonesia does not accept refugees permanently, being a non-signatory to the Refugee Convention, their motivation to continue their journey was also because of the difficulties they faced in Indonesia, such as long waiting times for UNHCR's RSD for resettlement to third countries and the poor conditions in which they found themselves while they were in Indonesia.[45] Thus, while the transit country narrative to some extent makes sense as a justification for not acceding to the Refugee Convention when it comes to the migration route of refugees in Indonesia who end up in Australia, it neglects the agency of refugees to choose the path they deem safe, including to remain in Indonesia in the long term.

The close cooperation between the two countries on this issue lasted until 2013 when Australia started the military-led Operation Sovereign Border by turning back intercepted refugees arriving by boat.[46] Moreover, in 2014, Australia announced a non-resettlement policy in which asylum seekers in Indonesia registered after July 1, 2014 cannot be resettled in Australia.[47] All these policies sought not only to discourage asylum seekers and refugees from making the maritime journey to Australia but also make them stuck in Indonesia by offering a very low number of resettlement quotas.[48] Some observers argue that this development means that Indonesia can no longer be considered as a transit country for refugees destined for Australia, but is now a de facto destination country.[49] Yet, the transit country narrative is still maintained to justify non-accession to the Refugee Convention. As Soemantri from MoFA states:

> We are not a destination country, we tend to be a transit country. By ratifying it [the Refugee Convention], it means that we open ourselves

45 See, for example, Sally Clark, 'Seeking Asylum: Factors Driving Irregular Migration from Indonesia to Australia during the Fifth Wave 2008–2013' (2019) 38(1) *Refugee Survey Quarterly* 83, 100–07.

46 Andreas Schloenhardt and Colin Craig, '"Turning Back the Boats": Australia's Interdiction of Irregular Migrants at Sea" (2015) 27(4) *International Journal of Refugee Law* 536, 548.

47 Anne McNevin and Antje Missbach, 'Luxury Limbo: Temporal Techniques of Border Control and the Humanitarianisation of Waiting' (2018) 4(1–2) *International Journal of Migration and Border Studies* 12, 18.

48 ibid.

49 Antje Missbach and Gerhard Hoffstaedter, 'When Transit States Pursue Their Own Agenda: Malaysian and Indonesian Responses to Australia's Migration and Border Policies' (2020) 3(1) *Migration and Society* 1, 3.

> to become a destination country while in terms of economy … we don't have that kind of capacity; we still have a lot of poor people that we have to deal with. Then from the sociocultural aspect, we also need to increase our capacity for social integration and other things, which is not easy … Even though we are not a state party to the Refugee Convention, we respect the principles and implement them properly and this Presidential Regulation (PR 125/2016) is an effort for us to be able to protect the human rights of refugees.[50]

The statement above leads us to the second implication of the transit country narrative, which underpins non-accession as Indonesia's policy of avoiding the unintended consequences of being a state party, especially the perceived economic and social burdens. These burdens would include the financial contribution expected from a state party as well as the capacity demands of conducting RSD:

> [If we become a state party] We have to contribute funds as a member and then process [asylum claims] ourselves. In terms of funding, we are not ready to process it ourselves; there must be people who are trained for that, and not all can … The process at UNHCR is not simple. They [asylum seekers] submit [asylum claims], then appeal, and so on; that's the process. Those are some considerations for us not to ratify …[51]

On the one hand, Indonesia's perceived inability to shoulder such burdens of acceding to the Refugee Convention to some extent reflects Davies's argument about Southeast Asian countries' "relatively honest" motivations for their non-accession attitude.[52] The burdens perceived by Indonesia would impede its treatment of refugees, so that accession to the Refugee Convention would not in fact improve the outcome for refugees. Yet, the burdens associated with being a state party can be eased by declaring reservations to the Convention. Among signatory states, such reservations are quite common: UNHCR notes that by 2024, almost half had declared reservations, including some on core refugee rights such as the right to decent work, freedom of movement, and

50 Interview with Soemantri (n 31). A similar narrative also appeared in my interview with other government officials (Interview with Wicipto Setiadi, former Director General of Legislation, Ministry of Law and Human Rights (online, December 15, 2021); Interview with Eriza (n 34); Interview with Indra (n 44).

51 Interview with Indra (n 44).

52 Davies (n 3) 135.

education.[53] Moreover, the perception that the processing of asylum claims automatically transfers to the state authority if Indonesia becomes a party is not entirely justified. UNHCR conducts RSD in many signatory states due to their unwillingness or lack of capacity. Thus, if Indonesia were to become a party to the convention but were unwilling or not ready to conduct RSD, this task could still be done by UNHCR or through cooperation.

In general, Indonesia's perceived role as a transit country is thus used to justify non-accession and to limit its obligations toward refugees. The government considers most responsibilities toward refugees to be borne by UNHCR in terms of protection and by IOM for financial assistance and accommodation. Its own responsibility, meanwhile, is simply to allow them to stay in Indonesia temporarily in cooperation with these two organizations.[54] These, among other duties, are regulated in PR 125/2016.[55] Thus, the drafting of the PR can be seen as Indonesia's effort to re-emphasize its role as merely a transit country, standardizing its treatment of refugees without having the onus of the responsibilities that come with being party to the Refugee Convention.[56]

4 Government Silos

Another factor influencing Indonesia's stance of non-accession is the prevailing silo tendency among government agencies – each promoting their own priorities and interests. In Indonesian, silos in the context of government are called *ego sektoral*[57] or *ego sentris*.[58] Such silos not only appear in refugee-related matters or migration governance,[59] but are prevalent in bureaucracy in general.[60] This silo tendency essentially entails each sector agency operating independently within rigid hierarchical structures, disregarding other sec-

53 UNHCR, 'Why to withdraw reservations to the 1951 Convention relating to the Status of Refugees and its 1967 Protocol', July 2024 <www.refworld.org/legal/modellaw/unhcr/2024/en/148327> accessed September 26, 2024.

54 Follow-up interview with Muhammad Indra, Acting Director General of Immigration 2009–2011 (Jakarta, Indonesia, February 14, 2022).

55 See especially arts 2, 13, 26.

56 Interview with Soemantri (n 31); Interview an official at MoFA (n 37).

57 Interview with Soemantri (n 31).

58 Interview an official at MoFA (n 37).

59 Wayne Palmer and Antje Missbach, 'Enforcing Labour Rights of Irregular Migrants in Indonesia' (2019) 40(5) *Third World Quarterly* 908, 918.

60 Mark Turner, Eko Prasojo and Rudiarto Sumarwono, 'The Challenge of Reforming Big Bureaucracy in Indonesia' (2022) 43(2) *Policy Studies* 333, 336.

tors' policies and regulations in the pursuit of its own interests.[61] In other words, it concerns bureaucratic infighting.[62] This section will show that there are indeed government actors who support Indonesia's accession to the Refugee Convention, but those opposing such accession hold more political power than those in favor. As I will discuss, there are some reasons why even those supporting accession appear unconvinced.

The silo tendency, when it comes to rejecting the accession to international refugee law instruments, is not something new. In the past, especially with regard to the treatment of Indochinese refugees, UNHCR actively encouraged the Indonesian government to accede to the Refugee Convention.[63] However, this effort faced a deadlock, mainly because the UN agency only managed to convince a limited number of governmental actors, such as the President and the MoFA. In a 1981 meeting between UNHCR's Director of International Protection, Michel Mousalli, and a sub-director of MoFA, Enny Soeprapto, the latter suggested that UNHCR needed to convince many government agencies in order for Indonesia to seriously consider accession to the instruments:

> UNHCR had perhaps not always tackled the problem right way. In Indonesia, one had to reckon with several interested quarters: there was not only the president and the Minister of Foreign Affairs, there was also the Army, State Security, etc., all of whom had to be convinced, not that there were *advantages* (material or otherwise) in adhering to the refugee instruments, but that it would be an ostentatious act of solidarity with the international community. We therefore needed to promote a *political will* rather than try and pull off a technocratic stunt.[64]

Taking account of the silo tendency, UNHCR and the government, through MoFA, then agreed to disseminate knowledge on international refugee law more broadly. Lectures were organized in universities and colloquiums so that national figures and officials from many agencies could familiarize themselves with this issue. This mission had one ultimate goal: Indonesia's acces-

61 Palmer and Missbach (n 59); Turner, Prasojo and Sumarwono (n 60).

62 Jacqueline Vel, Yando Zakaria and Adriaan Bedner, 'Law-Making as a Strategy for Change: Indonesia's New Village Law' (2017) 4(2) *Asian Journal of Law and Society* 454.

63 Davies (n 3) 134.

64 UNHCR, PM Moussalli (Director of International Protection), FE Krenz (Chief, General Legal Sections, 'Accession of Indonesia to the 1951 Convention and the 1967 Protocol Conversation with Mr Soeprapto (Confidential)', August 4, 1981; 671.1 INS, 671.2 INS 1 (emphasis in original).

sion to the Refugee Convention.[65] Although this kind of program continued until the 2000s and resulted in a very important step in the form of the NHRAP's accession plan, it had little effect on the concrete action for accession.[66] It is not the case that UNHCR does not have support for accession from government actors, but rather that actors who resist such encouragement have more supporters within the Indonesian bureaucracy.

As mentioned earlier, accession to the Refugee Convention was an official plan for the Indonesian government, appearing on the agenda in two periods of the NHRAP. Nevertheless, the silo tendency was one of the reasons why the government did not realize the plan and instead enacted PR 125/2016 as a compromise to tackle refugee issues. Not all government agencies involved supported the government's plan for accession, as Muhammad Hafiz from the Human Rights Working Group stresses in an interview with me: "The tendency within the government itself (to accede to the Refugee Convention) was not yet unanimous."[67]

Although there are nine government agencies and more than 400 regional governments involved in the implementation of the NHRAP,[68] the drafting of such planning, especially for accession to international human rights instruments, does not always involve all of them. In the case of the 2011–2014 NHRAP, the process was centered around three key ministries, namely the Ministry of Law and Human Rights as the coordinator, the Ministry of Home Affairs, and the MoFA.[69] As the NHRAP should be enacted by a presidential regulation, the drafting process involved many government agencies with different interests and a notable lack of public participation. Interestingly, in the 2010 drafting process of the NHRAP 2011–2014, most government agencies vetoed the plan to accede to the Refugee Convention, even though it was included in the final version.[70] It is unclear who proposed the plan to accede to the Refugee Convention. As Hafiz further explained:

> In the previous NHRAP [where the accession plan to the Refugee Convention was included], it [the accession plan] was either top-down [proposal] from the NHRAP Committee, Ministry of Law and Human Rights,

65 Soeprapto (n 21) 63.

66 ibid 63–65; Stephane Jaquemet,'Mandat dan Fungsi dari Komisariat Tinggi Perserikatan Bangsa-Bangsa Urusan Pengungsi (UNHCR)' (2004) 2(1) *Indonesian Journal of International Law* 1.

67 Interview with Hafiz (n 30).

68 Muthalib and others (n 26) 12.

69 ibid 44.

70 Fitria (n 12) 113.

> and others, or it was bottom-up from other related ministries/agencies. If we check, all the conventions ... were included, including the Convention on Protection from Enforced Disappearances and the Rome Statute. That's why I'm a bit doubtful who drafted [the accession plan] in the NHRAP.[71]

Based on his interaction with the MoFA, Hafiz suggested that the accession agenda in the NHRAP was not a priority, with various arguments put forward for why such a policy should not be pursued. The arguments sometimes came from the internal MoFA or from other ministries/agencies and focused on the social and economic burdens and the handover of RSD, as explained in the previous section.[72] MoFA's stance indicates a silo tendency not only in relation with other ministries but also within the MoFA itself. In a different context, tension within MoFA regarding the Refugee Convention can be seen in the initial process of drafting PR 125/2016. Febi Yonesta, who was involved in the process, reflected:

> In the deliberation, we argued more with [the Directorate of] Diplomatic Security than the Directorate of Human Rights. The Directorate of Human Rights has the same perspective as us. Previously, in the draft, the principle of *non-refoulement* was included, and the definition [of refugee] from the 1951 Convention was included ... The Directorate of Human Rights has an interest [in refugee protection]. However, when it comes to MoFA (in general), the interests are different ... Diplomatic Security (Directorate) is different. (Their) perspective is the security approach, [such as] handling, humanitarian response, emergency response, something like that.[73]

When I interviewed Mohammad Anshor, the former Director of Human Rights and Humanitarian Affairs–MoFA, who was also involved in drafting the 2004–2009 and 2011–2014 NHRAPs, he suggested that the plan to include all international human rights instruments was agreed upon by the key ministries, especially MoFA through its human rights directorate which is the national focal point for international human rights matters:

71 Interview with Hafiz (n 30).

72 ibid.

73 Interview with Yonesta (n 34).

> [B]efore I became Director of Human Rights, I was the head of the (human rights) sub-directorate ... We (planned) to ratify all the major human rights instruments. So, I started with the Disability [Convention], and it was ratified quickly ... Then, the Migrant Workers [Convention] had a unique process, but I was happy that I managed to get the support of the Ministry of Labor ... Then, Refugees [Convention and Protocol]. I didn't give top priority because, okay, it's important, but in principle, the Refugee Convention and Protocol have become customary international law and part of our national law, especially [the principle of] *non-refoulement*...[74]

The lack of priority given to accession to the Refugee Convention suggests not only that the Human Rights Directorate of MoFA was not confident that it could be realized because of lack of support from other departments, but that accession was not even really necessary: in his view, by virtue of its place in international law, the Convention was part of national law. This argument also emerged in other non-signatory states: in Lebanon, accession to the Refugee Convention was considered superfluous due to its perceived overlap with other human rights instruments.[75] The argument is valid in the case of the principle of *non-refoulement*, which has been recognized as a customary international law or even *jus cogens*.[76] Moreover, the principle is also considered a legal obligation, especially under the Convention Against Torture to which Indonesia is a party.[77] However, such a perception is not entirely correct because protection under the Refugee Convention has a much broader scope than simply the *non-refoulement* obligation, covering refugees' basic liberties, such as the permission to work and other fundamental rights.[78] Nevertheless, the opinion that customary international law or other international treaties impose legal obligations on Indonesia in its treatment of refugees is not commonly accepted within Indonesian bureaucracy. Most Indonesian officials instead believe that Indonesia has no legal obligation to refugees due to

---

74 Interview with Anshor (n 24).

75 Janmyr (n 6) 462.

76 Guy S Goodwin-Gill and Jane McAdam, *The Refugee in International Law* (4th edn, OUP 2021) 257.

77 Dio Herdiawan Tobing, 'Connecting the Obligation Gap: Indonesia's *Non-Refoulement* Responsibility Beyond the 1951 Refugee Convention' (2021) 8(3) *Asian Journal of Law and Society* 521, 523.

78 Interview with Eriza (n 34).

its non-signatory stance.[79] In general, the influence of government silos on non-accession has remained in place over time and is unlikely to be resolved in the near future.

5 The Selective Immigration Policy Principle Rooted in Indonesia's Colonial History

As explained in the introduction, the negative sentiment toward foreigners, especially refugees, is one of the reasons why many Asian countries, including Indonesia, have not acceded to the Convention or generally do not want to accord refugees more durable solutions.[80] In this section, I will unpack how, in Indonesia, this negative sentiment is related to the general immigration principle, the so-called *kebijakan selektif* [selective policy], which is intrinsically linked to the country's colonial history.

As the literature on international migration policy making in postcolonial states shows, the colonial experience has a significant influence. According to Koh, colonial legacies and, among other things, racial ideologies impact the daily lives of people in former colonies, including in migration governance.[81] Sadiq and Tsourapas argue that when postcolonial states developed their migration-control policies, they adopted many colonial or imperial practices, including regulatory frameworks and institutional borrowing due to lack of capacity in structures of state.[82] Although the intention of these newly independent states was to remove former colonial practices, a racialist approach toward different population groups often persisted.[83]

In current (Law 6/2011) and previous (Law 9/1992) immigration law, the selective policy principle is understood as a filter through which Indonesia only allows foreigners on its territory who "provide benefit" and "do not jeopardize national security and public order."[84] Law 9/1992 places a stronger emphasis on political stability as part of national security concerns by only ac-

79 Tobing (n 77) 522. This perception is also commonly found in my interviews with Indonesian officials.

80 Moretti (n 4) 27–30; Mathew and Harley (n 12) 15.

81 Sin Yee Koh, 'Postcolonial Approaches to Migration in Asia: Reflections and Projections' (2015) 9(8) *Geography Compass* 432, 434.

82 Kamal Sadiq and Gerasimos Tsourapas, 'The Postcolonial Migration State' (2021) 27(3) *European Journal of* International Relations 884, 890.

83 ibid 891; Sin Yee Koh (n 81) 434–36.

84 Explanatory Notes of Law 9/1992 on Immigration, para 6; Explanatory Notes of Law 6/2011 on Immigration, para 9.

cepting foreigners "who are not hostile to the Indonesian people and state" [*yang tidak bermusuhan terhadap rakyat dan negara … Indonesia …*]. This stems from when Indonesia was under Suharto's authoritarian regime, which was highly suspicious of foreign entities supporting democratization and human rights advocacy.[85] The wording of this principle changed slightly in Law 6/2011, which added an additional phrase: the selective policy "with respect for human rights values" intended "to [secure] the national interest."[86] The addition of "human rights values" in the new formulation of the selective policy is intended to balance the concept of national interest with the human rights instruments that have been adopted expansively in the Indonesian legal system since the 1998 political reform.[87] However, instead of broadly considering migrants, including refugees, within human rights frameworks, this new conceptualization of the selective policy was intended to protect Indonesian citizens from the prohibition of re-entering the country, a liberty that the previous law was accused of breaching.[88] Thus, the human rights aspect of the selective policy focuses more on citizens' rights than on people on the move in general.

However, the refugee issue was one of the topics debated in the process of making Law 6/2011, which related to Indonesia's stance as a non-signatory to the Refugee Convention. As the earlier version of the Bill drafted by the government had no provisions for refugees, some members of the House of Representatives proposed some clauses to take note of their specific circumstances.[89] However, the proposal was rejected without any extensive debates by the government or majority representatives, including those from the two biggest political parties in the House: the Democratic Party, a moderate-right political party, and the Indonesian Democratic Party of Struggle, a nationalist political party.[90] Thus, the final version of the Bill that became Law 6/2011 on

85 Daniel S Lev, 'Legal Aid in Indonesia' in Daniel S Lev (ed), *Legal Evolution and Political Authority in Indonesia: Selected Essays* (Kluwer International, 2000) 300.

86 Explanatory Notes of Law 6/2011 (n 84) para 9.

87 Irene Istiningsih Hadiprayitno, 'Defensive Enforcement: Human Rights in Indonesia' 11 *Human Rights Review* 373, 377–78.

88 Interview with Indra (n 44).

89 This includes Fahri Hamzah and Nazir Zamil from the Islamic Prosperous and Justice Party, Yahdil Abdi Harahap from the Islamic National Mandate Party, and Nudirman Munir from the Functional Group Party (Partai Golkar), the second largest center-right party in the House. Minutes of Meeting, Commission III of the House of Representative Meeting with the Minister of Law and Human Rights, April 27, 2010 11, 14, 18.

90 Interview with an expert member of staff of the House of Representatives (online, August 30, 2021); Interview with Benny K Harman, member of the Indonesian House of Representatives from Democrat Party (Jakarta, Indonesia, February 16, 2022).

Immigration does not contain any provisions for refugees or asylum seekers and frames them generally as illegal immigrants.

Interestingly, it is Indonesia's non-signatory status that appears to have prevented the 2011 Immigration Law from regulating refugees. When I asked why, Muhammad Indra, a former acting Director General of Immigration, explained: "We avoid getting in touch with the Refugee Convention … Maybe one day we will ratify [accede to it]."[91] Moreover, Deni Hariatna, an expert member of staff in the House of Representatives who helped with the law-making process, explained to me that "it was agreed that we skip [the discussion of] refugee arrangements [because] we have no binding obligations regarding refugee issues. In fact, if we regulate the details, it means that we are heading toward agreeing with the refugee law/Convention, right?"[92]

The interviews suggest that including any provision on refugees in the Immigration Law is considered an implicit adoption of the Refugee Convention. For the immigration authorities, rejecting any inclusion of provisions on refugees in such a law is influenced by the selective policy principle. When I asked further about refugees coming to Indonesia through regular channels, such as by airplane, Indra explained:

> Indonesia has not ratified (the Refugee Convention), so we can reject [refugees arriving by air] … the normal concept of immigration law [selective policy] applies to foreigners … [only for those] who are beneficial to development and do not disturb security and [public] order. It will disturb the order if they [refugees] come in droves.[93]

When I traced when and how the selective policy principle emerged, I found that it was adopted for the first time in Emergency Law 8/1955 regarding Immigration Criminal Offences, the first immigration law after independence that modified immigration criminal offenses from the Criminal Code of the Netherlands East Indies. In the Explanatory Memorandum of this law, the colonial's "open-door policy" aimed to "attract foreign capital" and, conse-

91 Interview with Indra (n 44).

92 Interview with Deni Hariatna, an expert member of staff of Commission III of the House of Representatives (online, March 8, 2022).

93 Follow-up interview with Indra (n 54).

quently, "needed foreign workers that competed with local workers so that labor wages could be further reduced."[94] It further summarizes the policy:

> [T]he more poor people who come from abroad, the more profitable for foreign capital ... Therefore, in the Netherlands East Indies Penal Codes, the punishment against people who were smuggled here is not so severe, and it is even very light, categorized as "*Overtredingen*" [light offense].[95] Our country no longer adopts an "*open deur*" [open door] or "*massale*" [massive] policy toward foreigners, but rather a "filter policy" or *selectief politiek* [selective policy] based on different interests, perspectives, and goals.[96]

The selective policy narrative was developed as a counter policy to colonial immigration policy following Indonesian independence. This took place after the (re)establishment of the Unitary State of the Republic of Indonesia in 1950, following the fall of the Republic of the United States of Indonesia, a federation established under the 1949 transfer of sovereignty agreement with the Kingdom of the Netherlands. According to the Directorate General of Immigration, the selective policy is based on protecting national interests and emphasizes the principle of providing greater protection to Indonesian citizens."[97] It can be suggested that the selective policy changed the direction of colonial policies, which had previously favored foreigners over Indonesian natives for economic reasons; the new policy empowered Indonesian citizens, echoing the anti-foreign spirit which was unsurprisingly dominant at the time.

The original character of the principle, which reflected anti-foreign sentiments in some respects, is still influential today. For example, in a discussion about the inclusion of refugee provisions in the 2010–2011 Immigration Bill, Fahri Hamzah, one of the initiators of such provisions and Chairperson of the House of Representatives' Working Group on Immigration Bill states:

> [W]hen I and some of my colleagues in the House wanted to take a stand [to accept and regulate refugees] ... we were accused of having

94 Explanatory Notes of Emergency Law 8/1955 regarding Immigration Criminal Offences, paras 1–2.

95 In the Dutch-Indies Criminal Code, migrants who came without a permit were only deported. Only repeated offenders were punished by a fine for the first offense and two months in jail for the second repetition.

96 Explanatory Notes of Emergency Law 8/1955 (n 102) paras 3, 4, 6.

97 Ramadhan Karta Hadimadja and Abrar Yusra, *Lintas Sejarah Imigrasi Indonesia* (Direktorat Jenderal Imigrasi, Departemen Hukum dan HAM RI, 2005) 45–46.

> international agendas … as now people suspect the entry of Chinese workers as the formation of the fifth [military] force[98] which will one day carry out a coup … so this fantasy has not yet gone away in the minds of our politicians …[99]

In addition, some nationalist representatives in the House also argued that accepting refugees would reduce the state's capacity to serve its citizens.[100] In very extreme words, one of the lawmakers stated during the parliamentary debates that "accepting one refugee means Indonesia sacrifices one citizen …"[101] It can be argued that although the selective policy has evolved significantly beyond a mere counterbalance to colonial policy, its roots in anti-foreigner sentiment mean that any effort perceived as a shift to a more supportive policy towards migrants, including accession to the Refugee Convention, is likely to be rejected.

Although the selective policy principle was established to counter the Dutch colonial immigration policy, it arguably mimics its colonial racial approach in the opposite direction. The Dutch East Indies policy gave more privileges to Europeans and "foreign Orientals," such as Chinese and Arabs, against *pribumi* [natives].[102] Although the subordinated people are now different, the anti-foreigner sentiment prevails in the new immigration policy, and underpins Indonesia's non-accession stance.

6 Conclusion

In this chapter, I have emphasized three factors that have influenced Indonesia's stance of non-accession to the Refugee Convention: the transit country narrative, silo mentality among government actors, and the selective

98 The fifth force was a proposal initiated by the Indonesian Communist Party's leader, DN Aidit in early 1965, supported by the Chinese government, to create a militia group of armed peasants and workers beside the existing four branches of the Indonesian armed forces: army, navy, air force, and police. Taomo Zhou, 'China and the Thirtieth of September Movement' (2014) 98 *Indonesia* 29, 30.

99 Interview with Fahri Hamzah, a former Indonesian House of Representatives member from the Prosperous and Justice Party (online, August 13, 2021).

100 Interview with an expert member of staff of the House (n 90); Interview with Harman (n 90).

101 Interview with an expert member of staff of the House, ibid.

102 See Upik Djalins, 'Becoming Indonesian Citizens: Subjects, Citizens, and Land Ownership in the Netherlands Indies, 1930–37' 46(2) *Journal of Southeast Asian Studies*, 227.

immigration policy stemming from its colonial history. These are intertwined with factors already identified in the existing literature, such as the perception that refugees are socio-economic burdens and that they threaten national security. As I demonstrated in the analysis, the country's persistent non-accession stance is a dynamic rather than a static issue: accession proposals were repeatedly included in the government's formal plans at the instigation of pro-human rights actors but had to be compromised when faced with the dominant voice of opposing actors. At the same time, the need for practical guidance so that all agencies could treat refugees in a standardized manner could not be ignored, resulting in the trade-off with non-accession that was PR 125/2016.

The analysis shows that a silo tendency among government actors determined the compromise – one between executing plans to accede to the Refugee Convention and creating a regulation on refugees justified by the narrative that Indonesia is just a country of transit. I demonstrate that this trend was not new, and that it was also a factor that prevented Indonesia from acceding to the Convention during the country's experience with Indochinese refugees. This is not the only historical factor influencing its non-accession stance: a selective immigration policy rooted in the anti-foreigner sentiment of the country's colonial history is also relevant to the discourse on Indonesian accession.

It is the legacy of this colonial history – affecting the perception of refugees as burdens, and deep-rooted anti-foreigner sentiment – that makes Indonesia's experience different from countries in the Global North. As Indonesia is not the only state that has experienced colonialism, its example might shine a light on other postcolonial states' attitude to the Refugee Convention or to refugees in general.[103] Although the reasons for non-accession may vary, these states' motives might be similarly shaped by their former colonial status. Further historical and empirical investigations are needed to examine how colonial-era factors continue to influence the evolvement of refugee policies in postcolonial states more generally, and accession to international refugee law instruments more specifically.

103 See, for example, chapter 6, for an analysis of the influence of Dutch colonialism in its two former colonies which impeded those countries from ratifying the Refugee Convention.

CHAPTER 6

"Disharmony" in the Kingdom of the Netherlands: (De)Colonization and Non-accession in Aruba and Curaçao

Natalie Dietrich Jones

1 Introduction

When the 1951 Convention relating to the Status of the Refugees (1951 Convention) was drafted,[1] the Caribbean was governed by colonial powers.[2] Sixteen years later, with the advent of the 1967 Protocol relating to the Status of Refugees (1967 Protocol),[3] this was still the case for most countries in the region. Today, while rates of ratification in the Caribbean are higher than the average for Asia, they are lower than the averages for Africa and Latin America.[4] Aruba and Curaçao, two former colonies of the Netherlands located in the Southern Caribbean, have not acceded to the 1951 Convention, or, in the case of Curaçao, the 1967 Protocol.[5] This chapter locates the reasons for non-accession in the continuity of colonial ties with their European metropole, the Netherlands.

The Kingdom of the Netherlands, hereafter "the Kingdom," is a loose confederation of four autonomous countries – Aruba, Curaçao, Sint Maarten, and the Netherlands. The intricacies of the constitutional arrangements governing

1 Convention Relating to the Status of Refugees (adopted July 28, 1951, entered into force April 22, 1954) 189 UNTS 137.

2 See Ulrike Krause, 'Colonial Roots of the 1951 Refugee Convention and its Effects on the Global Refugee Regime' (2021) 24 *Journal of International Relations and Development* 599.

3 Protocol Relating to the Status of Refugees (adopted January 31, 1967, entered into force October 4, 1967) 606 UNTS 267.

4 Natalie Dietrich Jones, 'Against the Tide? A Socio-Legal Review of Caribbean SIDS' (Non)-Compliance With International Agreements on Migrants and Refugees and the Protection of Vulnerable Migrants' in Lino Briguglio, Stefano Moncada, Wouter P Veenendaal and Jessica Byron (eds), *Handbook of Governance in Small States* (Routledge 2021).

5 Ministry of Foreign Affairs, 'The Kingdom of the Netherlands: One Kingdom – Four Countries; European an Caribbean' (2015) www.vn-vrouwenverdrag.nl/wp-content/uploads/Annex-1-Factsheet-Kingdom-of-the-Netherlands.pdf accessed March 23, 2021.

the relationship between the Netherlands and its former colonies[6] make Aruba and Curaçao distinct case studies among the cohort of non-signatory states examined in this collection. Aruba and Curaçao share with Indonesia the experience of colonization by the Dutch (see chapter 5); however, Indonesia's independence imbues it with autonomy to ratify international treaties. This is not the case for Aruba and Curaçao, which lack legal personality to ratify treaties.[7] In this regard, the two countries are more like Taiwan (see chapter 7), which also lacks capacity to engage in treaty ratification. Again, however, circumstances differ. Notwithstanding its experience of colonialism, Taiwan was not classified as "a territor[y] whose people have not yet attained a full measure of self-government" by the United Nations (UN).[8] Taiwan's autonomy to engage in diplomatic relations and ratify treaties is, however, constrained by its non-recognition as a state by several members of the international community.[9]

The position of Aruba and Curaçao contrasts, as well, with the Netherlands' historical relationship with the international refugee regime.[10] The Netherlands was one of the 26 states attending the Conference of Plenipotentiaries on the Status of Refugees and Stateless Persons in Geneva in 1951.[11] It is an original signatory state to the 1951 Convention, which it ratified on May 3, 1956,[12] and the 1967 Protocol, to which it acceded on

---

6 By the 19th century, the Netherlands' colonial empire included East Indies (Indonesia), Dutch Guiana (Suriname), and the Antilles (Aruba, Bonaire, Curaçao, Saba, Sint Maarten, and Sint Eustasius). For a detailed discussion of the Netherlands' colonial and decolonial history, see Gert Oostindie and Inge Klinkers, *Decolonizing the Caribbean: Dutch Policies in a Comparative Perspective* (Amsterdam University Press 2003).

7 Ministry of Foreign Affairs (n 5).

8 UN General Assembly (UNGA) res/66(1) (December 14, 1946). The Resolution identified territories that were classified as non-self-governing based on Chapter XI of the United Nations (UN) Charter.

9 See Pasha L Hsieh, 'The Taiwan Question and the One-China Policy: Legal Challenges with Renewed Momentum' (2009) 84(3) *Die Friedens-Warte: Journal of International Peace and Organization* 59.

10 The international refugee regime refers to the formalized system of "norms, rules, principles and decision-making procedures regulating the protection of refugees", which emerged in the early 20th century. See Alexander Betts, 'The Refugee Regime Complex' (2010) 29(1) *Refugee Survey Quarterly*, 17; David Scott FitzGerald, 'Refugee Regimes' in Marcelo J Borges and Madeline Y Hsu (eds), *The Cambridge History of Global Migrations: Volume 2, Migrations, 1800–Present* (CUP 2023) 441–42.

11 Paul Weis, *The 1951 Refugee Convention: Travaux Preparatoires analysed with a Commentary by Dr Paul Weis* (CUP 1995) 12.

12 UN Treaty Collection (UNTC), 'Multilateral treaties deposited with the Secretary-General: Status of the Convention Relating to the Status of Refugees (adopted July 28,

November 29, 1968.[13] The first High Commissioner to serve in the Office of the United Nations High Commissioner for Refugees (UNHCR), Gerrit van Heuven Goedhart, was Dutch.[14] Further, since 1955, the Netherlands has been a member of UNHCR's Executive Committee (ExCom).[15] In the contemporary era, the Netherlands' early positive contributions to the development of the international refugee regime can be juxtaposed against its former colonies' non-accession to the 1951 Convention and its 1967 Protocol.

Arguing for a (new) research agenda on the role of non-signatory states in the global refugee regime, Janmyr indicates that there is little known about states' motivation for non-accession.[16] Indeed, as pointed out by Ramasubramanyam, "dominant scholarship in the field does not capture the colonial roots of international refugee law."[17] Moreover, "very little of the history and evolution of international refugee law includes perspectives from formerly colonized states." While the study spans the experience of the metropole and former colonies of the Kingdom,[18] this chapter adopts a case study approach with emphasis on Aruba and Curaçao. Analysis of the experiences of these two Global South countries thus allows for the historization of cases not usually discussed in traditional international refugee law scholarship. The chapter therefore explains asymmetries in accession in the Kingdom through an interrogation of colonialism's influence on the shaping of the international refugee regime in the Dutch Caribbean.[19] This orientation thus locates the chapter within Third World Approaches to International Law (TWAIL) with

---

1951, entered into force April 22, 1954) 189 UNTS 137' <https://treaties.un.org/Pages/ViewDetailsII.aspx?src=TREATY&mtdsg_no=V-2&chapter=5&Temp=mtdsg2&clang=_en> accessed June 10, 2024.

13 UNTC, 'Multilateral treaties deposited with the Secretary-General: Status of the Protocol Relating to the Status of Refugees' (adopted January 31, 1967, entered into force October 4, 1967) 606 UNTS 267 <https://treaties.un.org/Pages/ViewDetails.aspx?src=TREATY&mtdsg_no=V-5&chapter=5&clang=_en> accessed June 10, 2024.

14 UNHCR, 'Previous High Commissioners: Gerrit van Heuven Goedhart' (2024) <www.unhcr.org/about-unhcr/who-we-are/high-commissioner/previous-high-commissioners/gerrit-jan-van-heuven-goedhart> accessed August 26, 2024.

15 UNHCR, 'The Netherlands (Kingdom of)' <https://reporting.unhcr.org/donors/netherlands-kingdom> accessed October 19, 2024.

16 Maja Janmyr, 'The 1951 Refugee Convention and Non-Signatory States: Charting a Research Agenda' (2021) 3(2) International Journal of Refugee Law 188.

17 Jay Ramasubramanyam, 'TWAIL, Archives, and Refugee Law' (2024) *Journal of Refugee Studies* 1–2 <https://doi.org/10.1093/jrs/feae013> accessed October 21, 2024.

18 Ministry of Foreign Affairs (n 5).

19 Tracy-Lynn Humby, 'Evaluating the Value of TWAIL, Environmental Justice, and Decolonization Discourses as Framing Lenses for International Environmental Law' (2016) 26(2) *Transnational Law and Contemporary Problems* 317.

grounding in a Global South voice.[20] In keeping with the methodological eclecticism of TWAIL,[21] the chapter addresses this gap by using a sociolegal approach that merges historical, legal, and international relations analyses.

To accomplish this task, the chapter creatively employs the term "disharmony" to discuss treaty non-accession in a postcolonial setting. The chapter advances three core arguments. The first is that there is a state of disharmony within the Kingdom based on the unevenness of treaty ratification/ accession in its four autonomous countries. Secondly, non-implementation of the territorial application clause (article 40) of the 1951 Convention in the Kingdom's former colonies,[22] while not an adequate justification for non-accession in Caribbean non-signatory states, helps contextualize autonomous decision making regarding non-accession among these postcolonial states. Finally, the constitutional arrangement in the Kingdom, itself a legacy of colonialism, provides a partial explanation of the current state of disharmony since it permits territorial differentiation in treaty ratification within the Kingdom.

The chapter proceeds as follows. Section 2 elucidates the concept of disharmony which grounds the chapter. Next, Section 3 contextualizes the past and present relationship between the Netherlands and its former colonies and explains the process of treaty accession. Drawing on *travaux préparatoires*[23] of the Convention and notices of depositary notifications for the Kingdom, Section 4 sheds light on the roots of disharmony by discussing treaty ratification in the metropole Netherlands *and* territorial application in the former colonies. Section 5, the penultimate section, discusses how the reality of disharmony shapes the current protection space in Aruba and Curaçao. Disharmony is discussed in that section against the background of the Venezuelan migration crisis, which has been affecting Aruba and Curaçao, and the wider Latin American and Caribbean region, since 2014. The chapter concludes with a summary of the chapter's contributions and reflections for future scholarship.

---

20 Bhupinder S Chimni, 'Three Approaches to the 1951 Convention: The Case for a Dialectical Approach' (2024) *Journal of Refugee Studies* <https://doi.org/10.1093/jrs/feae011> accessed October 17, 2024.

21 Humby (n 19).

22 According to art 40(1) of 1951 Convention, "[a]ny State may, at the time of signature, ratification or accession, declare that this Convention shall extend to all or any of the territories for the international relations of which it is responsible …". Also known as the "colonial clause," the provision allows for extension of the treaty to colonial territories held by metropole powers. Krause (n 2).

23 Weis (n 11).

2 On Disharmony

In this chapter, the concept of disharmony is used to describe the anomaly of uneven treaty ratification/accession in the Kingdom. Disharmony is therefore employed innovatively within the context of the refugee regime in the Dutch Caribbean, a sub-region where many legacies of colonialism linger. Through the lens of TWAIL, disharmony is a useful concept as it addresses the tension in complicity with the international refugee regime arising in the Global North (the Netherlands) and Global South (Aruba and Curaçao).

It is, however, not unusual to speak of disharmony within the context of the Kingdom. Scholars examining the relationship between the Netherlands and its Caribbean counterparts have communicated disharmony using varied terminology. The framing in the literature has, however, typically referred to the geopolitical and socio-economic concerns that divide the Kingdom. De Jong, for example, speaks to an imperfect union.[24] For Hoefte, aside from geographical distance, there are economic and sociocultural differences between the European part of the Kingdom and its Caribbean counterparts which are "thrust together."[25] The Caribbean countries are also characterized by "heterogeneity" due to variances in population and territorial size and disparate geographic location.[26]

Notwithstanding these differences, the Kingdom is bound together by a constitutional arrangement, which ensures unity in policy, especially that related to the protection of human rights (discussed further in Section 3).[27] The Statuut voor het Koninkrijk der Nederland [Charter of the Kingdom of the Netherlands, hereafter "Charter"] outlines eight areas (Kingdom affairs)

---

24 Lammert de Jong, 'The Kingdom of the Netherlands: A Not So Perfect Union with the Netherlands Antilles and Aruba' in Lammert de Jong and Dirk Kruijt (eds), *Extended Statehood in the Caribbean: Paradoxes of Quasi Colonialism, Local Autonomy and Extended Statehood in the USA, French, Dutch and British Caribbean* (Rozenberg Publishers 2005).

25 Rosemarijn Hoefte, 'Thrust Together: The Netherlands Relationship with Its Caribbean Partners' (1986) 38(4) *Journal of Interamerican Studies and World Affairs* 36.

26 Gert Oostindie and Rosemarijn Hoefte, 'The Netherlands and the Dutch Caribbean: Dilemmas of Decolonisation' in Paul Sutton (ed), *Europe and the Caribbean* (Macmillan 1991) 72.

27 Ministry of Foreign Affairs (n 5); Advisory Committee on Migration Affairs (Adviescommissie voor Vreemdelingenzaken/ACVZ), The Kingdom of the Netherlands and the International Protection of (Asylum) Migrants (ACVZ 2019) <www.adviesraadmigratie.nl/publicaties/publicaties/2019/03/19/the-kingdom-of-the-netherlands-and-the-international-protection-of-asylum-migrants> accessed June 26, 2024.

in article 3 that are managed jointly by the Kingdom.[28] These are: (a) maintenance of the independence and the defense of the Kingdom; (b) foreign relations; (c) Netherlands nationality; (d) regulation of the orders of chivalry, the flag, and the coat of arms of the Kingdom; (e) regulation of the nationality of vessels and the standards required for the safety and navigation of seagoing vessels flying the flag of the Kingdom, with the exception of sailing ships; (f) supervision of the general rules governing the admission and expulsion of Netherlands nationals; (g) general conditions for the admission and expulsion of aliens; and (h) extradition. The Charter is predicated on the autonomy of the four constituent countries of the Kingdom, as well as mutual cooperation, on matters concerning the Kingdom.

However, there is no unity across the Kingdom with respect to refugee policy. In 2019, an independent committee that advises the Kingdom on migration matters, highlighted this divergence: "International treaties relating to migration law apply in all countries of the Kingdom, *except in the Refugee Convention,* which is not in force in Curaçao and St Maarten."[29] This landscape of unevenness extends to the Caribbean autonomous countries of the Kingdom. During the most recent Universal Periodic Review (UPR) for the Netherlands, the Committee against Torture (CAT) noted its concern that "neither Aruba, Curaçao nor Sint Maarten had adopted its own refugee and asylum legislation, thereby creating a significant gap in the legal framework concerning protection against *refoulement.*"[30] This inconsistency had been highlighted in 2017 by UNHCR, which, during the third cycle of the UPR for the Netherlands, recommended that:

> Aruba, Curaçao and Sint Maarten develop and implement asylum legislation and procedures consistent with international standards and their various treaty obligations, including fair and efficient procedures for adjudicating asylum claims, as well as guaranteeing the rights of persons found to be in need of international protection.[31]

---

28 Statuut voor het Koninkrijk der Nederland [Charter of the Kingdom of the Netherlands] 2010, s 3 <https://wetten.overheid.nl/BWBR0002154/2024-01-01 Oostindie> accessed April 10, 2024.

29 Author emphasis. Advisory Committee on Migration Affairs (n 27) 17.

30 UN Human Rights Council Working Group on the Universal Periodic Review, Kingdom of the Netherlands Compilation of Information prepared by the Office of the United Nations High Commissioner for Human Rights UN doc A/HRC/WG.6/NLD/2 (August 9, 2022) para 92.

31 UNHCR, Submission by the United Nations High Commissioner for Refugees for the Office of the High Commissioner for Human Rights' Compilation Report Universal Periodic Review: 3rd Cycle, 27th Session (September 2016) 4.

This state of affairs contrasts with the Netherlands, which has well-developed asylum procedures.[32]

The concept of disharmony resonates with critiques of the state of human rights within the Kingdom. The Advisory Council on International Affairs emphasized the lack of "harmonization of international human rights standards within the Kingdom," based on the practice of territorial limitation in ratification of human rights treaties, as well as disparity in observance of international human rights standards in the Caribbean parts of the Kingdom and the Caribbean autonomous countries.[33] While acknowledging the need for greater harmony in the Kingdom, representatives of the Ministry of the Interior and Kingdom Relations argued that ultimately the responsibility for implementing human rights treaties belonged to the respective countries. The response is instructive for it underscores the principle of autonomy of the countries constituting the Kingdom.[34] As we see below, however, autonomy is a complicated concept in this (post)colonial context.

3 The Charter, Autonomy and Treaty Accession in the Kingdom

Aruba and Curaçao (along with Sint Maarten) are self-governing autonomous countries.[35] They therefore exercise autonomy over domestic issues (such as

32 Government of the Netherlands, 'Asylum Procedure' (2024) <www.government.nl/topics/asylum-policy/asylum-procedure> accessed August 26, 2024.

33 Advisory Council on International Affairs (AIV), Fundamental Rights in the Kingdom of the Netherlands: Equivalent Protection in All Parts of the Kingdom (AIV 2018) 6 <www.advisorycouncilinternationalaffairs.nl/documents/publications/2018/06/08/fundamental-rights-in-the-kingdom-of-the-netherlands> accessed October 21, 2024.

34 It should be noted that this disharmony in the human rights landscape is a feature of other colonial geographies. For example, Clegg discusses the lack of policy convergence in overseas territories of the United Kingdom. The difference here is that the United Kingdom has been actively engaging the territories to adopt human rights standards. Peter Clegg, 'The UK Caribbean Overseas Territories: Extended Statehood and the Process of Policy Convergence' in Lammert de Jong and Dirk Kruijt (eds), *Extended Statehood in the Caribbean: Paradoxes of Quasi Colonialism, Local Autonomy and Extended Statehood in the USA, French, Dutch and British Caribbean* (Rozenberg Publishers 2005).

35 Aruba and Curaçao are non-independent countries (NICs). Corbin identifies three categories of NICs: non-self-governing territories; self-governing autonomous countries, and integrated island jurisdictions, based on varying degrees of autonomy. Non-self-governing territories have no devolved powers and have limited authority over the internal matters delegated to them by the metropole. Integrated jurisdictions are managed by the respective metropole state. See Carlyle Corbin, 'Self-Governance Deficits in Caribbean Non-Independent Countries' in Peter Clegg and David Killingray (eds), *The*

economic planning, social policy, immigration, cultural affairs, and education); however, ultimately, the metropole holds responsibility over matters such as foreign policy and self-defense.[36] This classification places Aruba and Curaçao among a unique group of states in a modern state system dominated by independent nations. Within the Kingdom, they are distinguished from Bonaire, Saba, and Sint Eustasius, which are integrated as special municipalities into the Netherlands.[37] Aruba, Bonaire, Curaçao, Saba, Sint Eustasius, and Sint Maarten were administered jointly as the Netherlands Antilles until the secession of Aruba in 1986 and the eventual dissolution of the Netherlands Antilles in 2010.[38]

As indicated above, the Charter was promulgated in 1954 and established the nature of the relationship between the Netherlands and its colonies (then Suriname and the Netherlands Antilles).[39] The Charter was meant as a temporary mode of governance, as it was premised on the eventual independence of the Caribbean countries. While Suriname gained independence in 1975, discussion regarding the independence of the Antillean countries ensued for decades.[40] Oostindie notes that the decolonization process "halted in an apparent half house," since the idea of full independence for the Netherlands Antilles did not materialize.[41] However, the resistance to full autonomy reflects the agency of the local populations, and acceptance of new modes of political governance beyond independence. De Jong refers to these new

---

Non-Independent Territories of the Caribbean and Pacific: Continuity and Change (Institute of Commonwealth Studies, University of London 2012) 163 and Matthew L Bishop and others, 'Secession, Territorial Integrity and (Non)-Sovereignty: Why Do Some Separatist Movements in the Caribbean Succeed and Others Fail?' (2022) 21(5) *Ethnopolitics* 538.

36 Ministry of Foreign Affairs (n 5).

37 De Jong (n 24) 85.

38 ibid; Oostindie and Klinkers (n 6) 64–116.

39 This development was significant for the following year the UN released the Netherlands from its reporting obligations under art 73 of the UN Charter. Arjen van Rijn, 'Dimensions Under International Law linked to the Dissolution of the Netherlands Antilles' (2009) 40 *Netherlands Yearbook of International Law* 75; HG de Jong, 'Aruba: A Separate "Country" within the Kingdom of the Netherlands on its Way to Independence' (1989) 20 *Netherlands Yearbook of International Law* 73.

40 Oostindie and Klinkers (n 6) 64–116.

41 This is a complicated history to condense in this short chapter. In addition to Oostindie and Klinkers (n 6), see also Gert Oostindie, 'The Dutch Caribbean in the 1990s: Decolonization, Recolonization?' (1992) 11/12 *Annales des Pays d'Amérique Latine et des Caraïbes* 116; Gert Oostindie 'Dependence and Autonomy in Sub-National Island Jurisdictions: The Case of the Kingdom of the Netherlands' (2006) 95(386) *The Round Table: The Commonwealth Journal of International Affairs* 609.

modes of governance as "extended statehood," since the former countries of the Netherlands Antilles continue to retain constitutional links with the metropole Netherlands.[42]

An examination of the Charter's provisions aids in understanding the process of treaty accession in the Kingdom. Each of the four countries manage their internal affairs autonomously (article 41). However, foreign relations is a Kingdom affair (article 3(1)b). Thus Aruba and Curaçao are unable to independently negotiate and sign treaties or join international organizations (article 28).[43] Only the Kingdom of the Netherlands has legal personality and may conclude agreements for any or all its constituent parts.[44] However, Aruba, Curaçao, and Sint Maarten must be consulted on treaties that affect them (article 27(1)).[45] Article 28(c) ensures that the requisite conditions are in place to facilitate implementation of the treaty obligations for the concerned country. In the absence of a conducive legislative environment, the Kingdom will pass an act that provides instruction on how the treaty will be implemented.[46] Thus, implementation of a ratified treaty is the responsibility of the respective constituent country that has agreed to be bound; ultimately, however, the Kingdom is accountable for treaty implementation. The Kingdom has responsibility for adherence to international norms, especially the protection of human rights. The Kingdom also holds the responsibility to report on treaty obligations.[47]

The permanent connection to a Kingdom government does not thwart the agency of the states; that is, they may accede to any treaty that ensures continuity of Kingdom obligations and foreign policy, should they so desire. However, it is the Kingdom that ultimately enters into any such agreement, on behalf of the concerned country. Moreover, while some treaties may apply to the entire Kingdom, the constitutional arrangement allows for territorial differentiation. Thus, an agreement may be applicable to only one part of the Kingdom (the Netherlands), to the Caribbean countries in the Kingdom only, or to select parts of the Kingdom (European and Caribbean).[48] In this respect, the Charter is a creation of its time and is consistent with the general practice related to treaty obligations for non-self-governing territories, which

42 De Jong (n 24) 3.
43 Ministry of Foreign Affairs (n 5) 1–2.
44 Van Rijn (n 39).
45 Statuut (n 28).
46 ibid; Van Rijn (n 39).
47 Ministry of Foreign Affairs (n 5).
48 ibid; cf Van Rijn (n 39) 100–02.

emerged in the aftermath of the Second World War. During this period, non-self-governing territories were typically incorporated in treaties negotiated by metropole states through a clause on territorial application (the colonial clause). This type of clause was included in several international agreements negotiated under the auspices of the United Nations, including the 1951 Convention and 1967 Protocol.[49]

Of note, however, is that the Charter did not address the process of continuity of those treaty arrangements that predated *status aparte* in Aruba, Curaçao, and Sint Maarten. The change in status of Aruba and Curaçao to autonomous countries in the Kingdom, however, highlighted the issue of territorial validity.[50] In the context of *status aparte*, what would be the fate of treaties ratified by the Kingdom, but applicable solely to the Netherlands? The distinct paths taken in relation to the assumption of legal responsibilities for such treaties by Aruba on the one hand, and Curaçao and Sint Maarten on the other, reveal the roots of disharmony in relation to accession to the 1951 Convention and 1967 Protocol.

4 The Kingdom, the Colonial Clause and the Roots of Disharmony

4.1 *Treaty-Making and the Colonial Clause*

It is now acknowledged that the process to draft the 1951 Convention lacked the participation of representatives from non-self-governing territories, reflecting the power imbalances that defined the international system during that era.[51] The occlusion of non-independent states is manifest not just in the list of countries to which territorial application was subsequently applied, but in the many omitted from these lists.

The inherent exclusion of non-self-governing territories generally reflected colonial perceptions on treaty making, which was viewed as the sole preserve

49 United Nations, *Final Clauses in Multilateral Treaties Handbook* (United Nations 2003) 78–80. <https://treaties.un.org/doc/source/publications/FC/English.pdf> accessed June 25, 2024; Hanna Bokor-Szego, 'The Colonial Clause in International Treaties' (1962) 4 *Acta Juridica* 261

50 Van Rijn (n 39) 100–102. See also De Jong (n 24) 73.

51 Lucy Mayblin, 'Colonialism, Decolonisation, and the Right to be Human: Britain and the 1951 Geneva Convention on the Status of Refugees' (2014) 27(3) *Journal of Historical Sociology* 423; Krause (n 2).

State	The 1951 Convention	The 1967 Protocol
France	S: Sept. 11, 1952; R: Jun. 23, 1954	A: Feb. 3, 1971
French Guiana*	Territorial application (Jun. 23, 1954)	
Guadeloupe*	Territorial application (Jun. 23, 1954)	
Martinique*	Territorial application (Jun. 23, 1954)	
Saint Barthélemy*	Territorial application (Jun. 23, 1954)	
Saint Martin*	Territorial application (Jun. 23, 1954)	
Haiti (1804)	A: Sept. 25, 1984	A: Sept. 25, 1984
The United Kingdom	S: Jul. 28, 1951; R: Mar. 11, 1954	A: Sept. 4, 1968
Anguilla*		
Bermuda*		
Cayman Islands*	Territorial application by extension via Jamaica (Oct. 25, 1956)	
Montserrat*	Territorial application (Sept. 4, 1968)	Territorial application (Sept. 4, 1968)
Turks and Caicos Islands*	Territorial application by extension via Jamaica (Oct. 25, 1956)	
The Virgin Islands*		
Antigua and Barbuda (1981)	A: Sept. 7, 1995	A: Sept. 7, 1995
The Bahamas (1973)	Territorial application (Apr. 20, 1970) as Bahama Islands. A: Sept. 15, 1993	Territorial application (Apr. 20, 1970) as Bahama Islands. A: Sept. 15, 1993
Barbados (1966)	N/S	N/S
Belize (1981)	Territorial application (Jun. 19, 1957) as British Honduras. A: Jun. 27, 1990	A: Jun. 27, 1990
Dominica (1978)	Territorial application (Oct. 25, 1956) A: Feb. 17, 1994	A: Feb. 17, 1994
Grenada (1974)	Territorial application (Oct. 25, 1956) N/S	N/S
Guyana (1966)	N/S	N/S
Jamaica (1962)	Territorial application (Oct. 25 1956) D: Jul. 30, 1964	A: Oct. 30, 1980
Saint Kitts and Nevis (1983)	A: Feb. 1, 2002	N/S
Saint Lucia (1979)	Territorial application (Sept. 4, 1968) N/S	Territorial application (Sept. 4, 1968) N/S
Saint Vincent and the Grenadines (1979)	Territorial application (Oct. 25, 1956) A: Nov. 3, 1993	A: Nov. 3, 2003
Trinidad and Tobago (1962)	A: Nov. 10, 2000	A: Nov. 10, 2000
The Netherlands	S: Jul. 28, 1951; R: May. 3, 1956	A: Nov. 29, 1968
Aruba*	N/S	A: Jan. 1, 1986
Curaçao*	N/S	N/S
Sint Maarten*	N/S	N/S
Bonaire*		Territorial application (Jun. 22, 2011)
Saba*		Territorial application (Jun. 22, 2011)
Sint Eustatius*		Territorial application (Jun. 22, 2011)
Suriname (1975)	Territorial application (Jul. 29, 1971) D: Nov. 29, 1978	Territorial application (Jul. 29, 1971) D: Nov. 29, 1978

Listed countries are independent unless specified. The date of independence of former colonies is indicated in parentheses. Non-independent countries are indicated by asterisks (*). N/S: non-signatory state. S: Signature, R: Ratification, A: Accession, D: Succession. Compiled by author. The territorial application extended by the UK to Jamaica (25 October 1954) also applies to the Cayman Islands. TCI is not listed in the UN Treaties Database; however, territorial application by the UK has been confirmed for the TCI by way of an email received from the TCI Immigration Department to the author (17 May 2021). See also the Immigration (Amendment and Validation) Law 2002 (Law 24 of 2002).

FIGURE 6.1 Patterns of Ratification in Metropole States and Current or Former Colonies in the Caribbean

of independent states.[52] Yet, the addition of the colonial clause through article 40 of the 1951 Convention compelled metropole states to consider to which colonies, if any, they would extend territorial application.[53] As described in article 40(2), metropole states would declare such intentions in writing to the UN Secretary-General. Finally, article 40(3) indicates that:

> With respect to those territories to which this Convention is not extended at the time of signature, ratification or accession, each State concerned shall consider the possibility of taking the necessary steps in order to extend the application of this Convention to such territories, subject, where necessary for constitutional reasons, to the consent of the Governments of such territories.[54]

The content and mode of incorporation of article 40 into the 1951 Convention thus reflected global geo(colonial) politics. Only 26 (independent) states participated in the Conference of Plenipotentiaries. Declarations of territorial application by Australia, Denmark, France, the Netherlands, and the United Kingdom expanded the 1951 Convention's reach beyond the original 19 signatories to at least 24 colonies over which they exercised governance.[55] The majority of these states were in the Caribbean (see Figure 6.1).[56] In addition to the Netherlands, France and the United Kingdom extended territorial application to 12 non-independent countries within five years of signing the 1951 Convention, with much later extensions for two other colonies (the Bahamas and Suriname). Territorial applications were also extended under the 1967 Protocol, although the scope was much more limited than the 1951 Convention.[57]

---

52 Krause (n 2). The drafting of the 1951 Convention coincided with the first wave of decolonization in the Caribbean. It predates the Vienna Convention on Succession of States in Respect of Treaties (adopted August 23, 1978, entered into force November 6, 1996) 1946 UNTS 3. The Vienna Convention codified law regarding the practice of responsibility for treaty obligations in successor states. NS Rembe, 'The Vienna Convention on State Succession in Respect of Treaties: An African perspective on its Applicability and Limitations' (1984) 17(2) *Comparative and International Law Journal of Southern Africa* 131.

53 Rembe (n 52).

54 1951 Convention (n 1) art 40(3).

55 UNTC (n 12). See Section on Territorial Application.

56 ibid; Krause (n 2).

57 UNTC (n 13). See Section on Territorial Application.

The "guardianship" of the 1951 Convention by metropole states further underscores the asymmetry of the negotiation process.[58] Notifications of the desire to apply the 1951 Convention to non-independent countries meant that these states were (indirectly) incorporated into the international refugee regime by their metropole state.[59] Notwithstanding the above, implementation of this clause was potentially positive for the diffusion of the normative framework for refugee rights beyond the continent of Europe. Among former non-independent countries in the Caribbean, the pattern indicates that treaty ratification is more likely for countries where territorial application of the 1951 Convention and/or 1967 Protocol was applied by the metropole.[60] Diffusion would be particularly vital in a world that was being transformed by decolonial processes. Newly independent states would decide if they would assume the obligations of their predecessor metropole.[61]

4.2 *The Colonial Clause and (Non-)Accession in the Kingdom*

When the Netherlands signed the 1951 Convention, it did not immediately extend territorial application to the colonies within its realm. Neither did it notify an extension of territorial application on its accession, in 1956.[62] At

58 The UK representative (in favor of inclusion of the colonial clause) indicated that the "colonial clause was not a means of excluding non-self-governing territories from the application of any international agreement, but the only constitutional method to allow for extending its application to them." María-Teresa Gil-Bazo, 'Article 40: (Territorial Application Clause/Clause d'Application Territorial)' in Andreas Zimmerman, Jonas Dorschner and Felix Machts (eds), *The 1951 Convention Relating to the Status of Refugees and its 1967 Protocol* (OUP 2011) para 28. Contrarily, India and Pakistan (against inclusion of the clause) argued that the clause would give the metropole the right to impose its will and that the people of the non-self-governing territories should be consulted. UNGA, *Draft Convention Relating to the Status of Refugees. Memorandum Prepared by the Legal Department* UN doc A/CONF.2/21 (July 3, 1951).

59 Comments by France and the United Kingdom during the negotiation process suggest that the priority was not diffusion but ease of colonial administration. Exclusion of a clause on territorial application would have required these metropole states to politically engage with each of their (many) colonies. UNGA, *Conference of Plenipotentiaries on the Status of Refugees and Stateless Persons: Summary Record of the Twenty-Seventh Meeting*, UN doc A/CONF.2/SR.27 (November 27, 1951).

60 This pattern is also evident among the other countries where territorial application was extended outside of the region. María-Teresa Gilb-Bazo, 'The 1951 Convention Relating to the Status of Refugees and its 1967 Protocol Article 40 (Territorial Application Clause/ Clause d'Application Territorial)' in Andreas Zimmerman, Terje Einarsen and Franziska M Hermann (eds), *The 1951 Convention Relating to the Status of Refugees and its 1967 Protocol* (2nd edn, OUP 2024) para 58.

61 Rembe (n 52).

62 UNTC (n 12). See Section on Territorial Application.

the time, the Kingdom prioritized the Netherlands' ratification of the treaty and deferred notification of territorial application for its colonies.[63] Parliamentary approval for the Netherlands' ratification was obtained on March 22, 1956, but similar approval was not sought for the 1951 Convention for other parts of the Kingdom.[64] By this action, seven (Caribbean) colonies under the Netherlands' power were initially excluded from the 1951 Convention treaty process.[65] Differentiation in application of the treaty within the Kingdom was in keeping with the Convention and Kingdom Charter, as discussed above, as well as with the Constitution of the Kingdom of the Netherlands (articles 93 and 94).[66] Given the deficit position with respect to refugee protection in the colonies, the Netherlands would therefore be expected to assist the colonies in facilitating the necessary internal changes that would support the implementation of the Convention. It is worth noting that the question of prompt signature (and implementation) was a sticky point in negotiations on the colonial clause.[67]

Similarly, in 1969, when the Netherlands notified the UN Secretary-General about its accession to the 1967 Convention, it indicated that "the Netherlands accedes to the said Protocol so far as the *territory of the Kingdom situated in Europe is concerned.*"[68] The Kingdom, however, subsequently deposited a notification regarding territorial application of the 1951 Convention and 1967 Protocol for Suriname in 1971,[69] in the midst of discussions relating to its independence from the Kingdom. The notification for Suriname thus came within three years of the Netherlands' accession to the 1967 Protocol.[70] However, no similar notification was made for the Netherlands Antilles. At the time of the notification for Suriname, the government of the Netherlands Antilles had indicated, during parliamentary discussions, that it did not wish to request an extension. The rationale was the financial position in the countries constituting the Netherlands Antilles, and the perceived burden that would be

---

63 Letter from the Ministry of Foreign Affairs to author (September 19, 2024); 38 (1951) No 3 *Tractatenblad van Het Koninkrijk der Nederlanden Jaargang* 1957 No 21.

64 ibid.

65 UNTC (n 12). See Section on Territorial Application.

66 Van Rijn (n 39) 97.

67 Gil-Bazo (n 58) para 16, 26–28.

68 Author emphasis. CN/20U (1968) TREATIES 14 (Accession by the Netherlands) <https://treaties.un.org/doc/Publication/CN/1968/CN.204.1968-Eng.pdf> accessed April 10, 2024.

69 CN/134 (1971) TREATIES 3 (Notification by the Netherlands) <https://treaties.un.org/doc/Publication/CN/1971/CN.134.1971-Eng.pdf> accessed April 10, 2024; 38 (1951) No 3 Tractatenblad van Het Koninkrijk der Nederlanden Jaargang 1957 No 148.

70 UNTC (n 13).

placed on the labor market by the integration of refugee populations.[71] Therefore, until the territorial extension of the 1967 Protocol to Aruba in 1986 (discussed further below), there was no territorial extension to any of the countries in the Netherlands Antilles.[72]

The Netherlands was largely silent on the question of territorial application, owing to its "disintegration."[73] However, following its ratification of the European Convention on Human Rights (ECHR) in 1954, the Netherlands extended territorial application of the 1951 Convention to Suriname and the Netherlands Antilles.[74] There is therefore an apparent anomaly with respect to territorial application for the 1951 Convention (and the 1967 Protocol) as against the ECHR for the Antillean countries. Questions of limited capacity in the non-self-governing countries do not seem to be relevant in this instance considering this divergence.[75] The above suggests that the root of disharmony, reflected in disparate ratification statuses in the European and Caribbean autonomous jurisdictions of the Kingdom, lies partially in non-implementation of the colonial clause. The other explanation, however, is found in the constitutional arrangements and the impact of the colonial legacy on the autonomy of the Caribbean countries of the Kingdom.

4.3 *Decolonization and Treaty Accession*

Scholarship on state succession and treaty obligation is ambiguous despite over 50 years of debate on the subject. The question is divided between two alternate views regarding continuity and discontinuity (the "clean slate"). The former, grounded in automaticity of treaty obligations, holds that successor states take on the commitments of their predecessors. The latter suggests that states themselves must consent to the obligations of their predecessors; states are therefore free of these obligations where they did not consent to them pre-independence. For new states it is not either one or the other alternative, "since the law of state succession always takes place in highly politicized con-

---

71 Letter from the Ministry of Foreign Affairs to author (n 64); Zitting 1970–71 – 11 104 (R768).

72 UNTC (n 13).

73 Lawrence Cox, 'The Failure of the People's Republic of China to Extend the Refugee Convention to Hong Kong: The Contemporary Use of the Colonial Clause by a Non-Colonial Power to Circumvent Human Rights Obligations' (2003) 4(2) *Journal of Migration and Refugee Issues* 87.

74 Convention for the Protection of Human Rights and Fundamental Freedoms (adopted November 4, 1950, entered into force September 3, 1953).

75 See Cox (n 73).

texts, case-by-case arrangements and negotiations take place."[76] Aruba and Curaçao easily fall within this Rasulovian perspective.

De Jong notes that during the process of completion of Aruba's *status aparte*, an assessment was undertaken in respect of Aruba's treaty obligations. There were three considerations: (1) new treaties to be entered into by the Kingdom on Aruba's behalf; (2) applicability to Aruba of those existing treaties that applied solely to the Netherlands; and (3) renunciation of those treaties that applied to the Netherlands Antilles. There were no recissions. However, 58 treaties that were applicable to the Netherlands were extended to Aruba. 36 of these, which included the 1967 Protocol, required parliamentary approval. This was facilitated through special omnibus legislation in the Dutch parliament in December 1985.[77] Thus, in 1986, the Kingdom acceded to the 1967 Protocol for Aruba.[78] The extension of the treaty was retroactively applied on January 1, 1986, the effective date of *status aparte* in Aruba.[79]

The secession of Aruba, however, created some confusion. The Netherlands had initially indicated that the 1967 Protocol would apply to Aruba *and* the Netherlands Antilles.[80] However it subsequently issued one corrigendum indicating that it was withdrawing the 1967 Protocol from the list of treaties applicable to the Netherlands Antilles and Aruba, and a later notification specifying that the 1967 Protocol applied to Aruba.[81] The reasons behind this change are unclear. However, when the Netherlands Antilles was eventually dissolved, territorial application was extended to Bonaire, Saba, and Sint Eustasius, by way of a Depositary Notification dated June 23, 2011.[82]

---

76 Akbar Rasulov, 'Revisiting State Succession to Humanitarian Treaties: Is There a Case for Automaticity?' (2003) 14(1) *European Journal of International Law* 148–49.

77 De Jong (n 39) 79.

78 CN/49 (1986) TREATIES (Depositary Notification Declaration by the Netherlands Concerning Aruba); CN/49 (1986) TREATIES (Annex) <https://treaties.un.org/doc/Publication/CN/1986/CN.49.1986-Eng.pdf> accessed April 10, 2024.

79 *Status aparte* is the Dutch term used to refer to Aruba's political status in the Kingdom, after it seceded from the Netherlands Antilles.

80 CN/49 (1986) TREATIES (Depositary Notification) (n 78)

81 ibid; Application to Aruba CN/40 (1987) TREATIES-1/3/1/1/1 (Depositary Notification Corrigendum to Depositary Notification CN/49 (1986) TREATIES OF APRIL 7, 1986) <https://treaties.un.org/doc/Publication/CN/1987/CN.40.1987-Eng.pdf> accessed April 10, 2024.

82 CN/374 (2011) TREATIES-1 (Depositary Notification Protocol Relating to the Status of Refugees New York, January 31, 1967 Netherlands: Territorial Application to the Caribbean Part of the Netherlands (Bonaire, Sint Eustasius and Saba) <https://treaties.un.org/doc/Publication/CN/2011/CN.374.2011-Eng.pdf> accessed April 10, 2024. See also CN/673 (2010) TREATIES-4 (Depositary Notification) https://treaties.un.org/doc/Publication/CN/2010/CN.673.2010-Eng.pdf accessed April 10, 2024.

Glas and others argue that newly independent states are eager to integrate into the international system and to express their commitment to that system through treaty making as a practice of statehood.[83] Through the Kingdom, Aruba acceded to the 1967 Protocol, to which it had, "following its own interests, attached importance."[84] Curaçao and Sint Maarten, however, inherited the treaties where territorial extension had been previously applied to the Netherlands Antilles. These extensions did not include the 1951 Convention or the 1967 Protocol.

Curaçao and Sint Maarten, like Aruba, have the option to accede to the 1951 Convention and 1967 Protocol. However, they have yet to do so. In their case, decolonial autonomy has been prejudicial to the treaty accession process. Though not fully independent, they have observed principles of autonomy enshrined in the Vienna Convention, which indicates that:

> a newly independent state is not bound to maintain in force, or to become a party to, any treaty by reason only of the fact that at the date of the succession of States the treaty was in force in respect of the territory to which the succession of States relates.[85]

Their approach is consistent with customary principles of international law on state succession, as well as with provisions of the Charter allowing territorial differentiation.

The foregoing historical review explains the landscape of disharmony in the Kingdom, reflected in ratification of the 1951 Convention and accession to the 1967 Protocol in the Netherlands; accession to the 1967 Protocol in Aruba; territorial application in Bonaire, Saba, and Sint Eustasius; and non-accession in Curaçao and Sint Maarten. There is thus disharmony not just between the Netherlands and its Caribbean counterparts, but also within the Caribbean autonomous countries. The product of disharmony in the Kingdom is, therefore, limited engagement of the Caribbean autonomous countries with the international refugee regime.

83 Aarie Glas, Clifton van der Linden, Matthew J Hoffmann, and Robert Denemark, 'Understanding Multilateral Treaty-Making as Constitutive Practice' (2018) 3(3) *Journal of Global Security Studies* 339.

84 Van Rijn (n 39) 103 offers this assessment for all the treaties that were approved by the Dutch parliament.

85 Vienna Convention (n 52) art 16.

5 Disharmony in the Context of Crisis

As discussed in Section 2, refugee protection is weakened by the absence of legislation that would domesticize key principles of international refugee law.[86] This is notwithstanding the entry into force of key human rights agreements relevant to the protection of refugees – the International Covenant on Civil and Political Rights (ICCPR), the Convention against Torture (CAT), the Convention on the Rights of the Child (CRC), and the ECHR in *all* the Kingdom.[87] In the absence of legislation, local immigration laws that address admission and expulsion, but that do not include provisions on refugee protection, take effect.[88] In this regard Aruba stands out. There, the absence of legislation is significant given that the Charter provisions place express responsibility on Kingdom countries to implement legislation to give effect to international treaty obligations.[89]

Review committees of the respective human rights instruments have kept track of these deficits through periodic assessments.[90] However, with the Venezuelan migration crisis, there was a marked increase in claims for asylum in the four Southern Caribbean countries affected.[91] As a result, the challenges

86 *Refoulement* is not addressed in this chapter. See Natalie Dietrich Jones, 'The State Response to the Venezuelan Migration Crisis in the Dutch Caribbean' (Rutgers University Press forthcoming).

87 Advisory Committee on Migration Affairs (n 27) 18. See International Covenant on Civil and Political Rights (adopted December 16, 1966, entered into force March 23, 1976) 999 UNTS 171; Convention against Torture and Other Cruel, Inhuman or Degrading Treatment or Punishment (adopted December 10, 1984, entered into force June 26, 1987) 1465 UNTS 85; Convention on the Rights of the Child (adopted November 20, 1989, entered into force September 2, 1990) 1577 UNTS 3.

88 In Aruba, the National Ordinance on Admissions and Expulsion (LTU AB 1993 GT33) and in Curaçao the State Ordinance for Admissions and Expulsion (AB 2010 No 5). R4V, 'Caribbean RMRP Legal Framework Asylum and Migration' (2021) <https://data.unhcr.org/fr/documents/download/79225> accessed August 28, 2023. R4V, 'Legal Framework Asylum and Migration' (2023) <www.r4v.info/en/document/legal-framework-factsheet-caribbean-2023> accessed October 17, 2024.

89 See Van Rijn (n 39) and Advisory Committee on Migration Affairs (n 27).

90 See, for example, 'UN Human Rights Council, Universal Periodic Review – The Kingdom of the Netherlands' <www.ohchr.org/en/hr-bodies/upr/nl-index> accessed April 10, 2024.

91 The number of asylum applications increased exponentially from five in 2016 to 406 in 2019 in Aruba. IOM, 'Aruba Needs Assessment on Migration Governance' (2021) 18 <https://kmhub.iom.int/sites/default/files/2022-02/aruba-needs-assessment-migration-governance.pdf> accessed June 12, 2024. The four countries are Aruba, Curaçao, Guyana, and Trinidad and Tobago. On Curaçao, see Amnesty International, *Curaçao Little Improvement in the Protection of Venezuelans. Monitoring Report* (Amnesty International

faced by refugees, asylum seekers, and other vulnerable migrants have been placed under further scrutiny. One of the major concerns is the lack of transparency in procedures for refugee status determination (RSD). Prior to the crisis, RSD was in place in both Aruba and Curaçao. In Curaçao, UNHCR collaborated with the local Red Cross to conduct RSD until 2017, when, through a Ministerial Declaration, the government assumed responsibility.[92] Similarly, in Aruba, the government requested UNHCR to suspend its RSD procedures in 2018.[93] At present, UNHCR has an office in Aruba only.[94] There, an Asylum Action Team located within the Department for the Integration, Management and Admission of Foreign Nationals in the Ministry of Justice, Security and Integration was established in 2019, in response to the increase in claims for asylum.[95] This change highlights a lack of institutional capacity for handling high volumes of asylum applications, based on the limited experience of asylum processing in the country. It is unclear whether this new unit sufficiently addresses the gap created when the government requested UNHCR to suspend its RSD procedures.

With the onset of the crisis, local and international actors worked to highlight abuses by the state, organize legal representation for migrants, and launch advocacy campaigns regarding migrants' rights. In Curaçao, a new NGO – Human Rights Defence Curaçao (HRDC) – emerged in 2018 and is currently prioritizing support for Venezuelan refugees and migrants in crisis. HRDC has consolidated its position in the local landscape and has become a valuable partner of UNHCR and other members of the Inter-Agency Coordination Platform for Refugees and Migrants from Venezuela (R4V). However, at times, it finds itself constrained in its activities by the state. This obstruction includes the denial of visitation to migrants being detained.[96] An important

2023) <www.amnesty.org/es/wp-content/uploads/2023/02/AMR5640422023ENGLISH.pdf> and Amnesty International, Detained and Deported: Venezuelans Denied Protection in Curaçao (Amnesty International 2018) <www.amnesty.org/en/documents/eur35/8937/2018/en/> accessed June 12, 2024.

92 R4V (2021) (n 88) 3. Details regarding the change are not available to the public. However, it is possible that the increase in claims for asylum and pressure from the international community prompted the government to assume control over the process.

93 R4V (2021) (n 88) 3; Amnesty International (2018) (n 91) 30.

94 UNHCR, 'Factsheet Aruba and Curacao September to October 2023' <https://reliefweb.int/report/aruba-netherlands/aruba-and-curacao-fact-sheet-september-october-2023> accessed October 18, 2024.

95 IOM (n 91) 18.

96 Human Rights Defence Curacao, 'About' (2024) <https://humanrightsdefense.org/> accessed June 12, 2024; Dutch Council for Refugees, Human Rights Defense Curaçao denied access to immigration barracks once again." (June 12, 2024) <www.vluchtelingen

outcome of advocacy initiatives has been the approval of a procedure allowing for the assessment of violations of article 3 of the ECHR, in 2019.[97] In 2020, steps were taken to facilitate a speedier review of submissions.[98] Notwithstanding the formal changes that have been made to the policy environment to accommodate the processing of asylum applications, the lack of public information on successful claims suggest that the transformation has merely been nominal. As Amnesty International points out, there is significant space for transformation in this area, which is currently not in keeping with international standards regarding transparency, access, and due process for asylum seekers.[99]

6 Conclusion

This chapter demonstrates that disharmony is a useful concept with which to explore treaty accession processes in (post)colonial contexts. In addition, it shows the relevance of TWAIL to analyzing non-signatory states. In this regard, the chapter addresses the call to decolonize international refugee law scholarship through an examination of the role of colonialism in the shaping of the international refugee regime.[100] Its contribution is timely, since it tackles issues impacting respect for the human rights of refugees and vulnerable migrants in Global South countries not fully integrated into the international refugee regime and that continue to maintain a political relationship with a metropole state.

This retrospective look reveals that the architecture of the international refugee regime was not built to accommodate a neocolonial world. The chapter therefore affirms that although shaped by ongoing processes of decolonization, the international refugee regime did not compensate for the peculiarities of contemporary relationships between metropole states

werk.nl/en/articles/persbericht/human-rights-defense-curacao-denied-access-immigration-barracks-once-again> accessed October 3, 2021.

97 R4V (2023) (n 88) 1.

98 *Curaçao Chronicle*, 'Minister of Justice: Faster reply for refugees who request protection' (Willemstad, December 22, 2020) <www.curacaochronicle.com/post/main/minister-of-justice-faster-reply-for-refugees-who-request-protection/> accessed June 12, 2024.

99 Amnesty International (2023) (n 91).

100 See Martin Lemberg-Pedersen, Sharla M Fett, Lucy Mayblin, Nina Sahraoui and Eva Magdalena Stambøl, 'Introduction' in Martin Lemberg-Pedersen, Sharla M Fett, Lucy Mayblin, Mita Saharoui and Eva Magdalena Stambøl (eds), *Postcoloniality and Forced Migration* (Bristol University Press 2023) 17.

and former colonies. Thus, in the case of the Caribbean autonomous countries of the Kingdom, colonial legacies deter a smooth treaty accession process, especially as territorial application was not applied by the metropole state. The transformation of the refugee protection framework in colonized spaces is thus intricately tied to the resolution of colonial anomalies concerning treaty ratification. This discussion is especially meaningful for the Caribbean, but also for other (post)colonial spaces. The chapter thus points to the need for further research on the legacy of colonialism on accession to the 1951 Convention and 1967 Protocol in former and current colonial territories.

The experience of the self-governing autonomous countries of the Kingdom also suggests that treaty accession is not a seamless exercise. Indeed, the experience of the Dutch Caribbean shows that integration into the international refugee regime is challenging, given postcolonial continuities and the relative newness of their statehood. The quite recent vintage of the autonomy in these countries means that they have had a short timeframe over which to develop legislative, technical, and human resource capacity for migration policy generally, and refugee protection specifically. This has resulted in a deficit in the protection space for refugees. There are lessons here for other countries that face similar capacity constraints. Conditions in the local context will impact the degree to which these states can respond to the needs of refugees and contribute to the further development of the international refugee regime.

Representatives of the Kingdom have argued that notwithstanding article 43 of the Charter of the Kingdom of the Netherlands, the Caribbean autonomous countries are ultimately responsible for refugee protection in their respective jurisdictions. The Kingdom has therefore refused to intervene to settle concerns regarding the treatment of asylum seekers and other vulnerable migrants, a move that could be interpreted as a colonial maneuver.[101] Its provision of financial and technical assistance toward a policy of deterrence of the crisis in the Dutch Caribbean, however, underscores the region's dependence on the European metropole. Going forward, it will be important to settle the question of responsibility for refugee pro-

101 Intervention is not a popular option in the Caribbean autonomous countries. Where it has been employed, it has heightened tensions between the metropole Netherlands and its former colonies. Advisory Committee on Migration Affairs (n 27); Government of the Netherlands, 'Government response to Fundamental Rights in the Kingdom of the Netherlands' (2019) <www.advisorycouncilinternationalaffairs.nl/documents/government-responses/2019/04/04/government-response-to-fundamental-rights-in-the-kingdom-of-the-netherlands> accessed October 17, 2024.

tection, given the colonial legacies entrenched in the constitutional arrangement governing the relationship between the Netherlands and its former colonies.

Acknowledgements

I am grateful to staff at the Ministry of Foreign Affairs in the Netherlands for their invaluable assistance with sourcing archival material and for addressing my queries on treaty accession in the Kingdom. I would also like to thank the Law Library of the University of the West Indies (Mona, Jamaica) and the library of the University of Curaçao for facilitating access to reference materials.

CHAPTER 7

The Republic of China (Taiwan) and International Refugee Law: 1911–2024

Lili Song

1 Introduction

The Republic of China (ROC), also nowadays known as Taiwan, has dealt with refugees and asylum seekers since its establishment in 1911. It received around 60,000 White Russian refugees after the 1917 Russian Revolution[1] and around 20,000 Jewish refugees during the Second World War.[2] After it retreated from mainland China to the islands of Taiwan in 1949, the ROC has from time to time provided asylum to "defectors" from the People's Republic of China (PRC) and also accepted around 10,000 Indochinese refugees for resettlement between 1975 and 1990.[3] More recently, more than 1,000 Hong Kong activists have sought refuge in the ROC since 2019,[4] and several Ukrainians protested outside the Russian representative office in Taipei in 2022, calling on the ROC to enact a refugee law and assist Ukrainian asylum seekers.[5] The ROC has also received small numbers of refugees

1 Michael Marrus, *The Unwanted: European Refugees in the Twentieth Century* (OUP 1985) 60; Jishun Wang, 'Research on China's Participation in the League of Nations' Assistance of White Russian Refugees: 1921–1925' (Master's dissertation, Taiwan National Chengchi University 2011) 69, table 4.1.

2 Guang Pan, A Study of Jewish Refugees in China (1933–1945): History, Theories and the Chinese Pattern (Springer 2019) 29.

3 See Hao-Ming Lee, 'A Study of Taiwan's Asylum Policy' (Master's thesis, National Taiwan University 2017) 117 and 120 <https://doi.org/10.6342/NTU201700146> accessed October 11, 2024.

4 See Min-Yen Chiang and Candia Tong, 'From Non-Existence to Unrecognised Existence: The Evolution and Limitations of Taiwan's Hong Kong Asylum Mechanism After 2019' in Lara Momesso and Polina Ivanova (eds), *Refugees and Asylum Seekers in East Asia: Perspectives from Japan and Taiwan* (Palgrave Macmillan 2024).

5 Liam Gibson, 'Ukrainians in Taiwan Call for Asylum Law Outside Russian Representative Office: Protesters' Call Echoed by Taiwanese Civic Groups' *Taiwan News* (Taipei, March 1, 2022) <www.taiwannews.com.tw/news/4458701> accessed October 11, 2024.

and asylum seekers from other countries such as The Gambia, Colombia, and Uganda.[6]

The ROC is a somewhat peculiar case of a non-signatory to the 1951 Convention relating to the Status of Refugees and its 1967 Protocol (together and individually the Refugee Convention).[7] Following the adoption of the United Nations (UN) General Assembly Resolution 2758 on October 25, 1971,[8] the ROC lost its seat at the UN to the PRC and has not been recognized as a sovereign state by the UN. As a result, it has been generally excluded from the UN treaty system and could not become a signatory to the Refugee Convention even if it wanted to. Notably, the ROC is one of the few non-signatories that participated in the drafting process of the 1951 Convention.

The UN High Commissioner for Refugees (UNHCR) has not established any presence in the ROC and appears to have had limited interaction with ROC authorities since October 1971.[9] For example, UNHCR hardly engaged with ROC authorities during the Indochinese refugee crisis, has reportedly declined to be involved in the resettlement of PRC asylum seekers from the ROC to third countries, and appears to have had a very limited role in channelling ROC authorities' international aid to refugees outside the ROC.[10] In the absence of UNHCR's substantial involvement with and presence in

6 Ei-Leen Chiu, 'As a Human Being, Anywhere: Refugee Cases and Relevant Mechanisms in Taiwan' (2018) 4(4) *Taiwan Human Rights Journal* 155, 159.

7 Convention relating to the Status of Refugees 189 UNTS 137 (adopted July 28, 1951, entered into force April 22, 1954); Protocol relating to the Status of Refugees 606 UNTS 267 (adopted January 31, 1967, entered into force October 4, 1967).

8 *Restoration of the Lawful Rights of the People's Republic of China in the United Nations* GA Res 2758 (1971) <https://digitallibrary.un.org/record/192054> accessed October 11, 2024.

9 Lee (n 3) 139–49; Christine Lin, 'Examining Refugee Protection in Non-Signatories to the Refugee Convention and Protocol: Lessons Learned for the Taiwan Context' in Momesso and Ivanova (n 4) 63.

10 Lee (n 3) 141; Enben Lin, 'Taiwan's Experience and Current Situation Relating to Refugees and Asylum' (2022) <www.taiwansig.tw/index.php/政策報告/兩岸國際/8860-台灣處理難民及庇護經驗及現況>; Luan Sangguan, 'Mainland Political Refugees in Taiwan: Having 'Defected' to Democracy and Freedom And Still Without a Place to Settle' (2024) <www.wainao.me/wainao-reads/Mainland-Chinese-political-refugees-in-Taiwan-04222024> accessed October 15, 2024; Yi-Chen Wu, Shiuh-Shen Chien, 'Northernization for Breaking-through International Isolation: Taiwan's Trilateral Aid Cooperation in the Middle East Refugee Crisis and Beyond' (2021) 40(1) *Development Policy Review* e12556.

the ROC, civil society organizations such as the Taiwan Association for Human Rights and the ROC chapter of Amnesty International have long been a remarkable force in supporting refugees and advocating for a ROC refugee law consistent with the Refugee Convention.[11]

Indeed, the exclusion of the ROC from the UN treaty system does not mean that it cannot enact national laws consistent with the provisions of the Refugee Convention or voluntarily comply with those provisions in practice, if it wants to. For example, since 2002, the ROC has made notable efforts to draft a standalone refugee law with a view to incorporating provisions of the Refugee Convention into its domestic law (see Part 3 below).

This chapter examines the ROC's interaction with international refugee law (IRL), especially the Refugee Convention. It aims, primarily, to demonstrate that, despite the ROC's exclusion from the UN system since October 25, 1971, the Refugee Convention is nevertheless relevant and valued in the ROC. It also aims to show that the ROC vocally disagreed with Western-centered approaches during the drafting process of the 1951 Convention. A comprehensive examination of the ROC's current refugee law and policy and the underlying national political and social considerations, or a detailed historical analysis of the ROC's roles in the development of IRL, is beyond the ambition of this chapter.

The rest of this chapter proceeds in four parts. Part 2 offers observations about the ROC's participation in IRL making before 1971. Part 3 provides an overview of existing ROC law that incorporates or reflects IRL and the history and recent progress of the draft ROC Refugee Act. Part 4 considers ROC court cases in which arguments based on IRL were made. Part 5 concludes by situating the ROC experience within a wider context of the experience of other non-signatories to the Refugee Convention.

11 See chapter 4; Won Geun Choi, 'Advancing Refugee Protection from Bottom-Up: Case of the Asia Pacific Refugee Rights Network (APRRN)' (PhD dissertation, University of Hawai'i 2020) 12 and 137; Bonny Ling and Mariko Hayashi, 'Refugee Protection in Japan and Taiwan: Common Challenges and Ways Forward for Human Security' in Momesso and Ivanova (n 4) 38. See also Radio Free Asia, 'World Refugee Day: Taiwan Human Rights Groups Call for Refugee Legislation' (June 20, 2024) <www.rfa.org/mandarin/yataibaodao/gangtai/hx1-06202024105642.html> accessed October 11, 2024; Ann Maxon, 'Lawmakers, Groups Call for Passage of Refugee Act' *Taipei Times* (June 21, 2019) <www.taipeitimes.com/News/taiwan/archives/2019/06/21/2003717320> accessed October 11, 2024.

2 Participation in International Refugee Law Making before 1971

As a founding member of both the League of Nations (LN) and the UN, and a permanent member of the UN Security Council,[12] the ROC was involved in the drafting process of the Refugee Convention, the UNHCR Statute, the 1948 Universal Declaration of Human Rights (UDHR),[13] the 1967 Declaration on Territorial Asylum,[14] as well as the international refugee treaties concluded under the auspices of the LN.[15] It was represented on the 13-member Ad Hoc Committee tasked with drafting the 1951 Convention (Ad Hoc Committee)[16] and the UNHCR's Executive Committee (1958–October 1971).[17] ROC diplomat PC Chang, who was highly regarded for his work as Vice Chair of

---

12 When the Nationalist government was defeated by the Communist government in 1949, the ROC retreated to Taiwan but continued to hold the China seat at the UN.

13 Universal Declaration of Human Rights GA Res 217A (1948) (UDHR) <www.un.org/en/about-us/universal-declaration-of-human-rights> accessed October 11, 2024.

14 Declaration on Territorial Asylum GA Res 2312 (1967) <https://digitallibrary.un.org/record/203069> accessed October 11, 2024.

15 These treaties include: the Convention relating to the International Status of Refugees 159 LNTS 199 (signed October 28, 1933, entered into force June 13, 1935); the Arrangement Concerning the Extension to Other Categories of Refugees of Certain Measures Taken in Favour of Russian and Armenian Refugees 89 LNTS 63 (signed June 30, 1928, registered May 2, 1929); the Arrangement Relating to the Issue of Identity Certificates to Russian and Armenian Refugees 89 LNTS 47 (signed May 12, 1926, registered May 2, 1929); the Arrangement with Regard to the Issue of Certificates of Identity to Russian Refugees 13 LNTS 237 (signed July 5, 1922, registered November 16, 1922). See also *Plan for the Issue of a Certificate of Identity to Armenian Refugees* LN Doc CL 72(a) (May 31, 1924) <https://archives.ungeneva.org/plan-for-the-issue-of-a-certificate-of-identity-to-armenian-refugees-2> accessed October 11, 2024.

16 Ad Hoc Committee on Statelessness and Related Problems, later named Ad Hoc Committee on Refugees and Stateless Persons.

17 UNHCR, 'Executive Committee's Membership by Year of Admission of Members' <www.unhcr.org/media/excom-membership-date-admission-members> accessed October 11, 2024; *Increase in the Membership of the Executive* Committee of the Programme of the United Nations High Commissioner for Refugees ESC Res 682 (1958) <www.unhcr.org/publications/increase-membership-executive-committee-programme-united-nations-high-commissioner> accessed October 11, 2024; Sadruddin Aga Khan, 'Oral Statement of Prince Sadruddin Aga Khan, United Nations High Commissioner for Refugees, to UNHCR Headquarters Staff on 1 February 1972' (Geneva, February 1, 1972) <www.unhcr.org/3ae68fb314.html> accessed October 11, 2024: 'When the People's Republic became a member, it automatically had the right to avail itself of their seat on our governing body.' For background on the nomination of the ROC to the Executive Committee, see *Economic and Social Council Official Records, 26th Session: 1041st Meeting, Monday, 21 July 1958, Palais des Nations, Geneva* UN doc E/SR1041 (1958), paras 6, 23, and 27 <https://digitallibrary.un.org/record/817455> accessed October 11, 2024.

the drafting committee of the UDHR,[18] was influential in the drawing up of UDHR's article 14 (the right to seek and enjoy asylum).[19]

Janmyr rightly called for more scholarly attention to be paid to the stance and approaches taken by non-signatories that participated in the 1951 Convention's drafting.[20] This part responds to that call by offering three observations about the ROC's role, while also drawing upon its earlier involvement in the international refugee regime.

First, while it was absent from the Conference of Plenipotentiaries, the ROC actively participated in the drafting process of the 1951 Convention at all other stages. For example, 29 of the 43 meetings of the Ad Hoc Committee recorded remarks from the ROC representative.[21] At meetings of the Ad Hoc Committee, the UN Economic and Social Council, and the UN General Assembly, ROC representatives commented on the draft preamble, and draft articles 1 (refugee definition), 9 (provisional measures), 12 (personal status), 13 (movable and immovable property), 17 (wage-earning employment), 21 (housing), 29 (fiscal charges), 32 (expulsion), and 34 (naturalization).[22] The ROC was also one of the 58 states that provided a response regarding the proposed 1967 Protocol.[23]

---

18 See Eleanor Roosevelt, *On My Own* (Harper & Brothers 1958) 77; John Humphrey, *Human Rights and the United Nations: A Great Adventure* (Transnational Publishing 1984) 29.

19 See, for example, *Commission on Human Rights, Summary Record of the Fifty-Sixth Meeting* UN doc E/CN4/SR56 (June 2, 1948) 12 <https://documents.un.org/doc/undoc/gen/gl9/902/88/pdf/gl990288.pdf> accessed October 11, 2024; *Commission on Human Rights, Summary Record of the Fifty-Seventh Meeting* UN doc E/CN4/SR57 (June 3, 1948) 5 <https://documents.un.org/doc/undoc/gen/gl9/902/89/pdf/gl990289.pdf> accessed October 11, 2024.

20 Maja Janmyr, 'The 1951 Refugee Convention and Non-Signatory States: Charting a Research Agenda' (2021) 33(2) *International Journal of Refugee Law* 188, 193.

21 Summary records of those meetings are available at: <www.refworld.org>. See Ad Hoc Committee on Statelessness and Related Problems, First Session, January 16–February 16, 1950, New York; Second Session, August 14–25, 1950, Geneva.

22 See the summary records: ibid; Paul Weis (ed), The Refugee Convention, 1951: The Travaux Préparatoires Analysed, with a Commentary by the Late Dr Paul Weis (CUP 1995).

23 The ROC response was summarized in UNHCR, Proposed Measures to Extend the Personal Scope of the Convention relating to the Status of Refugees of 28 July 1951 UN doc A/AC96/346 (October 12, 1966) annex I, 2 <https://digitallibrary.un.org/record/3974488> accessed October 11, 2024. The discussion leading to the adoption of the 1967 Protocol (n 7) was relatively brief: Terje Einarsen, 'Background, Drafting History of the 1951 Convention and the 1967 Protocol' in Andreas Zimmermann, Felix Machts, and Jonas Dörschner (eds), *The 1951 Convention relating to the Status of Refugees and Its 1967 Protocol: A Commentary* (OUP 2011) paras 70–78.

Second, the ROC vocally objected to distinguishing between European and non-European refugees. For example, in 1950, it argued that:

> The definition proposed by the Economic and Social Council was too limited, both in space and time. It related mainly to certain categories of persons in Europe or regions bordering on Europe, other categories of IRO beneficiaries and victims of persecution which took place before 1 January 1951. Those restrictions were entirely arbitrary.[24]

Similarly, during deliberations of the International Refugee Organization's responsibilities in 1946, when some countries suggested postponing any detailed examination of non-European refugee situations because they considered European refugee situations to be more complicated and urgent, the ROC representative voiced his misgivings about any distinction being drawn between European and non-European refugees, arguing that the relevant UN resolution clearly obliged examination of non-European refugees' situations at the same stage.[25]

Third, from the 1920s to at least the early 1950s, the ROC's approach to IRL was significantly influenced by its experience of hosting White Russian and Jewish refugees and its familiarity with Western powers' extraterritorial consular jurisdiction, which existed in China from the 1840s to 1945.[26] For example, in 1921, the ROC representative emphasized that his government – while generally in agreement with other countries on assisting Russian refugees – strongly opposed the proposal of subjecting Russian refugees in China to another country's extraterritorial consular jurisdiction rather than to Chinese jurisdiction.[27] Similarly, in 1950, a ROC representative, agreeing that refugees should be treated in accordance with the laws of the host

24 *General Assembly, 5th Session, 3rd Committee, 329th Meeting, 29 November 1950* UN doc A/C3/SR329 (December 1950) para 16 <https://digitallibrary.un.org/record/819320> accessed October 11, 2024.

25 Special Committee on Refugees and Displaced Persons: Summary Record of 3rd Meeting, Held at Church House, Dean's Yard, London, on 9 April 1946 UN doc E/REF/11 (April 10, 1946) 2 <https://digitallibrary.un.org/record/843740> accessed October 11, 2024.

26 On extraterritorial consular jurisdiction in China, see Vi Kyuin Wellington Koo, *The Status of Aliens in China* (Columbia University 1912); Par Kristoffer Cassel, *Grounds of Judgment: Extraterritoriality and Imperial Power in Nineteenth-Century China and Japan* (OUP 2012).

27 Lee (n 3) 64–65.

country, stated that "[h]is own country would never agree to return to the practice of extraterritoriality, with which it had had bitter experience."[28]

The ROC did not become a party to the Refugee Convention before it lost representation at the UN.[29] The complicated legal and political issues surrounding the large numbers of PRC nationals seeking refuge in Hong Kong from the late 1940s to the early 1980s could have affected its readiness to ratify the Refugee Convention.[30] Incidentally, in 1949, the ROC lost effective control of mainland China and retreated to Taiwan, an island of about 36,000 square kilometers, bringing with it about one million mainlanders. The ROC's capacity to help refugees was thus significantly reduced after 1949, and the ROC representative made it clear in 1950 that his government was not in a position to accept refugees.[31]

---

28 UN Ad Hoc Committee on Statelessness and Related Problems, *First Session: Summary Record of the Eighth Meeting, 23 January 1950* UN doc E/AC32/SR8 (January 30, 1950) www.refworld.org/legal/leghist/ahcrsp/1950/en/43322 accessed October 11, 2024.

29 See Ministry of Foreign Affairs, Republic of China (Taiwan), 'List of International Human Rights and Humanitarian Treaties or Declarations Ratified by the ROC' (last updated October 11, 2024) <www.mofa.gov.tw/News.aspx?n=1159> accessed October 11, 2024. Some publications assert that the ROC signed the 1951 Convention (n 7) and the 1967 Protocol (n 7) in 1951 and 1967 respectively, but had not completed the UN procedure for depositing the instruments of ratification by October 1979: Meeting Minutes of the Committees of Internal Affairs and Foreign Relations and Defense, the Legislative Yuan, 9th Appointment, 1st session, 1st sitting, June 1, 2016; Guard of the Legislative Yuan, 105(45) 1 per Meinu You (member of the Legislative Yuan) <https://ppg.ly.gov.tw/ppg/download/communique1/work/105/45/LCIDC01_1054501_00005.doc> accessed October 11, 2024; Zhu-Han Lin, 'Why Does Taiwan Need a Refugee Act: Breaking Myths and Resolving Problems' (2013) 6(1) *Taiwan Human Rights Journal* 105, 107 <www.taiwanhrj.org/contents/399> accessed October 11, 2024; Taiwan Association for Human Rights, 'Joint Statement Calls the Legislative Yuan to Pass Refugee Act and NGO's Opinion on the Draft of Refugee Act in Taiwan' (August 28, 2012) 1 <www.tahr.org.tw/content/1112> accessed October 11, 2024.

30 The ROC's 'disinterest' in including the PRC refugees in Hong Kong in the proposed refugee definition under the 1951 Convention was noted: statement of Mr Robinson (Israel) in *Conference of Plenipotentiaries on the Status of Refugees and Stateless Persons: Summary Record of the 22nd Meeting, Held at the Palais des Nations, Geneva, on Monday, 16 July 1951* UN doc A/CONF2/SR22 (November 26, 1951) 7 <https://digitallibrary.un.org/record/696436> accessed October 11, 2024; Kazimierz Bem, 'The Coming of a "Blank Cheque": Europe, the 1951 Convention, and the 1967 Protocol' (2004) 16(4) *International Journal of Refugee Law* 609, 621. For discussion about relevant legal and political issues, see Edvard Hambro, *The Problem of Chinese Refugees in Hong Kong: Report Submitted to the United Nations High Commissioner for Refugees*, Leyden 1955; Glen Peterson, 'To Be or Not to Be a Refugee: The International Politics of the Hong Kong Refugee Crisis, 1949–55' (2008) 36(2) *Journal of Imperial and Commonwealth History* 171.

31 Weis (n 22) 18.

After the ROC's exclusion from the UN in 1971, it became impossible for it to accede to the Refugee Convention. Meanwhile, the ROC achieved rapid economic development in the 1970s and 1980s, lifted its martial law, and began its democratization process in 1987.[32] The ROC has faced shrinking diplomatic space and has devoted significant effort to gaining international recognition over the past few decades.[33] It is against this background that the discussion in Parts 3 and 4 should be understood.

3 Legislation Reflecting/Incorporating International Refugee Law

This section provides an overview of current ROC legal provisions relevant to refugee protection and the history of the draft Refugee Act. It demonstrates that the ROC has made notable efforts to incorporate the provisions of the Refugee Convention in its domestic law.

Currently, few ROC laws contain provisions specifically and explicitly mentioning refugees and asylum seekers. The Organization Act of the National Immigration Agency empowers the Agency to "determin[e] the status of potential refugees, and handl[e] matters relating to refugee asylum and sheltering."[34] According to the Employment Service Act,[35] refugees permitted to stay in the ROC "may, without their employers' initiation, apply on their own initiatives to the Central Competent Authority for permits to

32 See Hung-Mao Tien and Chyuan-Jeng Shiau, 'Taiwan's Democratization: A Summary' (1992–1993) 155(4) *World Affairs* 58.

33 See Cassandra Veney and Richard Payne, 'Taiwan and Africa: Taipei's Continuing Search for International Recognition' (2001) 36(4) *Journal of Asian and African Studies* 437; Anthony Van Fossen, 'The Struggle for Recognition: Diplomatic Competition Between China and Taiwan in Oceania' (2007) 12 *Journal of Chinese Political Science* 125; Theodor Tudoroiu, 'Taiwan in the Caribbean: A Case Study in State De-Recognition' (2017) 25(2) *Asian Journal of Political Science* 194.

34 Organization Act of the National Immigration Agency, Ministry of the Interior (adopted November 30, 2005, amended August 21, 2013) art 2(9), official English translation available at: <https://law.moj.gov.tw/ENG/LawClass/LawAll.aspx?pcode=D0000135> accessed October 11, 2024. This Act is very short, containing only eight concise articles.

35 Employment Service Act, Ministry of Labor (adopted May 8, 1992, last amended May 10, 2023) art 51, official English translation available at: <https://law.moj.gov.tw/ENG/LawClass/LawAll.aspx?pcode=N0090001> accessed October 11, 2024.

engage in work";[36] they are also exempt from a number of other restrictions that are normally applicable to foreign workers.[37] In practice, however, refugees are unable to fully enjoy the benefit of such Employment Service Act provisions because, in the absence of specific legal provisions on refugee status determination and refugee rights, they are issued the same identity document and receive the same treatment as stateless persons.[38]

Also worth mentioning are the 2009 Act to Implement the International Covenant on Civil and Political Rights and the International Covenant on Economic, Social and Cultural Rights (Implementation Act)[39] and article 16.4 of the Immigration Act.[40] The Implementation Act gives domestic legal status to human rights provisions in the ICCPR and the ICESCR.[41] As a result, the principle of *non-refoulement* under article 7 of the ICCPR has domestic legal status in the ROC.[42] Article 16.4 of the Immigration Act does not use the term "refugee;"[43] however, members of the Legislative Yuan (the ROC's highest executive organ) explicitly referred to the principle of *non-refoulement* in the Refugee Convention in their proposal to amend the

36 ibid art 51(2).

37 ibid art 51(1).

38 Lee (n 3) 115–16. No evidence suggests that things have changed since 2017.

39 Act to Implement the International Covenant on Civil and Political Rights and the International Covenant on Economic, Social and Cultural Rights, Ministry of Justice (adopted April 22, 2009) (Implementation Act), official English translation available at: <https://law.moj.gov.tw/ENG/LawClass/LawAll.aspx?pcode=I0020028> accessed October 11, 2024. For more discussion about the Implementation Act, see: Yu-Jie Chen, 'Isolated but Not Oblivious: Taiwan's Acceptance of the Two Major Human Rights Covenants' in Jerome A Cohen, William P Alford, and Chang-Fa Lo (eds), *Taiwan and International Human Rights: A Story of Transformation* (Springer 2019).

40 Immigration Act, Ministry of the Interior (adopted June 28, 2023), official English translation available at: <https://law.moj.gov.tw/ENG/LawClass/LawAll.aspx?pcode=D0080132> accessed October 11, 2024.

41 International Covenant on Civil and Political Rights 999 UNTS 171 (adopted December 19, 1966, entered into force March 23, 1976); International Covenant on Economic, Social and Cultural Rights 993 UNTS 3 (adopted December 19, 1966, entered into force January 3, 1976).

42 This was affirmed in the Taipei High Administrative Court, September 8, 2020, Minguo 109 (Quan) No 25 at 8.

43 Article 16.4 of the Immigration Act (n 40) states that a stateless person from India or Nepal who has entered the Taiwan Area before 29st June 2016 [sic] and cannot be repatriated shall be permitted to reside in the Taiwan Area by the National Immigration Agency if his/her status has been identified by the review committee meeting which convened by the central authorities for the Mongolian and Tibetan affairs.

article in 2009.[44] Courts[45] have also noted that article 16.4 of the Immigration Act was amended for the purpose of protecting refugees' basic human rights in accordance with the UDHR, the Refugee Convention, and the Declaration on Territorial Asylum.

In 2002, the Executive Yuan decided that a Refugee Act should be drafted, with a view of giving domestic legal effect to the Refugee Convention.[46] During the drafting process, consideration was also given to both the UDHR and the Declaration on Territorial Asylum[47] and comparative studies of refugee laws in eight countries – namely the United States, Canada, France, New Zealand, Australia, Japan, South Korea, and Brazil – were carried out.[48] For context, in 2000 the ROC government under the administration of the then newly elected Democratic Progressive Party declared human rights as an integral foundation of Taiwan's nationhood and began to seek to pass a series of human rights-related laws incorporating core international human rights treaties.[49]

Several drafts have since been submitted to the Legislative Yuan for deliberation.[50] The latest draft,[51] submitted in 2016, was accompanied by notes

44 Meeting Minutes of the Legislative Yuan, vol 98, issue 5, para 1 <https://judgment.judicial.gov.tw/FJUD/data.aspx?ty=JD&id=TPBA%2c109%2c%e5%85%a8%2c25%2c20200908%2c1> accessed October 11, 2024; Meeting Minutes of the Legislative Yuan, vol 98, issue 3 <https://tpa.judicial.gov.tw/tw/dl-108872-d7b2c88bfcb34f85a1fa5e24e433a3ce.html> accessed October 11, 2024.

45 Taipei High Administrative Court, March 10, 2020, Minguo 109 (Ting) No 12 at 10, 14, and 6; Supreme Administrative Court, May 21, 2020, Minguo 109 (Cai) No 789 at 8; Supreme Administrative Court, May 21, 2020, Minguo 109 (Cai) No 788 at 6; Supreme Administrative Court, May 21, 2020, Minguo 109 (Cai) No 787 at 7; Supreme Administrative Court, May 21, 2020, Minguo 109 (Cai) No 786 at 8.

46 Ministry of Interior, 'Research Project Report: The Progress of Establishing the Refugee Rules in Taiwan' (2010) app 5, 8 <www.immigration.gov.tw/media/6020/我國難民法制訂現況自行研究報告.pdf> accessed October 11, 2024.

47 ibid 6.

48 ibid app 5.

49 Fort Fu-Te Liao, 'Partly Virtual, Partly Real: Taiwan's Unique Interaction with International Human Rights Instruments' (2010) 16 *Asian Yearbook of International Law* 25, 29; Taiwan National Human Rights Commission, 'International Conventions' (2024) <https://nhrc.cy.gov.tw/en-US/cp.aspx?n=8693> accessed December 3, 2024.

50 For chronologies of the drafts, see Ministry of Interior (n 46); Kristina Kironska, 'Taiwan's Road to an Asylum Law: Who, When, How, and Why Not Yet?' (2022) 23(2) *Human Rights Review* 241; Kai-Xuan Lin, 'A Study on the Legislation of Refugee Law in Taiwan' (Master's thesis, National Taiwan University 2018), ch 3 <www.airitilibrary.com/Common/Click_DOI?DOI=10.6342%2fNTU201804316> accessed October 11, 2024.

51 <www.ly.gov.tw/Pages/ashx/File.ashx?FilePath=~/File/Attach/701/File_2644.pdf> accessed October 11, 2024.

expressly referring to the Refugee Convention, the UDHR, and the Declaration on Territorial Asylum. The notes specifically refer to articles 33, 28, and 1 of the 1951 Convention in relation to draft articles 8, 13, and 14. The draft defines a refugee as someone who satisfies the Refugee Convention definition or who flees wars or natural disasters (article 3).[52] It recognizes refugee status claimants' right to legal consultation, medical care, and adequate standards of living while their claims are being assessed (article 7); prohibits the deportation of refugee status claimants (article 8); excludes the application of relevant statutory provisions on penalization of unauthorized entry to refugees (article 11); requires relevant local authorities to issue identity documents to recognized refugees; and allows refugees to apply for permanent residence and naturalization (article 13). These draft provisions are generally in line with the Refugee Convention.[53]

However, the 2016 draft – only 17 articles long – contains no provision on remedies and appeal procedures and is silent on many refugee rights mentioned in the 1951 Convention, such as freedom of movement, the right to work, and access to public education. Draft article 10 allows exclusion from refugee protection under certain circumstances, including when the claimant passed through or traveled from a third country that could have processed their refugee status application (article 10.3). This exception has attracted criticism.[54] Draft article 12 also allows relevant authorities to impose a quota for how many people may receive refugee recognition. Thus, there is arguably room for improvement.

None of the drafts submitted to the Legislative Yuan were able to proceed beyond their second reading.[55] Lack of consensus on multiple crucial issues, including whether a standalone asylum law was necessary at all, made it

---

52 This does not include those from the PRC and Hong Kong. On the difficult and complex issue of the status of PRC, Hong Kong, and Macau asylum seekers in ROC law, see Lee (n 3) chs 4.2 and 5.2.2.

53 Some issues remain, eg draft art 8 does not mirror exactly art 33 of the 1951 Convention (n 7). For further discussion about issues with the draft provisions, see Taiwan Association for Human Rights (n 29). The statement critiques the 2012 draft Refugee Act, but many issues identified in it remain in the 2016 draft.

54 Longkuan Wang, 'A Few Issues About the Draft Refugee Act' (2017) 216 *Wangguo Falu* 24, 27; Ei-Leen Qiu, 'Refugee Asylum in Taiwan: Can the Administrative Mechanism Replace a Refugee Act?' (Initium Media, September 23, 2020) <https://theinitium.com/zh-hans/opinion/202000923-opinion-taiwan-refugee-protection> accessed October 11, 2024.

55 Ministry of Interior (n 46) 3; Kironska (n 50) 246. For information about ROC legislative procedure, see Legislative Yuan, 'Legislative Procedure' <www.ly.gov.tw/EngPages/Detail.aspx?nodeid=335&pid=43232> accessed October 21, 2024.

difficult for the drafts to move further in the legislative process.[56] Nevertheless, there has been some notable recent progress. In 2022, the ROC government identified refugee rights as one of eight prioritized human rights issues, and pledged to "[c]odify legal mechanisms for refugees to seek asylum and clarify related application procedures."[57] The National Immigration Agency conducted a further comparative study of refugee cases from several countries, such as South Korea, Japan, the United States, Canada, and the United Kingdom in 2023, and is expected to submit a new draft Refugee Act to the Legislative Yuan in the second half of 2024.[58]

Although the 2016 draft Refugee Act has not been enacted, it appears to have some persuasive value to ROC courts. In a 2020 decision, the Taipei High Administrative Court stated that the draft Act could serve as a point of reference for the relevant legal principles.[59] On appeal, the Supreme Administrative Court endorsed that statement[60] and further referred to article 10 of the draft Refugee Act when it discussed the notion of safe third country (see Part 4 below).[61]

4 International Refugee Law in ROC Domestic Courts

Since 2004, ROC lawyers have advanced arguments based on the Refugee Convention and the UDHR in nearly a dozen cases before ROC domestic courts,[62] including the Supreme Administrative Court, the final court for all administrative litigation matters in the ROC.[63] As the ROC has a civil law

56 Kironska (n 50) 257.

57 Executive Yuan, 'National Human Rights Action Plan' (May 18, 2022) <https://english.ey.gov.tw/News3/9E5540D592A5FECD/db879e12-f6bb-46d8-ba80-851185c963dd> accessed October 11, 2024.

58 Radio Taiwan International, '2nd Day of ICERD International Review: Committee Chairman Urged Taiwan to Pass Refugee Act as Soon as Possible' (April 23, 2024) <www.rti.org.tw/news/view/id/2203614> accessed October 11, 2024. As of December 3, 2024, no public information suggests that the new draft has been submitted.

59 Taipei High Administrative Court, August 19, 2020, Minguo 109 (Su) No 87 at 16.

60 Supreme Administrative Court, May 16, 2023, Minguo 110 (Shang) No 655 at 4.

61 ibid 18. Presumably, the Court was referring to the 2016 draft.

62 These cases may be found in the Judicial Yuan Judgment Online Database <https://judgment.judicial.gov.tw/FJUD/default.aspx> using the search phrase '難民地位公約' [Refugee Convention]. In all cases, IRL-based arguments were made supplementary to arguments based on domestic law.

63 For discussion about the ROC court system, see: Judicial Yuan, 'Understanding the Courts' (6 November 6, 2019, last updated 18 October 18, 2023) <www.judicial.gov.tw/

system, judicial decisions are generally not binding as precedent.[64] Nevertheless, as demonstrated below, these cases illustrate that IRL is valued by ROC human rights and immigration lawyers and, gradually and increasingly, by the ROC judiciary.

4.1 *Early Attempts in District Courts: 2004–2009*

The earlier cases happened to be criminal cases before district courts concerning PRC asylum seekers who were arrested and prosecuted for unauthorized entry into the ROC.[65] In a 2004 case before the Yilan District Court, counsel for the applicant provided copies of the UDHR and the 1951 Convention for the Court's consideration and submitted, inter alia, that the applicant had the right to seek asylum according to article 14 of the UDHR,[66] met the criteria for refugee status under the Refugee Convention, and therefore should not be deported or subjected to unnecessary restrictions of his freedom of movement.[67] Acknowledging that Taiwan had not, and could not, become a party to the Refugee Convention,[68] counsel for the applicant argued the following:

1. As a member of the international community, Taiwan should voluntarily abide by the human rights principles enshrined in the UDHR, in whose drafting Taiwan had participated.
2. Refugee protection is a matter of universal value where people's lives and freedom are at stake, and refugee rights should be regarded as fundamental human rights protected by the ROC constitution.
3. Given that President Chen Shui-bian had announced his government's determination to implement the human right ideals embodied in international treaties, in accordance with the principle of good faith, the

en/cp-1613-80062-a7043-2.html> accessed 11 October 11, 2024; Wen-Chen Chang, 'Courts and Judicial Reform in Taiwan: Gradual Transformations Towards the Guardian of Constitutionalism and Rule of Law' in Jiunn-Rong Yeh and Wen-Chen Chang (eds), *Asian Courts in Context* (CUP 2014).

64 A few decisions of the Supreme Court and the Supreme Administrative Court regarding the interpretation or application of certain laws or regulations have been given the status of binding precedents: see Chang (n 63) 164.

65 Taiwan Yilan District Court, November 19, 2004, Minguo 93 (Ti) No 2 Criminal Law Ruling; Fujian Jinmen District Court, June 30, 2009, Minguo 98 (Shang) No 8 Criminal Law Ruling.

66 Art 14.1 of the UDHR provides: "Everyone has the right to seek and to enjoy in other countries asylum from persecution."

67 Taiwan Yilan District Court (n 65).

68 "Taiwan" is the term used in the judgment's summary of counsel's arguments.

Taiwanese government should be seen as having undertaken an obligation to abide by relevant international human rights treaties.

The Court, in its relatively brief reasoning, made no reference to the UDHR or to the Refugee Convention, dismissing the application entirely based on ROC domestic law.

In a 2009 case before the Jinmen District Court, the applicant, citing article 14 of the UDHR and noting the ROC's longing for international recognition of its statehood, submitted that the ROC government had a "moral obligation" to provide him with asylum, claiming that only if the ROC did so would it earn respect from other countries.[69] He argued that as he was in danger for political reasons, he had a right to enter the ROC to seek asylum and should not be penalized for doing so. The Court stated, with little explanation, that regardless of whether the applicant could rely on the UDHR and the Refugee Convention to apply for asylum, his unauthorized entry was not legally justifiable.

It is possible that the Legislative Yuan's 2002 decision to draft a refugee law inspired the aforementioned cases, given the time proximity. While the IRL-based arguments did not succeed in any of the cases, the courts' reaction to those arguments differed. The Yilan District Court did not address the IRL-based arguments at all. In contrast, although the Jinmen District Court summarily dismissed the IRL-based arguments, it referred to the UDHR (which the applicant mentioned) as well as the Refugee Convention (which the applicant did not seem to mention), indicating that the Court probably saw some relevance of IRL.

4.2 *Two Cases in the Taipei High Administrative Court: 2010–2019*

The two cases discussed in this section were decided after the enactment of the Implementation Act in December 2009. In a 2010 case before the Taipei High Administrative Court,[70] the applicant was a PRC asylum seeker who entered the ROC using a false identity and who was seeking long-term residence in the ROC.[71] Counsel for the applicant advanced the following arguments. First, the applicant had a right to seek and enjoy asylum according

69 Fujian Jinmen District Court (n 65). This case was decided before the enactment of the Implementation Act in December 2009.

70 Taipei High Administrative Court, October 28, 2010, Minguo 99 (Su) No 1395.

71 In this particular case, he had been given permission to stay temporarily.

to article 14 of the UDHR. Counsel asserted that the UDHR had become part of customary international law and that the Overall Explanatory Notes for the Implementation Act recognized the UDHR as part of the International Bill of Human Rights.[72]

Second, the applicant was a refugee under the 1951 Convention as he was threatened and harassed by PRC authorities because of his pursuit for democracy and human rights. It was impossible for him to apply in the PRC for ROC entry permission. Those who are persecuted by their own government often struggle to obtain a passport, making it impossible for them to apply for pre-authorization to enter another country legally. That is why article 31 of the 1951 Convention requires states not to penalize refugees for their illegal entry or presence "provided they present themselves without delay to the authorities and show good cause for their illegal entry or presence." The applicant immediately handed himself in to ROC officials upon entry and explained his situation. He should not have been penalized for his initial unauthorized entry.[73]

Thirdly, and more importantly, the ROC had drafted a Refugee Act in accordance with the principles enshrined in the UDHR and the Refugee Convention. The draft Act provides that article 6 (on unauthorized entry) of the National Security Law should not apply to refugees from Mainland China, Hong Kong, or Macau and that rules governing naturalization and long-term residence of foreigners should apply to such refugees.[74] Thus, the applicant should not have been penalized for unauthorized entry and should have been eligible for long-term residence in the ROC.

The Taipei High Administrative Court did not comment on whether the applicant was a refugee. Noting that the applicant relied on the UDHR and the Refugee Convention to challenge the Ministry of Interior's decision to deny him long-term residence, the Court said that "what those instruments required was that regarding refugee determination and protection, states should have legislative and policy provisions favorable to refugees."[75] It fur-

72 Taipei High Administrative Court No 1395 (n 70) 5–6. The Explanatory Notes are available at: <https://law.kcg.gov.tw/human/human2.pdf> accessed October 11, 2024.

73 Counsel also argued that the illegality of his initial entry had been "cured" when the ROC authorities granted him permission to stay temporarily.

74 The applicant was penalized for illegal entry in accordance with art 6 of the ROC National Section Law.

75 Taipei High Administrative Court No 1395 (n 70) 13.

ther stated that the draft Refugee Act had not been passed and therefore could not be applied in the current case.[76] The Court declined to consider whether the applicant should be eligible for long-term residence had the draft Refugee Act been in force.[77]

In a 2015 case concerning the deportation of two PRC asylum seekers before the Taipei High Administrative Court,[78] the applicants' primary argument was that they would be subjected to torture or cruel, inhuman, or degrading treatment upon return and that their deportation would therefore violate of the principle of *non-refoulement* under article 7 of the ICCPR (which has been given domestic legal effect by way of the Implementation Act). They also argued that they were refugees as they were persecuted or feared being persecuted because of their political opinion, citing the Refugee Convention, the UDHR, the Declaration on Territorial Asylum, and article 3 of the draft Refugee Act.[79]

The Court did not explicitly address the refugee claim and made no express reference to the Refugee Convention (or to the UDHR or the Declaration on Territorial Asylum). However, in rejecting the torture argument, it gave two reasons in the following sequence:

1. Evidence before the Court showed no connection between the applicants' political opinion and the alleged persecutory measures taken by the PRC authorities.
2. There was no credible evidence showing that the applicants would be at risk of torture or cruel, inhuman, or degrading treatment in the PRC.

That the Court discussed the nexus issue first possibly suggests that it attached considerable weight to the issue. A nexus between persecution feared and one's political opinion is a key element of the Convention's refugee definition, whereas it is not a requirement for invoking the obligation of *non-refoulement* under the Convention against Torture[80] or the ICCPR. The

76 ibid 13.

77 ibid 13. On appeal, the Supreme Administrative Court allowed the appeal based on ROC domestic law and did not address the Refugee Convention: see Supreme Administrative Court, October 13, 2011, Minguo 100 (Pan) No 1813.

78 Taipei High Administrative Court, December 31, 2015, Minguo 104 (Ting) No 114.

79 ibid [2].

80 Convention Against Torture and Other Cruel, Inhuman or Degrading Treatment or Punishment 1465 UNTS 85 (adopted December 10, 1984, entered into force June 26, 1987).

fact that the nexus issue came up probably indicates that the judges saw the relevance of the refugee claim and had the Convention refugee definition on their mind even though they refrained from saying so.[81]

The IRL-based arguments advanced in the 2010 and 2015 cases involved more substantial legal articulation, compared to those advanced in the 2004 and 2009 cases mentioned above. The Taipei High Administrative Court appears to be more willing to engage with IRL than the Yilan and Kinmen district courts. In the 2010 case, the Taipei High Administrative Court gave an opinion – albeit a very brief one – on what the 1951 Convention generally required states to do; in the 2010 case, it effectively applied the nexus requirement in the refugee definition in the 1951 Convention.

4.3 *Tibetan Cases in the Supreme Administrative Court and the Taipei High Administrative Court: 2020–2024*

More recently, IRL-based arguments have also been advanced in a series of cases[82] concerning Tibetans facing deportation to India or Nepal (where they lived in exile for many years) who were found ineligible for ROC residency under article 16.4 of the Immigration Act.[83] In a 2020 case before the Taipei High Administrative Court,[84] the applicant, inter alia, submitted the following:

1. Certain principles enshrined in the Refugee Convention, most notably the principle of *non-refoulement*, had become part of customary international law, implying that the ROC was bound by such principles; if the deportation of the applicant would be inconsistent with the Refugee Convention, the deportation process should be terminated.[85]

81 Chiu, who attended the hearing virtually, opined that the Court dismissed the application based on the Refugee Convention and failed to sufficiently consider the risk of torture or cruel, inhuman, or degrading treatment: Chiu (n 6) 160–61.

82 Supreme Administrative Court No 655 (n 60); Supreme Administrative Court Nos 786–89 (n 45); Taipei High Administrative Court No 12 (n 45); Taipei High Administrative Court No 87 (n 59); Taipei High Administrative Court No 25 (n 42); Supreme Administrative Court, June 30, 2020, Minguo 109 (Cai) No 1082; Taipei High Administrative Court, March 6, 2020, Minguo 109 (Ting) No 13; Taipei High Administrative Court, July 13, 2023, Minguo 109 (Su) No 88.

83 For discussion about Tibetan asylum seekers in the ROC, see Mei-Lin Pan and Dolma Tsering, 'The Lived Experience of Tibetan Refugees in Taiwan: Contesting Rights to Work, Residence, and Citizenship' in Momesso and Ivanova (n 4).

84 Taipei High Administrative Court No 13 (n 82) 6.

85 ibid 7–8. The applicant did not seem to explain whether the deportation was inconsistent with those instruments.

2. The Overall Explanatory Notes to the draft Refugee Act prepared by the Executive Yuan acknowledged that everyone had the right to seek and enjoy asylum according to the UDHR, the Refugee Convention, and the Declaration on Territorial Asylum.[86]

In its judgment, the Court found that "the applicant ha[d] not explained whether she indeed qualifie[d] for refugee status; therefore, there [was] no issue of applying the relevant customary international law (eg the principle of *non-refoulement*),"[87] seemingly accepting that the principle of *non-refoulement* under the 1951 Convention was part of customary international law and that if the applicant proved to be a refugee, the principle of *non-refoulement* would apply.

In several decisions delivered in 2020,[88] the Supreme Administrative Court explicitly stated that deportation orders relating to the applicants should be considered in light of the amendment history of article 16.4 of the Immigration Act and the principle of *non-refoulement* in international law.[89] The Court noted that article 16.4 was amended in 2009 in accordance with the *non-refoulement* principle in the Refugee Convention and then in 2016 in accordance with the Implementation Act.[90] Referring to article 7 of the ICCPR and the UN Human Rights Committee's 1992 General Comment No 20,[91] it further noted that the *non-refoulement* principle had domestic legal effect in the ROC following the enactment of the 2010 Implementation Act.[92] In light of the above, the fact that article 16.4 specifically allows stateless Tibetans who were formerly in exile in India or Nepal to obtain ROC residency indicates that the Tibetans deserve protection against *refoulement*.[93] Thus, deportation of the applicants without verification of their nationality status may have violated the principle of *non-refoulement*.[94]

86 ibid 6.

87 ibid 11. No issues of torture or arbitrary deprivation of life were raised in this case.

88 Supreme Administrative Court Nos 786–89 (n 45).

89 Supreme Administrative Court No 789 (n 45) 7.

90 ibid 8.

91 Human Rights Committee, CCPR General Comment No 20: Art 7 (Prohibition of Torture, or Other Cruel, Inhuman or Degrading Treatment or Punishment) 44 (March 10, 1992) <www.refworld.org/legal/general/hrc/1992/en/11086> accessed October 11, 2024.

92 Supreme Administrative Court No 789 (n 45) 9.

93 ibid 10.

94 ibid 10.

In a decision delivered in 2023,[95] the Supreme Administrative Court provided more guidance on the principle of *non-refoulement* under article 33 of the 1951 Convention:

1. The principle of *non-refoulement* applies not only to refugees but also to asylum seekers.[96]
2. However, the principle of *non-refoulement* does not impose on states a duty to provide asylum, only a duty to guarantee the right to seek asylum and access to asylum procedures.[97]

The court noted the notion of safe third countries, referring, with approval, to article 10 of the draft Refugee Act, which authorizes the ROC to deny asylum to those entitled to protection elsewhere.[98] The Court found that, as the applicants' Nepalese citizenship had been verified and they enjoyed protection there,[99] deportation of the applicants would not amount to *refoulement*.[100]

In these most recent decisions, the Taipei High Administrative Court and the Supreme Administrative Court discussed the *non-refoulement* principle and the notion of a safe third country a lot more substantially – and seemingly in a more favorable light – than in any previous case. Such unprecedented extent of discussion, as well as the courts' readiness to acknowledge that article 16.4 of the Immigration Act reflected the *non-refoulement* principle in the Refugee Convention, may well be seen as the courts' increased receptiveness to IRL.

5 Conclusion

As this chapter has shown, the ROC's interaction with the Refugee Convention has occurred in two ways. On the one hand, it actively participated in the drafting process of the 1951 Convention. While the original text of the 1951 Convention may reflect Western dominance,[101] the ROC – as

95 Supreme Administrative Court No 655 (n 60).

96 ibid 13.

97 ibid 13.

98 ibid 18.

99 ibid 17–18.

100 ibid 19.

101 James Hathaway, 'A Reconsideration of the Underlying Premise of Refugee Law' (1990) 31(1) *Harvard International Law Journal* 129; Ulrike Krause, 'Colonial Roots of the 1951 Refugee Convention and Its Effects on the Global Refugee Regime' (2021) 24 *Journal of International Relations and Development* 627.

demonstrated in Part 2 above – was vocal in its disagreement to a Western-centered approach in the drafting process. This, when viewed together with the experience of other non-Western countries that participated in the drafting process such as Saudi Arabia, Pakistan, India, and Türkiye,[102] illustrates that non-Western participants – including those that remain non-signatories – did not passively accept, and were not complacent to, the views of their Western counterparts.

On the other hand, this chapter has also demonstrated how the Refugee Convention has influenced both domestic legislation and judicial decisions in the ROC over the past 25 years or so. As shown in Parts 3 and 4, the Refugee Convention is clearly relevant and valued. While the ROC's exclusion from the UN may be unique as a reason for non-accession to the Refugee Convention, the legislature's willingness to incorporate its key principles in domestic law, as well as the judiciary's recent endorsement of the principle of *non-refoulement*, are not exceptional among non-signatories. As shown in other chapters in this volume,[103] many non-signatories have been influenced by the Refugee Convention in various ways. The ROC case, however, illustrates in particular that the influence of the Refugee Convention is able to reach jurisdictions lacking substantial UNHCR presence and even UN membership.

The ROC's former president Tsai Ing-Wen once stated that "although the ROC is not a member of the UN, its people's desire to contribute to the international community is no less than that of the people from any [UN] member states."[104] Looking forward, in view of the recent progress in the draft Refugee Act and recent court cases mentioned above, there are reasons to believe that the Refugee Convention will continue to be relevant and valued in the ROC.

102 See Maja Janmyr and Charlotte Lysa, 'Saudi Arabia and the International Refugee Regime' (2023) 35(3) *International Journal of Refugee Law* 251–71; Jay Ramasubramanyam and Ulrike Krause, 'Need for Critical Reimagination: Colonial Legacy of the 1951 Refugee Convention' in Jane Freedman and Glenda Santana de Andrade (eds) *Research Handbook on Asylum and Refugee Policy* (Edward Elgar 2024) 39–51; Özlem Gürakar Skribeland, 'The Turkish Council of State's Engagement with International Refugee Law in Cases Involving "Non-European" Refugees' (2025) *International Journal of Refugee Law* <https://doi.org/10.1093/ijrl/eeae041> accessed February 2, 2025.

103 See chapters 4, 5, 8, and 3.

104 Office of the President, Republic of China (Taiwan), 'President: On Refugee Issues, Taiwan Should Not Isolate Itself from Other Countries' (2016) <www.president.gov.tw/NEWS/20485> accessed October 15, 2024.

CHAPTER 8

From Global Commitments to Local Implementation: A Legal Analysis of Thailand's National Screening Mechanism

Jittawadee Chotinukul

1 Introduction

The primary responsibility for refugee status determination (RSD) lies with states.[1] Nevertheless, the United Nations High Commissioner for Refugees (UNHCR) may conduct RSD under its mandate,[2] usually in states that have not ratified the 1951 Convention[3] and/or the 1967 Protocol,[4] or in states parties that lack a fair and efficient national asylum system.[5] Because effective refugee protection requires government action in tandem with UNHCR's own increasingly criticized RSD processes,[6] UNHCR has encouraged states to assume responsibility for the determination of refugee status.[7] Indeed, over the last 20 years, UNHCR has been involved in RSD transition processes

1 UNHCR, 'Note on Determination of Refugee Status under International Instruments', EC/SCP/5 (August 24, 1977) para 7; Executive Committee of the High Commissioner's Programme, 'Conclusion No 81 (XLVIII) on General Conclusion on International Protection' (1997) para (d); UNGA Res 57/187 (2003) UN doc A/RES/57/187, paras 7–8; UNHCR, 'Refugee Status Determination' EC/67/SC/CPR.12 (2016) paras 2, 14.

2 Statute of the Office of the United Nations High Commissioner for Refugees A/RES/428(V) (December 14, 1950) para 8.

3 Convention relating to the Status of Refugees (adopted July 28, 1951, entered into force April 22, 1954).

4 Protocol relating to the Status of Refugees (adopted January 31, 1967, entered into force October 4, 1967).

5 UNHCR, 'Refugee Status Determination' EC/67/SC/CPR.12 (2016) para 2.

6 See Michael Alexander, 'Refugee Status Determination by UNHCR' (1999) 11(2) *International Journal of Refugee Law* 251; Michael Kagan, 'The Beleaguered Gatekeeper: Protection Challenges Posed by UNHCR Refugee Status Determination' (2006) 18(1) *International Journal of Refugee Law* 1; Martin Jones, 'Refugee Status Determination: Three Challenges' (2009) 32 *Forced Migration Review* 53.

7 Executive Committee of the High Commissioner's Programme, 'Conclusion No 8 (XXVIII) on Determination of Refugee Status' (1977) para (d); Executive Committee of the High Commissioner's Programme, 'Conclusion No 11 (XXIX) General' (1978) para (i); UNHCR, 'Refugee Status Determination' EC/67/SC/CPR.12 (2016) para 14.

in more than 30 states, most of them states parties.[8] Instances of RSD transition from UNHCR to non-signatory states remain rare, with the notable exception of Hong Kong as a non-signatory territory.[9]

Since the adoption of the 2016 New York Declaration for Refugees and Migrants (New York Declaration),[10] the 2018 Global Compact on Refugees (GCR),[11] and the establishment of the Global Refugee Forum (GRF), we have nonetheless witnessed an increased intention of non-signatory states to assume responsibility for determining the status of individuals in need of protection. This has been expressed via voluntary pledges, made at global forums, to improve and strengthen national asylum systems, including through legislation.[12] Thailand is a case in point, and the focus of this chapter.

Following its global commitments to develop a screening mechanism, Thailand, for the first time in history, enacted the 2019 "Regulation of the Office of the Prime Minister on the Screening of Aliens Who Enter into the Kingdom and Are Unable to Return to the Country of Origin BE 2562"[13] (Regulation on the National Screening Mechanism (NSM)). This Regulation identifies persons in need of protection. Almost four years later, in March 2023, the government published the "Notification of the Protected Person Screening Committee on the Criteria, Procedures, and Conditions for Determining an Application for Protected Person Status"[14] (Notification on the

---

8 For the list of countries, see UNHCR, 'Refugee Status Determination' EC/67/SC/CPR.12 (2016) para 14; Wilbert van Hövell and others, 'Providing for Protection: Assisting States with the Assumption of Responsibility for Refugee Status Determination: A Preliminary Review' (2014) *UNHCR Policy Development and Evaluation Service* (PDES) PDES/2014/01, 23–24, footnote 43; Caroline Nalule and Derya Ozkul, 'Exploring RSD Handover from UNHCR to States' (2020) 65 *Forced Migration Review* 27, footnote 1.

9 See Rachel Li, Isaac Shaffer and Lynette Nam, 'Hong Kong's Unified Screening Mechanism: Form over Substance' (2021) 67 *Forced Migration Review* 48.

10 UNGA, New York Declaration for Refugees and Migrants, UN doc A/RES/71/1 (September 19, 2016).

11 Global Compact on Refugees, as contained in A/73/12 (Part II) (December 17, 2018) UN doc A/RES/73/151.

12 See UNHCR, 'Pledges and Contributions' <https://globalcompactrefugees.org/pledges-contributions> accessed March 11, 2024.

13 Regulation of the Office of the Prime Minister on the Screening of Aliens Who Enter into the Kingdom and Are Unable to Return to the Country of Origin BE 2562 (enacted December 25, 2019) *Royal Gazette* No 136, Special Section 314.

14 Notification of the Protected Person Screening Committee on the Criteria, Procedures, and Conditions for Determining an Application for Protected Person Status (adopted March 27, 2023 (BE 2566)). At the time of writing, the Notification is available only in Thai. All the provisions discussed in the analysis are translated by the author.

Eligibility Criteria) as a supplementary document in the *Royal Gazette*. The NSM was officially implemented in September 2023 and remains under development by the Thai government, with UNHCR support.[15] The establishment of a formal national screening mechanism marks a momentous step and makes Thailand a pioneer among non-signatory states in the Southeast Asian region.

This chapter takes as starting point these developments and seeks to examine the Thai domestic legislation governing the NSM – the Regulation on the NSM and the newly adopted Notification on the Eligibility Criteria – through the lens of international law. The aim is to determine whether Thailand's crucial move in establishing the historic screening mechanism is in line with international standards, represents good practice among non-signatory states in the region and beyond, and is a true step forward for enhanced protection for refugees on the ground.

The following section provides an overview of the legal and policy landscape of refugee protection and caseloads in Thailand. Part 3 discusses the timeline and the turning point that led to the creation of the NSM. This is followed by a critical evaluation of the NSM against international law, notably international human rights law. Finally, Part 5 concludes that Thailand's NSM as it is currently conceived falls short of international standards in terms of substantive rights and procedural guarantees. It further contends that while the fulfillment of global commitments by a non-signatory state like Thailand is to be applauded, robust and close monitoring is called for when evaluating success and impact on the lives of refugees and asylum seekers at the local level.

2 Thailand and Refugee Protection: A Tour d'Horizon

2.1 *Legal Frameworks*

At the international level, Thailand has not ratified the 1951 Convention or the 1967 Protocol.[16] Nonetheless, the country is a party to eight out of nine

15 UNHCR, 'UNHCR Multi-Country Office Thailand Operational Factsheet' (December 31, 2023) <https://reporting.unhcr.org/thailand-multi-country-office-operational-factsheet-7579> accessed March 14, 2024.

16 Reasons for non-accession include the fear that accession would restrict national sovereignty and security, and that it would oblige Thailand to accept an unlimited number of refugees for long-term settlement. See Vitit Muntarbhorn, *The Status of Refugees in Asia* (Oxford Clarendon Press 1992) 33, 132.

core human rights treaties that are applicable to refugees and asylum seekers.[17] Pertinent provisions include, among others, the prohibition of *refoulement* (article 3 CAT,[18] articles 6 and 7 ICCPR),[19] the protection against arbitrary expulsion (article 13 ICCPR), the prohibition of arbitrary arrest and detention and treatment of detainees (articles 9 and 10 ICCPR), and the principle of non-discrimination as well as the best interests of the child (articles 2 and 3 CRC).[20] In addition to the obligations under treaty law, Thailand, like other states, is also bound by the relevant rules of customary international law,[21] notably the principle of *non-refoulement*.[22]

At the regional level, Thailand has affirmed the Asian-African Legal Consultative Organization (AALCO)'s Bangkok Principles on the Status and Treatment of Refugees.[23] This regional instrument contains several articles similar to the 1951 Convention and, to some extent, offers more expansive protection than the latter.[24] However, in view of its non-binding character and the lack of political will, the Bangkok Principles have not carried strong persuasive force nor been incorporated in the national legislation of member states, including Thailand. Within the Association of Southeast Asian Nations (ASEAN) framework, while the ASEAN Human Rights Declaration

---

17 This includes the ICCPR, ICESCR, CAT, CRC, CEDAW, ICERD, CRPD, and ICPPED.

18 Convention against Torture and Other Cruel, Inhuman or Degrading Treatment or Punishment (adopted December 10, 1984, entered into force June 26, 1987).

19 International Covenant on Civil and Political Rights (adopted December 16, 1966, entered into force March 23, 1976).

20 Convention on the Rights of the Child (adopted November 20, 1989, entered into force September 2, 1990).

21 See Hélène Lambert, 'Customary Refugee Law' in Cathryn Costello, Michelle Foster and Jane McAdam (eds), *The Oxford Handbook of International Refugee Law* (OUP 2021).

22 Declaration of States Parties to the 1951 Convention and/or Its 1967 Protocol relating to the Status of Refugees, HCR/MMSP/2001/09 (2002), Preambular para 4; Elihu Lauterpacht and Daniel Bethlehem, 'The Scope and Content of the Principle of *Non-Refoulement*: Opinion' in Erika Feller, Volker Türk and Frances Nicholson (eds), *Refugee Protection in International Law: UNHCR's Global Consultations on International Protection* (CUP 2003); Guy S Goodwin-Gill and Jane McAdam, *The Refugee in International Law* (4th edn, OUP 2021) 300–06; Vincent Chetail, *International Migration Law* (OUP 2019) 119–24.

23 AALCO's 1966 Bangkok Principles on Status and Treatment of Refugees (adopted June 24, 2001). See also chapter 4.

24 For example, art I on the refugee definition, III(2) on temporary asylum, VI on the right to return, and IX on the right to compensation; See also Susan Kneebone, 'ASEAN and the Conceptualization of Refugee Protection in Southeastern Asian States' in Ademola Abass and Francesca Ippolito (eds), *Regional Approaches to the Protection of Asylum Seekers: An International Legal Perspective* (Ashgate Publishing 2014) 313–18.

2012 explicitly recognizes the right to seek and receive asylum in another state, the provision further stipulates "in accordance with the laws of such State and applicable international agreements."[25] This raises ambiguity about the realization of such right in practice, since most ASEAN states, including Thailand, are not party to the 1951 Convention and their domestic immigration laws are generally unfavorable to persons in need of international protection.[26] Regarding children, the commendable ASEAN Declaration on the Rights of Children in the Context of Migration was adopted in 2019. It acknowledges the need to enhance protection of all children in the context of migration, and recommends that ASEAN states develop alternatives to child immigration detention.[27]

At the domestic level, Thailand lacks a specific law on refugee protection. The primary law applicable to refugees is the Immigration Act BE 2522 (1979) governing aliens in general. Under the Immigration Act, no distinction is made between those entering the country for the purpose of seeking asylum and other groups of immigrants. Accordingly, refugees and asylum seekers who enter and/or stay in Thailand without valid documents or visas are categorized as illegal immigrants and, in principle, are subject to deportation.[28] While the 2019 inter-ministerial memorandum of understanding (MoU) on the Determination of Measures and Approaches Alternative to Detention of Children in Immigration Detention Centers is a welcome step toward ending the immigration detention of children, family separation and the exorbitant bail rate, among other issues, remain problematic.[29]

---

25 ASEAN Human Rights Declaration and the Phnom Penh Statement on the Adoption of the ASEAN Human Rights Declaration (adopted November 18, 2012) Principle 16.

26 Vitit Muntarbhorn, 'Regional Refugee Regimes: Southeast Asia' in Cathryn Costello, Michelle Foster and Jane McAdam (eds), *The Oxford Handbook of International Refugee Law* (OUP 2021) 429; Jittawadee Chotinukul, 'Association of Southeast Asian Nations' in Vincent Chetail (ed), *Elgar Concise Encyclopedia of Migration and Asylum Law* (Edward Elgar Publishing, forthcoming).

27 ASEAN Declaration on the Rights of Children in the Context of Migration (adopted November 2, 2019) paras 3, 9.

28 Immigration Act of Thailand BE 2522 (February 24, 1979) s 54.

29 See Asia Pacific Refugee Rights Network and others, 'Joint Statement on the Signing of the Memorandum of Understanding on the Determination of Measures and Approaches Alternative to Detention of Children in Immigration Detention Centers' (January 21, 2019); International Detention Coalition, 'It's Been 3 Years Since the Signing of the ATD-MoU in Thailand: Where Are We Now?' (*IDC*, March 31, 2022) <https://idcoalition.org/its-been-3-years-since-the-signing-of-the-atd-mou-in-thailand-where-are-we-now/> accessed March 19, 2024.

In a significant recent development, in 2022, Thailand promulgated the Act on the Prevention and Suppression of Torture and Enforced Disappearance BE 2565, which remarkably also endorses the principle of *non-refoulement*.[30] The new law has the potential to make a positive impact on the lives of refugees in Thailand but, as is often the case, enforcement is key to effective protection, and remains to be seen.[31] Parenthetically, the inclusion of the provision on *non-refoulement* in the Thai Anti-Torture and Enforced Disappearance Act illustrates the interplay between international refugee law and human rights law, and how universal refugee norms are transposed into the domestic legal sphere in non-signatory states.

2.2 *Caseloads and Policy Responses*

Thailand has been hosting forcibly displaced persons since the 1970s, and during this period it provided temporary refuge to the Indochinese from Vietnam, Cambodia, and Laos[32] as well as the Burmese.[33] Back then, an ad hoc screening procedure within the framework of the 1989 Comprehensive Plan of Action (CPA) was established to determine refugee status of the Indochinese,[34] whereas Provincial Admission Boards were initiated to temporarily screen those fleeing from Myanmar for the purpose of admission into the camps near the Thai–Myanmar border.[35]

On the basis of a Cooperation Agreement, Thailand has permitted UNHCR to operate in the country since 1975 to provide assistance to various groups of people displaced by the Indochina war.[36] Currently, UNHCR has three offices in Thailand: one multi-country office in Bangkok, which has also covered Cambodia, Laos, and Vietnam since 2020, and two field offices in Mae Sot and Mae Hong Son.[37]

---

30 The Act on the Prevention and Suppression of Torture and Enforced Disappearance BE 2565 (enacted October 24, 2022, entered into force February 22, 2023) s 13.

31 Intriguingly, the Act does not contain a provision on punishment for the violation of s 13.

32 See further Arthur C Helton, 'Asylum and Refugee Protection in Thailand' (1989) 1(1) *International Journal of Refugee Law* 20.

33 See further Vitit Muntarbhorn, 'Refugee Law and Practice in the Asia and Pacific Region: Thailand as a Case Study' (2004) UNHCR Research Paper 6–9.

34 UNGA, 'Declaration and Comprehensive Plan of Action of the International Conference on Indo-Chinese Refugees, Report of the Secretary-General' UN doc A/44/523 (1989).

35 Muntarbhorn (n 33) 6–7.

36 Agreement between the United Nations High Commissioner for Refugees and the Government of the Kingdom of Thailand (signed December 22, 1975).

37 UNHCR, 'UNHCR in Thailand' <www.unhcr.org/th/en/unhcr-in-thailand> accessed March 22, 2024.

Today, Thailand remains the country of first asylum for a considerable number of individuals seeking protection. As of December 2023, Thailand hosts 90,801 Myanmar refugees in the nine temporary shelters on the Thai–Myanmar border.[38] Registration of this group is led by the Royal Thai Government Provincial Admission Board (RTG-PAB) and since 2008 registration has only been open to exceptional serious protection and medical cases.[39] The role of UNHCR focuses primarily on protection and solutions, including identifying and referring cases to the RTG-PAB in close consultation with the Ministry of Interior, while humanitarian services for basic needs are provided by NGOs, given that Myanmar camp-based refugees are not allowed to move outside the camps.[40]

In the urban context, there are 5,213 urban refugees and asylum seekers from 47 countries, mainly Pakistan, Vietnam, Mali, and Iraq, residing in and around Bangkok.[41] UNHCR has played a pivotal role in providing protection to this group, not least conducting RSD. However, a registered or recognized status by UNHCR does not formally guarantee protection for these individuals.

In addition, there are approximately 5,000 Rohingya, many of whom are victims of trafficking.[42] As a policy and for reasons of national security, the Rohingya screened as victims of trafficking reside in shelters run by the Ministry of Social Development and Human Security with restricted freedom of movement and no right to work.[43] Those screened out and considered to be illegal immigrants are incarcerated in the Immigration Detention Centres (IDCs), often for prolonged periods.[44] Other groups include North Koreans and 48 Uyghurs who had been detained at the IDCs since March 2014.[45]

38 UNHCR (n 15).

39 ibid.

40 ibid.

41 ibid; UNHCR, 'Annual Results Report 2022: Thailand Multi Country' (May 3, 2023) 10, 12 <https://reporting.unhcr.org/sites/default/files/2023-06/Asia%20-%20Thailand%20Multi%20Country.pdf> accessed March 15, 2024; Parliamentary Committee on Legal Affairs, Justice and Human Rights, 'Study Report on Problems and Sustainable Solutions for Irregular Migration' (June 20, 2024) 10, 61.

42 Parliamentary Committee on Legal Affairs, Justice and Human Rights (n 41) 10, 61.

43 UNHCR, 'Submission by the United Nations High Commissioner for Refugees for the Office of the High Commissioner for Human Rights' Compilation Report Universal Periodic Review: 3rd Cycle, 39th Session: Thailand' (2021) 2.

44 ibid.

45 Parliamentary Committee on Legal Affairs, Justice and Human Rights (n 41) 61.

Since the 2021 military coup in Myanmar, those fleeing fighting represent a new caseload in Thailand. While the figure fluctuates due to the highly volatile situation, approximately 48,408 Myanmar individuals have crossed into Thailand to seek protection during several periods of movement between February 2021 and January 2024.[46] They were sheltered in Temporary Safety Areas (TSAS) under the control of the Royal Thai Army with limited access by humanitarian agencies, including UNHCR.[47] According to the government's standard operating procedures, these newcomers will be treated separately from the existing Myanmar camp population in that they will be initially received at TSAs and, if needed, relocated to holding areas organized by provincial authorities.[48] In addition to this group, there are 30,000–50,000 persons who reside in urban areas outside TSAs.[49] Among these are political activists and professionals, such as doctors and nurses.[50] At the time of writing, the Thai policy toward the latter group remains unclear.[51]

3 Participation in Global Forums on Refugees: A Turning Point

Despite not being a party to the international refugee instruments, Thailand has engaged with the international refugee regime in a number of ways. In addition to hosting UNHCR in the country, Thailand has been a member of UNHCR's Executive Committee since 1979. The country has actively participated in the annual plenary sessions, and importantly used this platform to express its stance and commitments toward refugee protection. For example, in 2022, Thailand reaffirmed that it would not force "Myanmar people fleeing unrest" to return to danger, and pledged to consider withdrawing its reservation to article 22 CRC related to refugee children.[52] In 2023, the

46 Thailand Inter-Agency Sector Working Group, '2024 Refugee Preparedness and Response Plan: Thai–Myanmar Border' (2024) 4 <https://reporting.unhcr.org/thailand-myanmar-border-refugee-preparedness-and-response-plan> accessed March 15, 2024.

47 ibid 5; UNHCR (n 15).

48 Thailand Inter-Agency Sector Working Group (n 46) 5, 15.

49 Parliamentary Committee on National Security, Border Affairs, National Strategy and National Reform, 'Report on Problems and Solutions for Persons Fleeing Fighting from Myanmar and Persons Fleeing Civil Unrest from Myanmar' (June 21, 2024) 11–12.

50 ibid.

51 ibid.

52 'Statement by Delegation of Thailand' 73rd Session of the Executive Committee of the High Commissioner's Programme (October 10–14, 2022).

country agreed to uphold the principle of *non-refoulement* enshrined in the Anti-Torture and Enforced Disappearance Act.[53] From a legal perspective, such an involvement indicates Thailand's influence on and cognizance of the adopted Executive Committee Conclusions.[54]

As previously mentioned, however, Thailand has long been reluctant to ratify the 1951 Convention or to establish its own national asylum systems. A turning point nevertheless came in September 2016 with the Leaders' Summit on Refugees. At the summit, Thailand – the only ASEAN state invited to attend – surprisingly pledged to develop a screening mechanism to "distinguish those with genuine protection needs from economic migrants."[55] It was suggested that Thailand make such a commitment because the then ruling junta saw the forum as an opportunity to restore its international legitimacy and global media attention following the public condemnation over the country's deportation of Uyghurs.[56] Not long after, in January 2017, Cabinet Resolution 10/01 BE 2560 – setting up a committee to develop policies concerning the screening mechanism – was adopted.[57]

In December 2018, Thailand joined the international community in adopting the GCR and its counterpart, the Global Compact for Migration. At the 2019 GRF, Thailand further pledged to "enhance capacity-building of officers involved in implementing the national screening system to differentiate persons in need of international protection from those seeking economic opportunities."[58] In parallel, at home, after years of concerted efforts, Thailand's global commitments came to fruition: on December 24, 2019, the Regulation on the NSM was approved by the Thai cabinet,

53 'Statement by Delegation of Thailand' 74th Session of the Executive Committee of the High Commissioner's Programme (October 9–13, 2023).

54 See also Maja Janmyr, 'The 1951 Refugee Convention and Non-Signatory States: Charting a Research Agenda' (2021) 33(2) *International Journal of Refugee Law* 188, 208–09; Guy S Goodwin Gill, 'The Office of the United Nations High Commissioner for Refugees and the Sources of International Refugee Law' (2020) 69(1) *International and Comparative Law Quarterly* 1, 8–9.

55 'Summary Overview Document Leaders' Summit on Refugees' (2016) <https://refugeesmigrants.un.org/sites/default/files/public_summary_document_refugee_summit_final_11-11-2016.pdf> accessed March 11, 2024.

56 Bhanubhatra Jittiang, 'Policy Entrepreneurship and the Drafting of Refugee Law in a Non-Signatory Country: The Case of Thailand's National Screening Mechanism' (2022) 35(4) *Journal of Refugee Studies* 1492, 1502.

57 Cabinet Resolution 10/01 BE 2560 (January 10, 2017).

58 UNHCR, 'Pledges and Contributions: Government of Thailand, submitted December 12, 2019' <https://globalcompactrefugees.org/pledges-contributions> accessed March 24, 2024.

and the Notification on Eligibility Criteria for individuals seeking protection under the NSM was adopted on March 27, 2023. On the international plane, Thailand continues to actively engage in global forums on refugees. At the latest GRF, the country committed to strengthen the NSM by, inter alia, investing in data and interpretation systems, developing protection and referral frameworks, conferring appropriate legal status to the "Protected Person," and cooperating with partner countries, UNHCR and the Asylum Capacity Support Group, as well as by improving the use of alternatives to detention.[59]

Thailand's participation in global forums on refugees from 2016 onwards represents a watershed moment in the history of refugee protection in the country. It is against this backdrop that the NSM was established, turning Thailand's global commitments into local implementation. We will now examine this mechanism in closer detail.

4 Thailand's National Screening Mechanism: A Legal Examination

Bearing in mind that the NSM's implementation is – at the time of writing – under development by the Thai government, with UNHCR technical support and advocacy,[60] this section scrutinizes key elements of Thai legislation through the lens of international law to assess its compliance with the relevant international standards applicable to asylum procedures.[61]

The NSM Regulation consists of 30 clauses divided into five chapters: i) Protected Person Screening Committee; ii) Screening of Protected Persons; iii) Arrangements for Protected Persons; iv) Evaluation and Review; and v) Transitory Provision. Although the Regulation does not provide substantive eligibility criteria for determining the status of "Protected Person," it envisages and confers power on the Committee to lay down criteria, procedures, and conditions for status determination.[62] Pursuant to this, the Notification on the Eligibility Criteria was subsequently issued and entered

59 'Statement by Thailand' Global Refugee Forum 2023 (December 14, 2023); UNHCR, 'Pledges and Contributions: Government of Thailand, submitted December 21, 2023' <https://globalcompactrefugees.org/pledges-contributions> accessed March 25, 2024.

60 Including providing training on interviewing techniques, the use of COI, and assessment drafting.

61 For early analysis, see Jittawadee Chotinukul, 'Thailand and the National Screening Mechanism: A Step Forward for Refugee Protection?' (2020) *Global Migration* Research Paper No 25, Global Migration Centre.

62 cls 9(1) and 20 para 1.

into force in September 2023. The Notification consists of 10 sections detailing the criteria, procedures, and conditions for assessing a request to be a Protected Person as well as an application for Protected Person status. To examine and understand how the NSM operates, the two instruments must thus be read in tandem.

Before proceeding to a detailed analysis, three preliminary observations should be shared. First, the NSM was established by Regulation, which is the lowest form in the hierarchy of Thai laws. This means that the Regulation is subordinated to the 1979 Immigration Act as the primary law governing aliens generally, as seen in several clauses of the Regulation where the applicability of immigration law is referred to. Second, although the Regulation was enacted for the purpose of screening those in need of international protection, the term "refugee" or "asylum seeker" is not mentioned anywhere. Instead, the Regulation uses "Protected Person" and "Person under Screening." Such deliberate avoidance emphasizes the long-standing position of Thailand of preventing any formal affiliation with the international refugee instruments to which it has not acceded.

Third, there are concerns with the composition of the Screening Committee. The Committee is comprised of 12 members from different government agencies – with the Commissioner-General or Deputy Commissioner-General of the Royal Thai Police as the Chairperson – and no more than four experts, appointed by the Commissioner-General of the Royal Thai Police.[63] The disproportionate number of expert members compared with *ex-officio* members raises concern over the exercise of the Committee's discretion when it comes to balancing national security and the rights of individuals.[64] This concern cannot be overstated, particularly given that several clauses governing the NSM contain the phrase "as determined by the Committee" and allow exceptions on the grounds of "national security" – the vague term subjected to interpretation by the Committee.

---

63 cl 5.

64 Similar concern is also expressed by the National Human Rights Commission of Thailand. Its recommendation to increase six more expert members in the Committee has, however, been discarded. See 'Summary Report by the Royal Thai Police' (October 12, 2023) <https://resolution.soc.go.th/PDF_UPLOAD/2567/P_410171_6.pdf> accessed April 9, 2024; 'News on the Cabinet Meetings' (January 2, 2024) <www.thaigov.go.th/news/contents/details/76940> accessed April 9, 2024.

4.1 *The Prohibition of* Refoulement

The principle of *non-refoulement* is at the heart of the international protection of refugees. This cardinal principle is guaranteed in article 33 of the 1951 Convention. Further, as mentioned earlier, it is also endorsed either explicitly or implicitly in the human rights treaties and is a well-established norm of customary international law.

Examining the Thai legislation, it is commended that the prohibition of *refoulement* is recognized in the Regulation for both those seeking protection and those granted Protected Person status.[65] Such protection against forced return is, however, not absolute and may be refused where "national security is threatened." While the exception on the grounds of national security can be invoked, like in article 33(2) of the 1951 Convention, it should be noted that, as with any exception to a principle, a carve-out for "national security" must be interpreted restrictively, specifically when fundamental rights of individuals are at stake such as in this case, and its threshold remains relatively high, mainly involving terrorism, espionage, or other related activities aimed at overthrowing the country's institutions.[66] Moreover, in view of the absolute characteristic of the principle of *non-refoulement* in the human rights treaties which Thailand has ratified as well as Section 13 of the Thai Anti-Torture and Enforced Disappearance Act, due regard must be given to the broadened scope of protection against *refoulement* when implementing the relevant provisions.

4.2 *The Right to Seek Asylum*

The right to seek and to enjoy asylum is enshrined in article 14 of the UDHR,[67] which Thailand has affirmed. Although the UDHR is a non-binding instrument, arguably, article 14 has acquired the status of customary international law.[68] While the right to seek asylum does not warrant a substantive right to be granted asylum, for to grant or reject asylum remains a

---

65 cls 15 and 25(1) respectively.

66 Chetail (n 22) 189.

67 Universal Declaration of Human Rights, GA Res 217A (III), UN doc A/810 (December 10, 1948).

68 Subrata Roy Chowdhurry, 'A Response to the Refugee Problems in Post Cold War Era: Some Existing and Emerging Norms of International Law' (1995) 7(1) *International Journal of Refugee Law* 100, 105–06; Rainer Hofmann and Tillmann Löhr, 'Introduction to Chapter V: Requirements for Refugee Determination Procedures' in A Zimmermann (ed), J Dörschner and F Machts (assistant eds), *The 1951 Convention relating to the Status of Refugees and its 1967 Protocol: A Commentary* (OUP 2011) 1088.

sovereign right of states,[69] it does require a procedural right – the right to an asylum procedure.[70] This right imposes a corresponding obligation on states to grant access to status determination procedures without discrimination.[71] Access to a fair and efficient asylum procedure is further reinforced by the principle of *non-refoulement,* since to comply with the obligation of *non-refoulement*, states are obliged to assess an individual's asylum claim in order to avoid sending him/her back to persecution.[72]

The importance of ensuring access for all persons seeking international protection to determination procedures has additionally been reiterated in other instruments, namely the UNHCR Executive Committee Conclusions[73] and the ILA Declaration on International Minimum Standards for Refugee Procedures.[74] In essence, everyone seeking international protection should have access to fair and efficient procedures for the determination of refugee status or other mechanisms, and access to the procedures should be granted without discrimination on the grounds of racial or ethnic origin, status, or country of origin, among others.

In the domestic context, attention should be drawn to Section 2 of the Notification, which prescribes that an alien eligible to submit a request to be Protected Person shall *not* be: aliens whom the Ministry of Interior has specific measures to deal with,[75] or migrant workers from neighboring

69 Declaration on Territorial Asylum, A/RES/2312(XXII) (December 14, 1967) art 1(1); Alice Edwards, 'Human Rights, Refugees, and the Right to "Enjoy" Asylum' (2005) 17(2) *International Journal of Refugee Law* 293, 300.

70 Thomas Gammeltoft-Hansen and Hans Gammeltoft-Hansen, 'The Right to Seek – Revisited. On the UN Human Rights Declaration Article 14 and Access to Asylum Procedures in the EU' (2008) 10 *European Journal of Migration and Law* 439, 446.

71 ibid; María-Teresa Gil-Bazo and Elspeth Guild, 'The Right to Asylum' in Cathryn Costello, Michelle Foster and Jane McAdam (eds), *The Oxford Handbook of International Refugee Law* (OUP 2021) 876–77.

72 Gammeltoft-Hansen and Gammeltoft-Hansen (n 70) 446–47; Nikolas Feith Tan and Jens Vedsted-Hansen, 'Catalogue of International and Regional Legal Standards: Refugee and Human Rights Law Standards Applicable to Asylum Governance' (2021) ASIL Global Asylum Governance and the European Union's Role, 16–17.

73 For example, Executive Committee of the High Commissioner's Programme, 'Conclusion No 74 (XLV) General' (1994) para (i); Executive Committee of the High Commissioner's Programme, 'Conclusion No 82 (XLVIII) Conclusion on Safeguarding Asylum' (1997) para (d)(iii); Executive Committee of the High Commissioner's Programme, 'Conclusion No 99 (LV) General' (2004) para (l).

74 ILA, Resolution 6/2002 on Refugee Procedures (Declaration on International Minimum Standards for Refugee Procedures) (2002) paras 1, 2.

75 s 2(2).

countries, namely Myanmar, Laos, Cambodia, and Vietnam.[76] Whereas the former does not specify the category of aliens, considering the Thai policy responses to different refugee caseloads, it is understood that the provision excludes the Myanmar camp population.

Examining these clauses that automatically exclude some groups of individuals from accessing to the NSM, the analyses are as follows. First, the exclusionary clauses, acting as a legal hurdle, are in flagrant violation of the fundamental right to seek asylum which guarantees access for everyone to an asylum procedure without discrimination. By arbitrarily denying some categories of persons access to the NSM, Thailand, in turn, risks violating its obligation of *non-refoulement* under international law and its own domestic law.

Second, such exclusionary clauses also contravene the principle of equality before the law in article 26 of the ICCPR. While the right to seek asylum is not recognized in the ICCPR, the Human Rights Committee (HRC) has made clear that the application of the principle of non-discrimination contained in article 26 is not limited to the rights provided for in the Covenant.[77] Rather, article 26 in itself provides an autonomous protection, which "prohibits discrimination in law or in fact in any field regulated and protected by public authorities."[78] Therefore, "when legislation is adopted by a State party, it must comply with the requirement of article 26 that its content should not be discriminatory."[79] Based on this, the Thai provisions that exclude some individuals from accessing the NSM on account of their race, national origin, migrant status, or any 'other status' are not in line with article 26 of the ICCPR.

Finally, it should also be mentioned that denying outright access to the NSM to some individuals based solely on their ethnicity or migrant status appears to discard the concept of refugee *sur place*, which acknowledges that a person may become a refugee after he/she has left his/her country of origin due to circumstances arising in the country of origin during his/her absence, or as a result of his/her own actions while in the country of residence.[80]

76 s 2(3).

77 HRC, 'General Comment No 18: Non-Discrimination' (1989) para 12.

78 ibid.

79 ibid.

80 See UNHCR, Handbook on Procedures and Criteria for Determining Refugee Status and Guidelines on International Protection under the 1951 Convention and the 1967 Protocol Relating to the Status of Refugees (1979, reissued 2019) paras 94–96. The concept is also recognized in art I(3) of the Bangkok Principles.

4.3 *Non-penalization Due to Illegal Entry or Stay*

Since refugees presumably flee their country of origin from persecution that is committed or condoned by their home state authorities, they are unlikely to comply with the requirements for legal entry. Based on this rationale, article 31 of the 1951 Convention exempts, under some preconditions, refugees from penalties on account of their illegal entry or presence. The protection from penalties is a right exclusively guaranteed in the 1951 Convention, although there has been a debate about non-penalization being an emerging general principle of law.[81]

Where Thai legislation is concerned, the Regulation only warrants protection from deportation, but is mute on other penalties, notably arrest and detention.[82] Even if persons pending status determination are entitled to the issue of identity documents,[83] their lawful stay or legal status is not recognized. Furthermore, the equivocal wording which stipulates that subject to immigration law, the authorities "may" allow Persons under Screening to stay at a place "as deemed appropriate,"[84] leaves wide discretion to the authorities and fails to categorically rule out detention. This is further exacerbated by the subordinate status of the Regulation to the Immigration Act. Without an explicit provision exempting penalization on account of illegal entry or stay, refugees and asylum seekers who enter and/or stay in Thailand illegally remain subject to arrest, detention, and prosecution under the Immigration Act even before undergoing the NSM process.[85] In fact, as per current practice, to be eligible to apply to the NSM, persons have to be "irregularly present": either they must have previously been arrested and released on bail, or must submit themselves for arrest and prosecution. This evidently discourages most asylum seekers from coming forward to seek protection under the NSM.

Related to this, and crucially, even though the Thai Immigration Act authorizes detention in this case, Thailand is under the obligation of article 9 ICCPR to ensure that detention is not arbitrary, that is it must be justified as

---

81 Cathryn Costello and Yulia Ioffe, 'Non-Penalization and Non-Criminalization' in Cathryn Costello, Michelle Foster and Jane McAdam (eds), *The Oxford Handbook of International Refugee Law* (OUP 2021) 929–32.

82 cl 15.

83 cl 19 para 1.

84 cl 19 para 2.

85 See also 'Joint Letter to Mr. Sretta Thavisin Prime Minister of Thailand, Re: Request to Exempt National Screening Mechanism Applicants from Prosecution under the Immigration Act' (December 12, 2023) <www.fortifyrights.org/tha-inv-let-2023-12-12/> accessed April 17, 2024.

"reasonable, necessary and proportionate in the light of the circumstances and reassessed as it extends in time."[86] Apart from the prohibition of arbitrary detention, Thailand is also bound by article 10(1) ICCPR, which requires that all persons deprived of their liberty shall be treated with humanity and with respect for human dignity.

4.4 *Who Qualifies as "Protected Person"?*

The international definition of refugee is provided in article 1A(2) of the 1951 Convention. As pointed out, Thai law does not accept the term "refugee," but has in lieu adopted the new label "Protected Person." The Regulation defines "Protected Person" as "an alien who enters into or resides in the Kingdom and is unable or unwilling to return to his/her country of origin since there is a reasonable ground to believe that he/she would face harm from persecution as determined by the Committee, and is granted status as a Protected Person under this Regulation."[87]

Examining this provision, it is noteworthy how similar the definition of "Protected Person" is to that of "refugee." It even incorporates the core element of persecution. That said, the Thai definition does not contain reasons for persecution, but rather refers to the phrase "as determined by the Committee." Arguably, the absence of the nexus requirement can be double edged. The apparent drawback is, of course, that it leaves the definition ambiguous subject to broad discretion of the Committee, which could pose a risk of restrictive interpretation. But, at the same time, it has the advantage of making the definition more flexible, which could in effect encompass persons fleeing generalized violence or situations of armed conflict. This is particularly meaningful for the new arrivals fleeing fighting in Myanmar and seeking protection in Thailand, assuming that they can access the NSM. Having analyzed this, the Committee later issued the Directive on a Reasonable Ground to Believe that the Individual Would Face Harm from Persecution (adopted July 11, 2023) to include the five grounds of persecution as an additional element.

The Notification further offers guidance when assessing "a reasonable ground to believe that the applicant would face harm from persecution" by requiring that the relevant facts and other circumstances in the country of origin, such as a consistent pattern of serious, gross, or widespread human rights violations or events seriously disturbing public order in either part or the whole of the country of origin, be taken into consideration.[88] It should

86 HRC, 'General Comment No 35: Article 9' (2014) para 18.

87 cl 3.

88 s 5 para 2. The same is included in the Directive, s 3 para 2.

be observed that the list of objective elements provided in the provision is non-exhaustive, and serves merely as examples of factors to be taken into consideration when determining "persecution." In other words, it would be wrong to infer that persecution is confined only to the listed situations. The notion of "persecution" itself hence remains to be determined by the Committee. In this regard, the Directive provides useful interpretive guidance: it elaborates and adopts the widely accepted meaning of persecution in international law understood as comprising a threat to life or freedom, or other serious violations of human rights, among others.[89]

Finally, on the subjective element stipulated in the Notification:[90] while it is welcomed that the applicant's personal circumstances are to be taken into account when determining his/her application for Protected Person status, there are concerns about how the applicant's political circumstances[91] would be used by the Committee. Besides, other factors, namely national security, and "any other information, documents or evidence as determined by the Committee"[92] obviously raise questions about the objectivity and predictability of the criteria.

4.5 *The Right to an Effective Remedy*

The right to an effective remedy is endorsed in article 16(1) of the 1951 Convention. It guarantees a refugee free access to the courts, which presumably includes for the purposes of reviewing any rejection of refugee status by asylum seekers.[93] In the realm of human rights law, although the HRC does not accept that procedural standards of the right to a fair trial (article 14 ICCPR) apply to RSD procedures,[94] it views RSD as intrinsically related to *refoulement* or expulsion and, as a result, governed by human rights standards

89 Directive, s 2. See also UNHCR (n 80) paras 51–53; James C Hathaway and Michelle Foster, *The Law of Refugee Status* (2nd edn, CUP 2014) 193–208. Interestingly, the draft notification contained some of these elements, but in the final version they were removed and replaced by 'as determined by the Committee' and s 5 para 2 was added.

90 s 6.

91 s 6(2).

92 s 6(4).

93 Vincent Chetail, 'Are Refugee Rights Human Rights? An Unorthodox Questioning of the Relations between Refugee Law and Human Rights Law' in Ruth Rubio-Marín (ed), *Human Rights and Immigration* (OUP 2014) 52.

94 HRC, 'General Comment No 32, Article 14: Right to Equality before Courts and Tribunals and to a Fair Trial', UN doc CCPR/C/GC/32 (2007), para 17; HRC, *AC and Other v Netherlands*, Communication No 1494/2006 (2008) para 8.4; HRC, *X v Denmark*, Communication No 2007/2010 (2014) para 8.5.

concerning due process.[95] According to the HRC, the legal bases for these procedural standards are primarily found in article 13 of the ICCPR (specific procedural guarantees governing expulsion), article 2(3), coupled with articles 7, 6 of the ICCPR (the right to an effective remedy, combined with the substantive provisions triggering protection against *refoulement*), or in a combination of both.[96]

Leaving aside the unclear position on the legal bases for due process guarantees in asylum procedures, what is evident is that such procedural safeguards, including the right to appeal against first-instance negative decisions, are firmly guaranteed in the ICCPR. Beyond treaty law, the right to appeal or review to an independent body in RSD procedure is further affirmed by soft law standards, such as the UNHCR Executive Committee Conclusion No 8 (1977) (para (e)(vi)), the UNHCR Handbook on Procedures,[97] and the ILA Declaration.[98]

Looking at the domestic provisions, while appeal is warranted at the admissibility stage where a request to be a Protected Person is dismissed by the authorities,[99] it is alarming that the right to appeal on the merits of the claim is precluded.[100] Appeal or review against other adverse decisions made under the NSM either internally to the Committee or externally to a court of law is also barred.[101] This includes where the status of Person under Screening or of Protected Person is revoked by the Committee[102] and where Protected Person status is denied on the grounds of national security, despite all criteria being met.[103] While Clause 24 of the Regulation allows aliens whose status is rejected or revoked to "resubmit another request to the Committee for reconsideration," this can by no means be a substitute for the right to appeal. Moreover, the remedial action provided for in Clause 24

95 David Cantor, 'Reframing Relationships: Revisiting the Procedural Standards for Refugee Status Determination in light of Recent Human Rights Treaty Body Jurisprudence' (2015) 34(1) *Refugee Survey Quarterly* 79, 89.

96 ibid.

97 UNHCR (n 80) para 192 (vi).

98 ILA (n 74) para 13.

99 cl 17 of the Regulation.

100 cl 20 para 3.

101 Such clauses also appear inconsistent with the Thai Administrative Procedure Act, since the Committee's decision is an administrative order and thus rejected applicants can appeal before the Administrative Court. See Darunee Paisarnpanichkul and Kornkanok Wattanabhoom, 'Report on Thai Legislation and Policies Review relating to New Arrivals from Myanmar' (September 2023) *Myanmar Response Network* (*MRN*) 42–43.

102 cl 21 para 2.

103 s 9 of the Notification.

is contingent upon vague and subjective conditions: "if there is information or fact as prescribed by the Committee."

Within this ambit, Clause 18 para 2 deserves a mention. It talks about abandonment of requests: if the alien fails to file an application for Protected Person status within 60 days after the notification date, the alien shall be deemed to have abandoned the request and legal action pursuant to immigration and other relevant laws shall be taken against him/her. As one of the main guarantees ensured by the right to an effective remedy, non-fulfillment of formal requirements, including late submission of an asylum request, cannot lead to a request being excluded from examination of the merits of the claim.[104] The same also finds support in the UNHCR Executive Committee Conclusion No 15 (1979) (para (i)) and in a Guide to International Refugee Protection and Building State Asylum Systems.[105]

4.6 *Rejecting Protected Person Status on the Grounds of National Security*

Under Thai legislation, despite having satisfied all the criteria and conditions set forth in Section 5 of the Notification, the Person under Screening may still be denied Protected Person status if the Committee considers that granting the status to the alien may threaten national security (Section 9 para 1). The Committee's decision shall be final and be treated as undisclosable information pursuant to article 15(1) and (2) of the Official Information Act BE 2540[106] (Section 9 para 2).

The provision gives broad discretionary powers to the Committee to deny the applicant Protected Person status even if he/she meets all the criteria on the grounds of the ill-defined term "national security." What is more, as discussed, the right to appeal against such negative decision and access to information, including the reasons for rejection, is precluded. This clearly raises issues of the transparency and conformity of the Thai screening process to international standards. The invocation of Section 9 should not be underestimated, particularly when looking at the drafting history of the Regulation,

104 Chetail (n 93) 53.

105 UNHCR and Inter-Parliamentary Union (IPU), A Guide to International Refugee Protection and Building State Asylum Systems: Handbook for Parliamentarians No 27 (2017) 178.

106 Official Information Act BE 2540 (1997). Art 15(1) prohibits the disclosure of official information that will "jeopardise the national security, international relations, or national economic or financial security," while art 15(2) prohibits the disclosure of information that will "result in the decline in the efficiency of law enforcement or failure to achieve its objectives."

which suggests that persons with "specific national security concerns" in the eyes of the Thai government could include persons fleeing fighting from Myanmar, Rohingya, Uyghurs, and North Koreans.[107] Concerning those fleeing generalized violence from Myanmar, assuming that they could access the NSM and while they may be eligible to Protected Person status based on the flexible definition in Clause 3 of the Regulation as analyzed above, these individuals could regrettably be rejected the status by virtue of Section 9.

4.7 *Durable Solutions and Rights Accorded to Protected Person Status*

Finally, Clause 25(2) of the Regulation provides for voluntary repatriation and resettlement – the solutions already available to those recognized as refugees by UNHCR in Thailand. What is novel is Clause 25(3) which for the first time paves the way for the possibility of local integration. It stipulates that when an alien is granted Protected Person status, the relevant agencies shall authorize the Protected Person "to stay in the Kingdom on an exceptional basis or temporarily, and refer the case for further action in accordance with immigration law, provided that the screening outcome under the Regulation is taken into consideration."

As can be seen, the provision is ambiguous and demonstrates that even when granted Protected Person status and authorized to stay in Thailand, the legal status of these individuals remains volatile and, critically, may still be subject to immigration law. Such provision not only appears incompatible with the international notion of local integration,[108] but also shows that the NSM was designed to continue a policy of temporary refuge, making the Thai government responsible for status screening, in exchange for eventual resettlement by third countries.[109] Certainly, Thai law offers no prospect of naturalization. The way in which the provision on local integration is formulated unavoidably raises doubts about the viability of this solution in practice.

On the accompanying rights to individuals granted Protected Person status, they are meagre. Only the right to education and access to healthcare

---

107 Letter from the Office of the Council of State to the Cabinet (December 18, 2019) <https://resolution.soc.go.th/PDF_UPLOAD/2562/9933420829.pdf> accessed April 15, 2024.

108 See James C Hathaway, *The Rights of Refugees under International Law* (2nd edn, CUP 2021) 1206.

109 Adam Severson, 'Thailand's Changing of the Guard: Negotiating the Transition from UNHCR Refugee Status Determination to a National Refugee Screening Mechanism' (*Refugee Law Initiative,* November 19, 2020) <https://rli.blogs.sas.ac.uk/2020/11/19/thailands-changing-of-the-guard-negotiating-the-transition-from-unhcr-refugee-status-determination-to-a-national-refugee-screening-mechanism/> accessed April 22, 2024.

are explicitly guaranteed (Clause 25(4)). It is strongly urged that other substantive rights, notably the right to legal recognition and the right to work, be secured.

5 Conclusion

The establishment of the national screening mechanism to identify persons in need of protection by Thailand as a non-signatory state is undoubtedly a milestone in the history of refugee protection – not only in the country but also the region.

On the surface, the pioneering case of Thailand appears to be a success story deserving applause, for the country did fulfill its global commitments. But an in-depth legal analysis reveals that several provisions of the domestic legislation governing the NSM are not in line with the relevant international standards in terms of both substantive rights and procedural guarantees. In light of the findings, it would not be difficult for one to perceive the Thai screening mechanism more as a deterrent than a protection tool and to call into question whether these new developments truly contribute to better protection for refugees and asylum seekers. Drawing on insights from the case of Thailand, it is further argued that the fulfillment of pledges at the global level does not necessarily mean better protection for refugees at the local level, but can regrettably be a mere mirage of enhanced protection in the absence of rigorous monitoring.

That said, moving forward, it is never too late for Thailand to put things right and set a good example to other states, not least non-signatory states in Southeast Asia that are considering following in Thailand's footsteps. The NSM was only launched in September 2023 and currently runs in parallel with UNHCR RSD procedure. Its implementation remains under development by the Thai government, with engagement by relevant stakeholders, including UNHCR and civil society organizations to ensure the required procedural standards.

While it would be premature to predict for certain the future direction and long-term impact of Thailand's NSM, much can be done now to improve the rights of these vulnerable individuals on the ground. Recognizing legal status of persons seeking protection under the NSM and guaranteeing their right to an independent appeal or review would be a good start. This is an opportunity for Thailand to prove that its global achievements are not just an illusion, but a genuine reflection of meaningful progress and enhanced protection for refugees in the country.

CHAPTER 9

Mechanisms of Enrollment: How the Network of International Protection Grows

Georgia Cole

1 Introduction

In recent years, a new field of academic research has started to provide critical insights into the ways in which states that are not signatories to the 1951 Convention or its 1967 Protocol[1] have nonetheless been affecting the production, enactment and future of international refugee law and protection. This has coincided with an increasing recognition that refugee protection has long been, and continues to be, promoted through an international regime of institutions, laws, actors, and ideologies other than the post-1951 system overseen by the United Nations High Commissioner for Refugees (UNHCR).

In this chapter I nonetheless focus on the approaches employed by UNHCR to encourage increased state engagement with the 1951 Convention and with the organization itself. While states, civil society actors and refugees themselves have played a pivotal role in the promotion of international protection in non-signatory states, UNHCR's Statute clearly states the organization's roles in "promoting the conclusion and ratification of international conventions for the protection of refugees"[2] and in "promoting through special agreements with Governments the execution of any measures calculated to improve the situation of refugees and to reduce the number requiring protection."[3] As an example, in its recent celebrations to mark the 73rd anniversary of the 1951 Convention, the organization again "urge[d] the remaining 46 UN Member and Observer States to accede to it."[4] Beyond the direct provision of support

1 Convention relating to the Status of Refugees (adopted July 28, 1951, entered into force April 22, 1954) 189 UNTS 137; Protocol Relating to the Status of Refugees (adopted January 31, 1967, entered into force October 4, 1967) 606 UNTS 267.

2 Statute of the Office of the United Nations High Commissioner for Refugees, UNGA Res 428 (V) (December 14, 1950) ch 2, art 8(a).

3 ibid 2, art 8(b).

4 'UN Refugee Agency marks 73 years of the Refugee Convention, urging universal accession' (UNHCR 2024) <https://www.unhcr.org/news/briefing-notes/un-refugee-agency-marks-73-years-refugee-convention-urging-universal-accession> accessed August 15, 2024.

to refugees, UNHCR is therefore explicitly tasked with extending this network of international protection through both legal and operational means.

This raises the question as to how UNHCR *assembles* various entities into the international refugee regime given the "hard work required to draw heterogeneous elements together, forge connections between them and sustain these connections in the face of tension."[5] The organization does not, for example, have the authority to operate through sovereign control over states' actions; it cannot simply coerce non-signatory states into acting or engaging with international refugee law. It must instead exercise power in other ways, building an assemblage of actors to enact and affirm legal principles and protection practices, even if understandings of these principles and practices are not entirely aligned across the different stakeholders and forums it engages with, or even within the organization itself.

In the chapter that follows, I thus first analyze the growing body of literature on the relationship between UNHCR and non-signatory states to identify common mechanisms and stages through which UNHCR attempts to enroll these actors, their practices and citizens into networks of international protection. To do so, I apply a basic framework derived from Science and Technology Studies (STS) because of its emphasis on explaining *how* networks grow, with growth as the key motivator and endpoint, rather than necessarily on *why* this happens or on what *the effects* of this might be on the actors and entities enrolled. In this sense, I chose this interdisciplinary framework because it provides an implicit critique of how UNHCR's actions appear at times to prioritize expansion without critical, or even strategic, engagement with what the trade-offs of this might be. In the second half of this chapter, I then make this critique more explicit by using further frameworks from STS to highlight what effects UNHCR's varied, and sometimes fragmented, efforts to expand the international refugee regime in non-signatory states might have on the future governance, sites and experiences of protection.

2 Building Associations and Assemblages

In his path-defining study on the scallop industry of St Brieuc Bay, Callon sought to explain how a group of researchers built a broad consensus around how to conserve these creatures and the fishing industry that rested on them. The researchers' aim, he shows, was to establish a group of actors who were

5 Tania Murray Li, 'Practices of Assemblage and Community Forest Management' (2007) 36(2) *Economy and Society* 263, 264.

aligned around their particular understanding of the industry's situation, and committed to their proposed course of action for responding to it.[6] To elucidate how this consensus was assembled, Callon elaborated on four forms of what he called "translation." He saw this as a process through which entities are continually displaced, transformed and reassembled into an assemblage "during which the identity of actors, the possibility of interaction and the margins of maneuver are negotiated and delimited."[7] The desired end goal is that all the actors are then "obliged to remain faithful to their alliances"[8] and committed to an aligned set of outcomes.

Callon identified the four at times overlapping and coincident stages of "translation" as follows. First came *problematization,* whereby the researchers defined the contours of the problem and then positioned themselves and their proposed course of action as an "obligatory passage point" through which the other actors, namely the scallops and the fishermen, had to pass to resolve the issue. Next was *interessement,* during which the researchers sought to manoeuvre, modify and "lock" these other actors into the roles and subject-positions that aligned with the researchers' assessment of the problem and how to solve it. Drawing on the idea of "interesting" other actors sufficiently to secure their loyalty, this stage hence captured those mechanisms through which the researchers aimed to ensure that the other actors' identities and actions were primarily aligned with them and their agenda rather than with any competing alliances. Then there was *enrollment,* as the researchers attempted to ensure that all other actors within the network were securely interconnected to each other as well as them. Finally, he notes a process of *mobilization,* which entailed the researchers working to ensure that the representatives for the various groups enrolled in this coalition (eg the fisherman tasked with being a spokesperson for their peers) could maintain the support of those they spoke on behalf of.[9]

For Callon, this framework provided a way to understand "the establishment and evolution of power relationships" and to show that "the capacity of certain actors to get other actors – whether they be human beings, institutions or natural entities – to comply with them depends on a complex web of interrelations."[10] While in some ways it may appear jarring to apply a fram-

6 Michel Callon, 'Some Elements of a Sociology of Translation: Domestication of the Scallops and the Fishermen of St Brieuc Bay' (1984) 32(1) *The Sociological Review* 196.

7 ibid 203.

8 ibid 224.

9 ibid 196.

10 ibid 201.

ework originally intended for managing natural "things" to a system oriented around people, this is arguably another reason *for* using it. As an analytical tool, it mirrors the fact that much like Callon's scallops, displaced populations are attributed agency within and by these assemblages. However, this is largely as errant bodies that need to be controlled rather than as political actors with preferred solutions of their own.

In this chapter, I thus draw upon Callon's structure to explore some of the ways in which UNHCR enrolls non-signatory states into the international refugee regime. This approach draws attention to mechanisms that are commonly identified in socio-legal studies of UNHCR's promotion of the 1951 Convention, namely socialization and norm promotion, but it importantly goes beyond these ideas (see chapter 1). In particular, it takes seriously those instances and acts of enrollment that are seemingly without any intent to transform states by socializing them into new courses of behavior. This opens up questions about what the longevity, risks and purposes of these actions might be, which I then explore in the penultimate section of the chapter by drawing on critiques of particular assemblages from within this field of scholarship.

As an example, Li uses this assemblages framework in her work on community management initiatives to illustrate how the focus on building and maintaining assemblages can reinforce the anti-politics machine. She highlights how international organizations are required to maintain amicable relationships with states in order to continue operating there. Fierce disagreement and explicit critiques by them are hence dulled and assemblages are maintained by what Li terms "harmony language, pointing to a way forward defined by more coordination, consultation, participation, constructive debate and mutual learning by all parties."[11] The result is often the avoidance of any calls for major structural change, or explicit condemnation of national policies, and a focus instead on either using the "carrot" to elicit political shifts or adopting the familiar and ahistorical position that "any engagement is better than nothing."

While allowing UNHCR to be foregrounded as the central actor forging these networks, frameworks from STS also push one to reflect on the other relationships, ideas and actors exerting pressure both within and upon a network, as well as how representative and stable these actors are. Through using it, I thus seek to affirm the importance of situating international refugee law as only one part of a broader network of actors and institutions providing inter-

11 Li (n 5) 283.

national protection, as well as some of the dangers of pushing convergence and growth around too narrow an assemblage of representatives and approaches.

2.1 *Problematization*

For Callon, problematization involves an actor delimiting their own and others' identities in such a way as to make themselves indispensable. We see this through UNHCR's varied attempts to establish its incommensurable role as an "obligatory passage point" in refugee protection, which includes negotiating an expansive array of roles in, and agreements with, non-signatory states. In Türkiye, for example, Gürakar Skribeland describes the "ever-changing role of UNHCR" in supporting international protection applicants, including through monitoring foreigners in removal centers and providing entrepreneurship support to young refugees lacking employment opportunities.[12] Importantly, it executes these roles in a context where its ability to support individual's initial access to international protection has been severely curtailed. In the case of Saudi Arabia, Janmyr and Lysa note the pragmatic compromises that UNHCR has made to sustain a relationship with the Kingdom, which has included promoting "protection space" to support displaced populations in the country instead of a more assertive agenda to secure accession to the 1951 Convention.[13]

In terms of agreements negotiated by UNHCR to carve out a role in particular locations, this includes a wide range of Special Agreements and Cooperation Agreements (often collectively referred to as Memoranda of Understanding (MoUs)). These, respectively, establish mechanisms to support refugees or to reduce the numbers of refugees requiring assistance, and establish UNHCR's presence in a state (see chapter 10). The former may, therefore, as Janmyr, Hossain and Turner state, "compensate for the fact that the host state is not a party to any of the relevant refugee law instruments" through affirming states' commitments to refugee protection and permitting UNHCR to perform a relatively expansive suite of activities on these state's territories.

An example of this "enrollment through agreements" can be seen in Zieck's work looking at the history of UNHCR's support to Afghan refugees in Paki-

12 Özlem Gürakar Skribeland, 'Turkey: party or non-party state?' (2021) 67 *Forced Migration Review* 46.

13 Maja Janmyr and Charlotte Lysa, 'UNHCR's Expansion to the GCC States: Establishing a UNHCR Presence in Saudi Arabia 1987–1993' (2024) 33(1) *Middle East Critique* 45, 48; Maja Janmyr and Charlotte Lysa 'Saudi Arabia and the International Refugee Regime' (2023) 35(3) *International Journal of Refugee Law* 251, 265.

stan.[14] She charts how UNHCR encouraged, framed and facilitated the repatriation of Afghan refugees over the course of eight different agreements with the Pakistani and Afghan governments, and assesses the evolution in the meaning of terms and practices across them. While this allowed UNHCR to consolidate a working relationship with the Pakistani government as a non-signatory to the 1951 Convention, Zieck notes the general confusion that this convoluted process entailed. Janmyr et al's work similarly flags the many dangers of this *ad hoc* approach, not least in terms of their lack of transparency and accountability to displaced populations (see chapter 10). The network of international protection may thus expand or thicken through these documents, but this is largely oriented toward protection through *management* – with refugees objectified and corralled much like Callon's scallops – rather than through changes to structural norms or refugees' participation.

Alongside UNHCR's efforts to carve out new operational niches and agreements for itself, the physical presence and legal needs of large numbers of displaced people can serve as an initial entry point for UNHCR to enroll states into the purview of the international refugee regime. Eritrea, for example, is not a signatory to the 1951 Convention but has, since it gained de facto independence from Ethiopia in 1991, had an almost continuous UNHCR presence in the country. This was first because the newly formed Eritrean government requested UNHCR's assistance with the large number of Eritrean refugees wishing to repatriate in the early years of independence and then, more recently, it has emphasized UNHCR's responsibility to support Somali, Ethiopian and Sudanese refugees within its borders. The large number of Eritrean refugees claiming asylum outside of the country, and the Eritrean government's scathing opposition to the "UNHCR Eligibility Guidelines for Assessing the International Protection Needs of Asylum-Seekers from Eritrea,"[15] has also ensured a continuous engagement – however negative – between the Eritrean government and UNHCR.

The expansion of UNHCR's activities in Saudi Arabia was similarly greatly enabled by an acute humanitarian situation when Iraqi refugees in the demilitarized zone between Iraq and Saudi Arabia were airlifted to the Kingdom

14 Marjoleine Zieck, 'The Legal Status of Afghan Refugees in Pakistan, a Story of Eight Agreements and Two Suppressed Premises' (2008) 20(2) *International Journal of Refugee Law* 253.

15 'UNHCR Eligibility Guidelines for Assessing the International Protection Needs of Asylum-Seekers from Eritrea' (UNHCR 2009) <https://www.refworld.org/policy/countrypos/unhcr/2009/en/66801> accessed March 27, 2024.

during the Gulf War.[16] While the Saudi authorities could pay for the camps in which the Iraqi refugees were placed, they lacked expertise in administering these spaces and in securing durable solutions. UNHCR was quick to point out its critical role in negotiating repatriation and resettlement on their behalf. The High Commissioner during this period also made an explicit link between the organization's support for the timely resettlement of the Iraqi refugees, and what they expected in return from an indebted Saudi Arabia in terms of future funding for UNHCR's activities elsewhere. This was seen as particularly important as UNHCR saw support from Saudi Arabia as opening the door to wider recognition of UNHCR in the Gulf Cooperation Council (GCC) region.[17] Displaced populations themselves thus also help to bind states to UNHCR: whether it is refugees that arrive on a territory, or refugees from that territory, they bring states into a discussion about rights, responsibilities and solutions that create an opening for further consolidation of UNHCR's role (eg Saudi Arabia) even if via a point of collision (eg the Eritrean government). In other words, the basic act of hosting or creating refugees can be enough to establish an identity for states that initiates a point of entanglement with the assemblage of the international refugee regime.

Finally, however, UNHCR's attempt to position itself as a key intermediary in non-signatory states may nonetheless require a more active process of definition: UNHCR may need to (re)define the identities of others in ways that render the nature of the network and its inter-relationships both beneficial and unquestionable. In the case of UNHCR then, we can ask: how does it define the identities of the actors that it is seeking to engage in ways that make these roles and agreements possible? To what extent do these identities align with the core operational or legal roles of UNHCR? And are there common or more successful strategies for (re)defining the identities of each actor, and why?

Importantly, we can see that UNHCR does not see all non-signatory states as a homogenous collective, or as monolithic entities,[18] but instead seeks to expound different features of their humanitarian identities. Part of this is because UNHCR is itself not a homogeneous entity with one coherent global

16 Janmyr and Lysa (n 13).

17 ibid.

18 Janmyr and Lysa's work shows how UNHCR's efforts to consolidate their position within Saudi Arabia required different strategies when approaching the Ministry of Foreign Affairs versus the Ministry of Defense. This indicates the need to also be aware of the scale at which enrollment happens, which may well be nuanced at a sub-national level. See Janmyr and Lysa (n 13).

strategy and intent. Different employees, offices and eras of staff have clearly adopted and prioritized different approaches to promoting the organization's role in international protection. As suggested above, however, I would contend that these have often converged around protecting more people in more places with more budget, ie around more growth.

A clear example of this can be seen through UNHCR's engagement with wealthy non-signatory states in the Gulf, where the organization's focus seems to be on enrolling these states as humanitarian donors rather than socializing them into becoming hosting states or signatories. This fundraising strategy also exemplifies UNHCR's assertive and explicit attempts to position itself as an obligatory passage point for the effective protection of refugees. In recent years, it has courted wealthy non-signatory states and their populations (including, in UNHCR's words, "tech-centric Muslim Millennials")[19] to define them as vital donors to the international protection regime, while positioning itself as an essential conduit to ensure that these funds reach the most vulnerable. In particular, UNHCR has encouraged the private sector and state-sponsored NGOs in the Gulf states and Indonesia to channel their Zakat contributions through UNHCR to "maximize the power"[20] and impact of these millennia-old donations, and publicly encouraged high net worth individuals in the Middle East and Islamic Finance players to uphold their "responsibilities" to displaced Muslims through channeling donations to UNHCR.[21]

To encourage this support, UNHCR has nonetheless had to adapt some of its practices to ensure that the recipients of these funds and the forms of their disbursal are Zakat-compliant, with implications for who the organization is able to support, how and where. Improved relationships with politicians and prominent businesspeople in these locations may therefore open the door for other protection-oriented conversations in places like Indonesia and Saudi Arabia that are being targeted for zakat. This practice may also, however, silence more assertive lobbying for protection "in situ" as UNHCR wishes to avoid antagonizing these much-needed "growth markets" for plugging UNHCR's "funding gap."[22]

---

19 'Refugee Zakat Fund: 2019 Mid-Year Report' (UNHCR 2019) <https://zakat.unhcr.org/wp-content/uploads/2019/08/UNHCRs-Refugee-Zakat-Fund-Mid-Year-Report-2019-FINAL-v1.pdf> accessed May 12, 2024.

20 'Ramadan' (USA for UNHCR) <https://www.unrefugees.org/how-to-help/islamic-philanthropy/ramadan/> accessed May 14, 2024.

21 Georgia Cole, 'Non-signatory Donor States and UNHCR: Questions of Funding and Influence' (2021) 67 *Forced Migration Review* 56.

22 'UNHCR unveils the Refugee Zakat Fund, a global Islamic finance structure to help displaced populations worldwide' (UNHCR 2019) <https://www.unhcr.org/hk/news/

This has appeared to suit these states well. Since its international isolation in 2017, for example, Qatar has sought to enhance its collaborations with United Nations (UN) institutions as part of a campaign of what Barakat calls "legitimacy through association."[23] In 2018, this resulted in the Qatari government signing the QC4HCR agreement with UNHCR to expand opportunities for partnership and coordination, while significantly scaling up its disbursal of public funds through multi-lateral organizations. A similar trend has been seen over the past two decades in Dubai, which has successfully positioned itself as a key player in the global humanitarian architecture, particularly through the expansion of the International Humanitarian City first established in 2003. UNHCR's largest global stockpile of humanitarian assistance is now located there.[24] In the United Arab Emirates, "humanitarian diplomacy" has indeed been a key part of foreign policy since the 1970s, which, as Gökalp argues, is aimed at gaining "international acknowledgement, leverage, recognition and relevance."[25]

UNHCR has played off these projected identities to leverage support. In the case of Saudi Arabia, it suggested to the Saudi authorities that their failure to commit to supporting the administrative costs of a more permanent UNHCR presence in the country might result in them being publicly shamed, with an associated loss in international legitimacy, as UNHCR would be forced to ask the international community for financial support.[26] A similar opportunity to buttress support accompanied the Saudi authorities' request to UNHCR to help them defend an incident of deadly violence in the Iraqi refugee camps in 1993. For UNHCR, the Saudi government's dependence on the organization for its "legitimacy on the international plane" presented an opportunity to affirm the value of the international refugee regime – not least as a key international forum for furnishing state's reputations – as it sought to formalize its presence within the country.[27] There is no guarantee, however, that UNHCR's political opportunism in response to these

---

unhcr-unveils-refugee-zakat-fund-global-islamic-finance-structure-help-displaced-populations> accessed May 14, 2024.

23 Sultan Barakat, 'Priorities and Challenges of Qatar's Humanitarian Diplomacy' (2019) 07 Chr. Michelsen Institute 1.

24 'United Arab Emirates' (UNHCR) <https://www.unhcr.org/asia/countries/united-arab-emirates> accessed April 11, 2024.

25 Deniz Gökalp, 'The UAE's Humanitarian Diplomacy: Claiming State Sovereignty, Regional Leverage and International Recognition' (2020) 01 Chr. Michelsen Institute Working Paper 1.

26 Janmyr and Lysa (n 13).

27 ibid 58.

windows of opportunity has any enduring effects on state's identities and practices.

2.2 *Interessement and Enrollment*

These stages are ultimately related to stabilization: once actors have their identities and goals defined and aligned, work needs to be done to maintain this situation. This can be tricky. Actors span networks, with no guarantee that their identities and goals in one network will be compatible with their position in another, and actors outside of these networks may be looking to define the identities of those actors within them in ways that threaten any alignment. In the field of transnational law, Canfield highlights this, noting that it "is constituted by networks of states, international institutions, multinational corporations, and transnational activists struggling for power by producing competing norms" while hoping to attain "interpretive authority."[28] Force, seduction, solicitation and other strategies may be required to cut off these competing alliances, with "fuzziness, adjustment and compromise" key to holding these assemblages together.[29] For Callon, these strategies constitute enrollment as this is "the group of multilateral negotiations, trials of strength and tricks that accompany the interessements and enable them to succeed."[30]

We see this clearly within the international refugee regime, with a perfect example from the Indonesian context detailed by Dewansyah in this volume (see chapter 5). UNHCR is looking to shape the identities of states and other actors toward various goals at the same time that other states, political elites, the private sector, the voting public, multi-lateral organizations, etc. are also attempting to define them, potentially in mutually exclusive ways. The organization must therefore understand: which entities are trying to seduce states parties away? What are they trying to "interest" states parties (not) to do? What identities are these "spoilers" seeking to define for governments and states? What networks are they trying to promote? What strategies do they have in their arsenal to do so? And how might these be challenged by UNHCR and other actors seeking to hold together the assemblage of international refugee protection?

Here, I focus on the various strategies adopted by UNHCR in its attempts to lock actors into identities and courses of action, and to ensure that those within these networks remain tightly interconnected. UNHCR appears to

28 Matthew Canfield, 'Banana Brokers: Communicative Labor, Translocal Translation, and Transnational Law' (2019) 31(1) *Public Culture* 69, 69.

29 Li (n 5) 279.

30 Callon (n 6) 211.

undertake much of this work through socialization, be it through the convening of particular spaces, partnering with certain institutions, or through the direct transmission of norms and values.

In terms of spatial mechanisms, UNHCR organizes key international forums in which signatory and non-signatory states, as well as a wide range of other actors, converge to be socialized in international refugee law and protection norms, and to contribute toward their development. UNHCR's Executive Committee (ExCom) is one such example, where states adopt non-binding but highly influential conclusions on refugee protection. Membership is determined based "on the widest possible geographical basis from those states (members of the United Nations and Others) with a demonstrated interest in, and devotion to, the solution of refugee problems."[31] As a result, Bangladesh, India, Jordan, Lebanon, Pakistan and Venezuela are members of ExCom without being signatories to the 1951 Convention.[32] The Global Refugee Forum is another key space, as were the multitude of events leading up to the adoption of the New York Declaration for Refugees and Migrants in 2016 and the Global Compact on Refugees (GCR) signed in December 2018.[33] Within the GCR, the UN acknowledges the "generous approach to hosting refugees" exhibited by non-signatory states, while using this as an opportunity to encourage them to consider accession.[34]

Limited evidence indeed shows the power of these spaces in encouraging non-signatory states to improve the provision of protection to refugees. Chotinukul's work, for example, attests to the significance of these global forums for driving conversations around protection in the Thai context (see chapter 8). At the 2016 Leaders' Summit that ran adjacent to the UN Summit for Refugees and Migrants, Thailand's Prime Minister publicly committed to various mechanisms that would allow refugees to remain lawfully in the country with expanded rights to protection. Three years later, and after sus-

31 UNGA, 'International assistance to refugees within the mandate of the United Nations High Commissioner for Refugees 1166 (12)' (26 November 1957) <https://www.unhcr.org/uk/publications/international-assistance-refugees-within-mandate-united-nations-high-commissioner-1> accessed 12 April 2024.

32 Ovacık and Johny's work in this volume also details how these ExCom Conclusions and UNHCR's Country of Origin Reports are drawn upon by legal actors, including domestic courts, in non-signatory states as respected sources of knowledge to advance refugee protection (see chapter 3).

33 Maja Janmyr, 'Non-Signatory States and the International Refugee Regime' (2021) 67 *Forced Migration Review* 39.

34 UNGA, 'Global Compact on Refugees' (United Nations 2018) para 6 <https://www.unhcr.org/media/global-compact-refugees-booklet> accessed March 21, 2024.

tained lobbying from civil society organizations to uphold these commitments and affirm the GCR, the government established the National Screening Mechanism to ensure that those in need of protection could remain in the country on a temporary basis.[35]

Similarly, albeit perhaps optimistically, Alexander and Singh suggest that India's role in drafting the GCR and then endorsing it "demonstrates her willingness to usher in a uniform, fairer, and stronger course of action and procedure to accommodate and deal with large refugee movements."[36] As the authors themselves then note, however, the GCR is a non-binding instrument with no enforcement mechanisms that is contradictory in terms of whether it is political or not. As such, it was an easy thing for governments to commit to in principle, in spaces conducive to collective action, without providing a clear and enforceable pathway to improving refugees' access to protection. In Arnold-Fernandez's view, the GCR may even have worsened refugees' abilities to access protection by allowing states to over-write their commitments to the 1951 Convention with new pledges to non-binding, and ultimately weaker, principles that states themselves had developed.[37] Chotinukul's conclusions on the introduction of the National Screening Mechanism in Thailand certainly echo this note of caution.

In terms of socialization through other institutions, the literature points to attempts by UNHCR to buttress the assemblage through aligning its goals with other actors or networks promoting similar priorities. Janmyr and Lysa's work shows that UNHCR's early attempts to establish a presence in Saudi Arabia involved collaboration and networking with influential regional players such as the GCC, the Organization of Islamic Cooperation (OIC) and the Islamic Development Bank (IDB).[38] Very recently, UNHCR has attempted to link the Sustainable Development Goals (SDGs) with the Global Compact on Refugees. UNHCR has sought to leverage states' commitments within the SDGs to "leave no one behind" to ensure that refugees are effectively included, supported and monitored through national governments' SDG plans.[39] To do so, however, it

35 Naiyana Thanawattho, Waritsara Rungthong and Emily Arnold-Fernández, 'Advancing Refugee Rights in Non-signatory States: the role of civil society in Thailand' (2021) 67 *Forced Migration Review* 61.

36 Atul Alexander and Nakul Singh, 'India and Refugee Law: Gauging India's Position on Afghan Refugees' (2001) 11(2) *Laws* 31, 33.

37 Emily E. Arnold-Fernández, 'The Global Compact on Refugees: Inadequate Substitute or Useful Complement?' (2023) 5 *Frontiers in Human Dynamics*.

38 Janmyr and Lysa (n 13) 39.

39 Mai Wardeh and Rui Cunha Marques, 'Measuring the SDGs in Refugee Camps: An Insight into Arab States Bordering Syria' (2003) 15(1) *Sustainability* 15, 1720.

has first had to tackle the "refugee gap"[40] so that refugees are not only addressed through the non-specific indicator "well-managed migration policies."[41] Furthermore, while this may provide a route through which UNHCR can encourage states to engage with refugee protection, they are, much like the GCR, ultimately unenforceable goals and few states submit annual monitoring reports on their progress toward attaining them.

Finally, UNHCR works directly with institutions, universities (see chapter 11), government representatives, civil society actors and refugees to encourage their continued engagement with the network of international protection, and to ensure that numerous different actors are capable of exerting pressure on states parties to uphold key protection norms.[42] In Bangladesh, for example, UNHCR has worked to socialize the government into key hard and soft law mechanisms pertaining to international protection. This, buttressed by national judicial decisions, has contributed to the government largely adhering to the principle of *non-refoulement* with the Rohingya refugees since 2017.[43] Suyastri et al's study of legal protection in Indonesia highlights the role that refugees who have received information from UNHCR and their peers about their legal entitlements have played in pushing for greater state provision of international protection.[44] In their work on Thailand, Thanawattho et al suggest that while the success of civil society organizations in lobbying the Thai government has rested on local formulations of rights and responsibilities (see below), these initiatives have relied on funding from UNHCR.[45] The widespread socialization of key actors on the central norms of international refugee law indeed clearly diffuses responsibility for defining and maintaining the identities of states in more pro-refugee ways.

This then relates to an important final point on enrollment, which is that actors other than UNHCR are of course playing critical roles in keeping the assemblage of international protection together, as extensively detailed in

40 International Rescue Committee, *Missing Persons: Refugees Left Out and Left Behind in the Sustainable Development Goals* (2019) <https://www.rescue.org/sites/default/files/document/4121/missingpersonreport100319.pdf> accessed April 16, 2024.

41 Chiara Denaro and Mariagiulia Giuffre, 'UN Sustainable Development Goals and the "Refugee Gap": Leaving Refugees Behind?' (2022) 41(1) *Refugee Survey Quarterly* 79.

42 Janmyr (n 33).

43 M Sanjeeb Hossain, 'Doing Legal History in Refugee Law: A Snapshot of Bangladesh's Engagement with Non-Refoulment' (2023) 36(4) *Journal of Refugee Studies* 1030.

44 Cifebrima Suyastri, Mohammad Thoriq Bahri, and Marhadi Marhadi, 'Legal Gap in Refugee Protection in Non-Signatory Countries: An Evidence from Indonesia' (2023) 14(3) *Danube* 193.

45 Thanawattho et al (n 35).

the Asian context by Barbour (see chapter 4). This includes refugees, through their sustained lobbying of non-signatory states to uphold the rights of displaced populations, and sub-national bodies, such as provincial courts. These courts may not have the authority to overturn national level laws and policymaking, but, as Ovacık and Johny detail in the case of India (see chapter 3), they do hold states to account for often highly politicized and inconsistent decision-making vis-à-vis asylum.[46] It also includes non-signatory states themselves. As Fakhoury discusses, non-signatory states playing host to large numbers of displaced people in the Middle East have leveraged their position as "containers" of refugees to extract concessions from Global North countries whose political capital rests on these populations remaining on distant shores, as well as to strengthen alliances with the European Union and UNHCR.[47] Veiled threats to change the hosting arrangement in non-signatory states have thus ensured that signatory states in the Global North cannot entirely withdraw from the delicate global system of responsibility-sharing.

2.3 *Mobilization*

In Callon's final stage of translation, that of mobilization, he asks us to consider: "who speaks in the name of whom? Who represents whom?" And how effective are they in this position? This is because in any assemblage, spokespeople are designated to represent what the "masses" want and need. It is only when the representatives or spokespeople go unchallenged that we see the construction of a reality in which a "constraining network of relationships has been built," whereby "the margins of maneuver of each entity will then be tightly delimited."[48] Conversely, if the masses within these networks do not remain faithful to their representatives, or other representatives upset this equilibrium, the whole alignment falls apart.

This raises questions within the system of international protection. What, or who, are the representatives of non-signatory states, and the displaced people residing within them, within the network of the international refugee regime? Who are the "masses" that they claim to represent? Do these masses follow their representatives, or do these masses instead enact or challenge

---

46 Aishwarya Birla, 'Evaluating the Indian Refugee Law Regime: How Has the Judiciary Responded to Refugee Claims in Light of International Law Obligations, and How Can It Do Better?' (2023) 35(1) *International Journal of Refugee Law* 81, 87.

47 Tamirace Fakhoury, 'Refugee Return and Fragmented Governance in the Host State: Displaced Syrians in the Face of Lebanon's Divided Politics' (2021) 42(1) *Third World Quarterly* 162.

48 Callon (n 6) 218.

international refugee law through alternative channels and means? This might include displaced populations themselves, who contest the assumption that UNHCR should be their spokesperson or mediator in contexts where more substantive rights might be better demanded through alternative channels.

Across the literature on non-signatory states there is indeed widespread evidence of the weaknesses of certain "representatives" and "spokespeople," who may be promoting networks of international protection in one arena while they are being simultaneously ignored or disassembled in another. Kneebone et al's work on Indonesia details the limits of regulations designed to offer protection to displaced populations when the immigration and legal institutions tasked with upholding them are not sensitized to their content. They argue that the introduction of Presidential Regulation No. 125 of 2016 concerning the Treatment of Refugees in Indonesia has not translated into meaningful and effective protection because of the political economic context at the level of local government, which is the main body responsible for providing services to refugees, as well as a lack of financial support and rights-based commitments from the national government.[49]

A recurrent theme therefore is the breakdown in alignment between legal "representatives" at an international level and the bureaucratic, judicial and political "masses" that surround them. In Birla's work on India they state that though the Indian Constitution provides protection to refugees through Article 21 (the right to life), and protection against *non-refoulement* through the Universal Declaration of Human Rights (UDHR),[50] the International Covenant on Civil and Political Rights (ICCPR),[51] the Convention Against Torture (CAT),[52] and the UN Convention on the Right of the Child (CRC),[53] this is repeatedly ignored in Indian Courts. On the one hand, Birla suggests that despite this patchwork of protections for displaced populations, the judiciary remains unable to consistently and reliably extend support toward refugees without an explicit legal framework to underpin their actions, ie without rati-

49 Susan Kneebone, Antje Missbach and Balawyn Jones, 'The False Promise of Presidential Regulation No. 125 of 2016?' (2021) 8(3) *Asian Journal of Law and Society* 431.

50 Universal Declaration of Human Rights (adopted December 10, 1948) UNGA res 217 A (3).

51 International Covenant on Civil and Political Rights (adopted December 16, 1966, entered into force March 23, 1976) 999 UNTS 171.

52 Convention against Torture and Other Cruel, Inhuman, and Degrading Treatment or Punishment (adopted December 10, 1984, entered into force June 26, 1987) 1465 UNTS 85 (CAT).

53 Convention on the Rights of the Child (adopted November 20, 1989, entered into force September 2, 1990) 1577 UNTS 3.

fying the 1951 Convention. On the other hand, they imply that the country's commitment to key refugee law principles will always be largely determined by politics. As Birla states, India's "tumultuous relationship with refugee protection" is "exacerbated by the control that the executive branch and, by extension, the ruling party's politics have over the matter."[54]

Li, Shaffer and Nam's assessment of the success of mobilization in the Hong Kong context is much the same. There, the Court of Final Appeal held in *C & Ors v the Director of Immigration and Another* that as the Government voluntarily complies with the 1951 Convention despite not ratifying it, it must abide by its high standards of fairness and establish a Unified Screening Mechanism to prevent *non-refoulement*.[55] While praised by some as a possible model for refugee protection in states that are not signatories to the 1951 Convention, Li, Shaffer and Nam note that less than 1 percent of claims are accepted. This, they argue, shows the precariousness of a system that lacks "moral commitment," "the Refugee Convention's normative foundations," "a whole-of-society approach" and, critically, "political buy-in."[56] In other words, these examples show the potential precariousness of ad hoc approaches to building assemblages that focus on specific, rather than systemic, commitments to international protection.

3 The Risks of Assemblages

Contained throughout this brief discussion of how UNHCR undertakes processes of "translation" vis-à-vis non-signatory states have thus been some of the pitfalls of the organization's approach, including with regards to the long-term sustainability of a network built on short-term expediencies. We see this clearly in the work of Janmyr, Hossain and Turner on MoUs (see chapter 10). They highlight the risks for refugee protection of this fragmented parallel system of often opaque and unenforceable documents, as well as some of the unforeseen consequences of the pragmatic compromises involved in securing them.

While these agreements may enroll states into the international refugee regime at a particular location at a particular time, thus temporarily growing

54 Birla (n 46) 100.

55 Brian Barbour, 'Beyond Asian Exceptionalism: Refugee Protection in Non-signatory States' (2021) 67 *Forced Migration Review* 42.

56 Rachel Li and Isaac Shaffer and Lynette Nam, 'Hong Kong's Unified Screening Mechanism: Form over Substance' (2001) 67 *Forced Migration Review* 48.

the network, there are nonetheless questions around to what end. Where is UNHCR hoping that these agreements will take the organization and refugee protection in general? Are they part of any long-term strategy or purely indicative of short-term pragmatism? What is the afterlife of these compromises? And what are the implications for refugees themselves of the concessions accepted to secure these agreements, particularly given these affected populations have very little idea about what they contain? In concluding their piece on how UNHCR consolidated its position in Saudi Arabia, Janmyr and Lysa indeed call for further research into the longer-term impacts of the pragmatic compromises that UNHCR accepted in the early 1990s to consolidate its position in the country.[57]

There are also numerous operational examples of UNHCR "sacrificing principles at the altar of pragmatism"[58] to try to maintain a foothold in non-signatory states. With regards to the Gulf states, UNHCR has partnered with these governments in the provision of humanitarian assistance that has furthered these states' political, diplomatic and social objectives in neighboring countries, such as Yemen, in ways that may have actually exacerbated displacement in the region.[59] When the Lebanese government started trying to induce Syrian refugees to return in 2017, UNHCR began investigating whether it would be safe for these returnees in Syria. Threatened with the revocation of their staff's residency permits by the Lebanese authorities, however, UNHCR rowed back on this fundamental aspect of its protection mandate.[60]

This raises further questions about what the real purpose – or consistent principles – of this assemblage are, and whether UNHCR even always knows. In seeking to get Bangladesh to accede to the 1951 Convention in 1978, the High Commissioner at the time, Poul Hartling, wrote that getting more states to accede to international refugee law instruments was "an important factor in resolving refugee problems."[61] UNHCR indeed promotes international refugee law within the 1951 Convention as critical in providing solutions to the "problem of refugees," albeit without any unified agreement as to what that problem might be. In her study of building assemblages around forest conservation and management, Li suggests that a weakness of that approach was that it started from a proposed solution – that those who live in closest proximity to forests are in the best position to protect it – rather than from any agreed

57 Janmyr and Lysa (n 13).

58 Michael Barnett, *UNHCR and the ethics of repatriation* (Forced Migration Review 2001) <https://www.fmreview.org/barnett/> accessed December 9, 2024.

59 Cole (n 21).

60 Fakhoury (n 47).

61 Cited in Hossain (n 43).

definition amongst the numerous stakeholders of what the problem actually was.[62] The same might be said of the international refugee regime. With no explicit, shared understanding of what the "refugee problem" is, the assemblage seems oriented to *managing* numerous "problems" and not *resolving* them or it.

There is also ample evidence of where formal involvement in the network of the international refugee regime does not necessarily equate to better protection. Clearly many signatory states who technically abide by refugee law outsource their non-conformity to other states, with externalization allowing states to unravel the assemblage while appearing to be a strong part of it. We see this through Kneebone, Missbach and Jones' work on Indonesia. The Indonesian government's very limited response to refugees was replaced by an approach focused almost exclusively on stopping "irregular migrants" travelling onwards to Australia, following heavy pressure from the Australian government.[63] Chimni has indeed long cautioned against Asian states acceding to the 1951 Convention until it becomes a much more effective mechanism for sharing global responsibility rather than shifting it.[64] As Janmyr states, "while there is a widespread and entrenched assumption that refugee protection is superior in signatory States when compared with non-signatories, there are no systematic and comparative studies supporting an argument that accession to the 1951 Refugee Convention automatically means better protection … and in some cases protection may even be better in non-signatory States than in signatory States."[65] Some of the alternatives promoted in these spaces may at the least become increasingly important as asylum systems around the world become more restrictive.[66]

3.1 *Complementary and Contingent Networks*

Here, the theoretical literature on assemblages helps deepen and extend this critique. As Callon states, his approach permits "an explanation of how a few

62 Li (n 5).

63 Kneebone et al (n 49).

64 B. S. Chimni, *The Law and Politics of Regional Solution of the Refugee Problem: The Case of South Asia* (Regional Centre for Strategic Studies, 1998).

65 Janmyr (n 33).

66 Georgia Cole 'Sampling on the Dependent Variable: An Achille's Heel of Research on Displacement?' (2021) 34(4) *Journal of Refugee Studies* 4479; Charlotte Lysa 'Governing Refugees in Saudi Arabia (1948–2022)' (2023) 42(1) *Refugee Survey Quarterly* 1. Of course, social scientists are well aware of many of these discontents. As Li suggests, however, they often put forward a form of 'contained critique' to avoid 'unravel[ing] the assemblage' (Li (n 5) 13).

obtain the right to express and to represent the many silent actors of the social and natural worlds they have mobilized."[67] When this process of translation has been successful, "only voices speaking in unison will be heard,"[68] and other aspects or alternative approaches may be rendered "invisible or irrelevant."[69] Espeland and Stevens' note the same dangers inherent to the related process of "commensuration," which refers to the process of establishing common metrics, frameworks, approaches and discourses to enable the alignment of diverse actors. They suggest that in establishing commonalities and comparability between previously disparate things, this hugely political act can "radically transform the world by creating new social categories and backing them with the weight of powerful institutions"[70] all while significantly changing, or as Callon suggests, invisibilizing, their prior meanings and significance.[71] Put plainly, there are always costs to be identified and questioned whenever any single network is being established and promoted.

Numerous studies touch on the shortcomings of transforming the multiplicity of displaced people into the legal-bureaucratic category of "refugees" given refugee law can be seen "as a quintessential tool of commensuration."[72] This is precisely the point made by Mohammed and Jureidini.[73] They discuss how *ummatic* principles[74] and institutional collaborations practiced in Islamic, non-signatory States could enhance more secular understandings of refugee protection provided they are not simply collapsed into mainstream refugee law approaches. In their view, the ideologies associated with the bordered nature of the modern nation-state and the prominence accorded to national sovereignty are some of the most powerful forces in *disassembling* the networks of actors and spaces that could best protect displaced populations, and yet both of these principles are strongly reinforced by the 1951 Convention. As such, they suggest that the OIC could col-

67 Callon (n 6) 224.

68 Callon (n 6) 223.

69 Wendy Nelson Espeland and Mitchell L. Stevens, 'Commensuration as a Social Process' (1998) 24(14) *Annual Review of Sociology* 313, 314.

70 ibid 323.

71 ibid 324.

72 Canfield (n 28).

73 Hossameldeen Mohammed and Ray Jureidini, 'Umma and the Nation-state: Dilemmas in Refuge Ethics' (2022) 7 *Journal of International Humanitarian Action* 1, 17.

74 Lysa provides historical examples of how the claim to asylum through the "Umma" has worked, such as with Uzbeks fleeing Soviet repression in the 1950s and Uighurs fleeing China two decades later to the Hijaz. See Charlotte Lysa, 'Governing Refugees in Saudi Arabia (1948–2022)' (2023) 42(1) *Refugee Survey Quarterly* 1.

laborate with UNHCR to promote the principles of *umma* alongside international refugee law, importantly while retaining the critical differences between these approaches. In terms of how this might be done practically, Kazmi and Shah discuss how university students as the influential "lawyers of tomorrow" can be taught creative approaches to enhancing international protection without elevating one conception of refugee law over other ways of protecting displaced populations (see chapter 11).

For De Sousa Santos, this requires a different form of "translation" rooted in a belief in "negative universalism."[75] This entails every actor recognizing both that their institutional culture is incomplete and can be enriched by dialogue and confrontation with others, and that there is no all-encompassing, singular approach to social transformation and justice that can ever feasibly work. Instead, they suggest that actors should be offering "a point of porosity" that makes them permeable to the practices, discourses and knowledges of others without destroying, redefining or homogenizing any identities in the process.

The work by Thanawattho et al in Thailand shows the value of this "negative universalism" for promoting international protection.[76] They draw on the experiences of a coalition of refugee-focused organizations in the country, mainly led by Thai nationals and called the Coalition for the Rights of Refugees and Stateless Persons (CRSP), to show the limits of commensuration. They detail the hostility that Thai government officials have shown toward transnational alliances seeking to push new policies and practices through the language of international human rights. In contrast, the CRSP has managed to more successfully "enroll" the Thai government in protection initiatives by drawing on a high degree of contextual knowledge and local embeddedness, speaking in languages, values and discourses that these officials understand, and through appeals to CRSP members' rights as concerned citizens. While the CRSP has drawn on pledges made by the Thai government at various international refugee forums, they have not called for ratification of the 1951 Convention given their uncertainty as to what this would achieve in the absence of political will to action it. Herein thus lies one of the benefits of localization when conceived of in terms of mutual learning and partnership, as opposed to the absolute convergence of identities in too tightly bounded an assemblage.

75 Boaventura De Sousa Santos, 'The Future of the World Social Forum: the work of translation' (2005) 48(2) *Development* 2.

76 Thanawattho et al (n 35).

4 Conclusion

The focus in the first half of this chapter on schematizing the roles played by UNHCR in its attempts to build and maintain assemblages of international protection in non-signatory states should thus in no way be treated as an endorsement of these activities. As detailed, these strategies differ from socialization in that they often entail short-term compromises and pragmatic alliances to ensure a combination of protection, relevance and growth. They risk both jeopardizing alternative ways of supporting displaced populations and unravelling over time. Callon indeed notes that the actors in his story worked "incessantly … defining and associating entities, in order to forge alliances that were confirmed to be stable only for a certain location at a particular time."[77] The assemblage he studied was extremely fragile and the process of interessement was always threatened due to the wide array of different actors, technologies, discourses, laws, populations and objects drawn together within it.

In reality, however, we see this fragility across the literature on the international refugee regime. There is evidently a marked lack of consistency in how states respond to displaced populations whether they have acceded to the 1951 Convention or not.[78] This provides a further reason to analyze the provision of international protection as largely about contingent assemblages, with fragile bonds rooted in history, culture, funding, etc. that to some extent have to be forged afresh with each new caseload, drawing on the discursive, moral and legal resources available. International refugee law and UNHCR may play key roles in these assemblages, but their limitations are certainly not the limits of the network of international protection broadly conceived and operationalized. As shown in this chapter, critiques derived from STS help to highlight what the possible risks of their further expansion might be, as well as the sorts of pluralistic and complementary assemblages that we might instead seek to encourage.

77 Callon (n 6) 222.

78 For examples from India see Alexander and Singh (n 36) 31; from Türkiye see Kemal Kirişci and Ayselin Yıldız, 'Turkey's asylum policies over the last century: continuity, change and contradictions' (2023) 24(3–4) *Turkish Studies* 1; and from Lebanon see Maja Janmyr, 'Sudanese Refugees and the "Syrian Refugee Response" in Lebanon: Racialised Hierarchies, Processes of Invisibilisation, and Resistance' (2022) 41(1) *Refugee Survey Quarterly* 1.

CHAPTER 10

UNHCR-Host State Agreements as Alternative Protection Regimes

Maja Janmyr, M Sanjeeb Hossain and Lewis Turner

1 Introduction

As this volume explores, many states across the world are not signatories to the 1951 Convention relating to the Status of Refugees and its 1967 Protocol (together and individually "the Refugee Convention"),[1] nor do they have any national laws pertaining to asylum-seekers and refugees. In place of a clear legal framework, agreements between UNHCR and the host state (and, occasionally, a third party) are often negotiated. This chapter focuses on the two kinds of agreements most foundational to UNHCR's presence and role in non-signatory refugee hosting states, namely, *cooperation* agreements[2] and *special* agreements. Both types of agreements are also commonly referred to as Memoranda of Understanding (MoUs).[3]

Having their basis in the UNHCR Statute, agreements between UNHCR and refugee-hosting states are integral to the international refugee law regime.

1 Convention relating to the Status of Refugees 189 UNTS 137 (adopted July 28, 1951, entered into force April 22, 1954); Protocol relating to the Status of Refugees 606 UNTS 267 (adopted January 31, 1967, entered into force October 4, 1967).

2 Cooperation agreements were referred to as "branch office agreements" or "field office agreements" before 1989. Today, UNHCR refers to them broadly as host-state or host-country agreements.

3 This chapter uses the terms "agreements" and "MoUs" interchangeably. An agreement can be defined as "mutual consent by participants to a commitment regarding future behavior." See The Guidelines of the Inter-American Juridical Committee for Binding and Non-Binding Agreements and the related *travaux préparatoires,* guideline 1.1. Available at <https://www.oas.org/en/sla/iajc/themes_recently_concluded_Binding_and_Non-Binding_Agreements.asp> accessed December 9, 2024. While some suggest that the use of the label MoU signifies an intention to create a politically binding but not legally binding instrument, based on the practices of states and international organizations, others are less certain. Aust, for example, has argued that one must be "extremely careful" when evaluating the status of the MoU, for "sometimes one will find a treaty called a Memorandum of Understanding." See Anthony Aust, *Modern Treaty Law and Practice* (2nd edn, 2007) 25; Jan Klabbers, 'Governance by Academics: The Invention of Memoranda of Understanding' (2020), 80(1) *Zeitschrift für ausländisches öffentliches Recht und Völkerrecht* 35.

They may also create an important link between non-signatory states and the Refugee Convention, covering questions such as protection, emergency response, durable solutions, and advocacy. In some cases, an agreement may remedy the fact that a state in question has no formal ties to key refugee law instruments, while in others, as we will explore in this chapter, they may undermine key protection principles. For refugees, the importance of these agreements cannot be overstated. Apart from functioning as the backbone of the refugee response in a given context, the agreements are sometimes the sole document that spells out refugees' rights and/or how and by whom they will be governed.

Yet despite the crucial role they play in shaping the protection landscape in many host states, MoUs are rarely the focus of scholarly inquiry.[4] This chapter posits that these agreements may function as alternative protection regimes to the Refugee Convention. Based on our original research on the contexts of Bangladesh, Jordan, Lebanon, and Saudi Arabia, as well as discussions of agreements from other contexts, this chapter explores the features of these agreements, their roles in non-signatory states, and their strengths and weaknesses as protection instruments.

The chapter begins with an overview of cooperation and special agreements, placing them within the broader context of UNHCR's work with host governments. It subsequently explores the agreements as alternative protection regimes in lieu of the Refugee Convention, as well as their role in protecting refugees in non-signatory states. The chapter concludes by zooming in on contemporary concerns and critiques of these agreements, focusing on issues relating to their content, participation and transparency, legal status and enforceability, practice and implementation, and fragmentation. This chapter's overarching argument is that the use of cooperation and special agreements can constitute a shift away from, toward, or even beyond the protection offered by the Refugee Convention.

2 The Development and Rationale of UNHCR-Host State Agreements

UNHCR's provision of international protection invariably depends upon a presence in the territory of states, and under the UNHCR Statute, the organization's competence concerning refugees is universal in nature, without any

4 For an important exception, see Marjoleine Zieck, *UNHCR's Worldwide Presence in the Field: A Legal Analysis of UNHCR's Cooperation Agreements* (Wolf Legal Publishers 2006) 160.

geographical limitation.[5] Articles 8 and 16 of the UNHCR Statute provide the basis for UNHCR's presence in a state's territory through "special" and "cooperation" agreements. Cooperation agreements are concluded based on article 16 of the UNHCR Statute:

> The High Commissioner shall consult the governments of the countries of residence of refugees as to the need for appointing representatives therein. In any country recognizing such need, there may be appointed a representative approved by the government of that country. Subject to the foregoing, the same representative may serve in more than one country.

"Special agreements," on the other hand, find their basis in article 8 of the UNHCR Statute. This obliges the High Commissioner to "provide for the protection of refugees falling under the competence of his Office" by "[p]romoting through special agreements with governments the execution of any measures calculated to improve the situation of refugees and to reduce the number requiring protection."[6]

Although many of the agreements we focus on in this chapter provide UNHCR with a legal footing on a refugee hosting state's territory, in numerous instances, the agency's offices operate without any formal legal agreement with the host state.[7] While this does not mean that UNHCR is present in those territories without consent,[8] its relationships with host states are not always formalized through agreements. For instance, demonstrating the precarity of UNHCR's legal status in some non-signatory states, in 2010 UNHCR was expelled from Libya and had its offices closed despite informally operating there from 1991. A government communiqué stated that it did not recognize UNHCR's presence because Libya is not a party to the Refugee Convention.[9] By contrast, UNHCR has operated in Lebanon since 1962, yet it was only in 2003 that a government entity formally entered into an agreement with the organization. Similarly, while UNHCR has operated in Bangla-

---

5 Statute of the Office of the United Nations High Commissioner for Refugees A/RES/428(V) (December 14, 1950) ch 2 art 6

6 ibid 2, art 8(b).

7 Zieck (n 4) 160.

8 ibid 294.

9 'Allow UNHCR Back into Libya, MDE 19/010/2010' (Amnesty International 2010) <https://www.amnesty.org/en/wp-content/uploads/2021/07/mde190102010en.pdf> accessed December 9, 2024.

desh since its independence in 1971, a cooperation agreement was negotiated only in 1993.[10]

The aforementioned UNHCR agreements with Lebanon and Bangladesh demonstrate that the agreements can alleviate the agency's legal precarity and can therefore form a key part of the framework for UNHCR's work in a given state, especially non-signatory states. Of the 89 UNHCR-Host State agreements concluded between 1951 and 2005, 24 were with states who were not party to any of the relevant refugee law instruments at the time.[11] These include non-signatory states from several regions but with notably high numbers from the Middle East, such as Jordan, Lebanon, Kuwait and Saudi Arabia; and from Asia, such as Bangladesh, Indonesia, Pakistan, Thailand and Vietnam. As Zieck observed in her seminal study of these agreements, in several cases, states acceded to the 1951 Convention and 1967 Protocol just prior to (or shortly after) concluding a cooperation agreement with UNHCR.[12]

The manifest purpose of cooperation agreements is to establish a UNHCR office in the host state. Special agreements, by contrast, are meant to focus on measures which improve the situation of refugees (eg assistance, protection) and/or seek to reduce the number of refugees requiring protection (eg voluntary repatriation). In some instances, for example in Jordan, the initial cooperation agreement lays the groundwork for a special agreement, which might follow relatively quickly thereafter.[13] In other cases, like Lebanon, a special agreement exists without there being a cooperation agreement in place.[14]

In theory, there is a clear distinction between cooperation and special agreements, which – as noted above – are concluded based on different articles of UNHCR's Statute. In practice, however, this ostensibly neat distinction can be very blurred, to the extent that it is sometimes unclear whether an agreement is a cooperation agreement or special agreement. In

10 'Submission by the United Nations High Commissioner for Refugees (UNHCR) for the Office of the High Commissioner for Human Rights' Compilation Report – Universal Periodic Review: Bangladesh' (UNHCR 2012); See also M Sanjeeb Hossain, 'Doing Legal History in Refugee Law: A Snapshot of Bangladesh's Engagement with *Non-Refoulement*' (2023) *Journal of Refugee Studies* <https://doi.org/10.1093/jrs/fead025> accessed March 15, 2024.

11 Zieck (n 4) 259.

12 Examples include Papua New Guinea, the Russian Federation, Turkmenistan and East Timor. See ibid.

13 ibid 287–88.

14 'The Memorandum of Understanding between the Directorate of the General Security (Republic of Lebanon) and the Regional Office of the UN High Commissioner for Refugees, Concerning the Processing of Cases of Asylum-Seekers Applying for Refugee Status with the UNHCR Office (2003).' On file with authors.

many instances, cooperation agreements do not simply establish UNHCR's presence within a state, but also include substantive normative content, including key elements of the Refugee Convention. Indeed, UNHCR itself may use a range of language to describe an agreement, ranging from a "framework agreement,"[15] a "joint cooperation agreement,"[16] and, as mentioned, an MoU.[17] Therefore, although we describe two different kinds of agreements below, for the purposes of outlining how different kinds of agreements are discussed, these "ideal type" agreements, and the distinctions between them, are often not reflected in practice.

2.1 *Cooperation Agreements*

Since 1989, UNHCR's cooperation agreements with host states have officially been based on a regularly updated model agreement,[18] governing both the legal questions concerning the establishment and operation of a representative presence in a state's territory and, proceeding from UNHCR's mandate, the more substantive issues of UNHCR's relations with states.[19] This means that while the agreement typically details the rights and obligations of both parties in terms of privileges, immunities, exemptions and facilities, as Zieck has observed, "they transcend the contents of host state agreements on account of the way in which their provisions, including those on status and matching entitlements, are tied to Statutory and other tasks of the High Commissioner."[20] These agreements therefore set standards with respect to the substance of UNHCR's work in a given state. This is reflected in how the cooperation is based on a certain normative content, as the 2009 model cooperation agreement provides in Article 3(1):

15 'UNHCR Global Appeal 2011 (Update) – Egypt' (UNHCR 2011) <https://www.unhcr.org/media/unhcr-global-appeal-2011-update-egypt> accessed March 15, 2024.

16 'UNHCR, Ministry of Health Agree to Strengthen Cooperation' (UNHCR Egypt 2019) <https://www.unhcr.org/eg/12775-unhcr-ministry-of-health-agree-to-strengthen-cooperation.html> accessed March 15, 2024.

17 'Refugee Context in Egypt' (UNHCR Egypt) <https://www.unhcr.org/eg/about-us/refugee-context-in-egypt> accessed March 15, 2024.

18 'Model UNHCR Co-Operation Agreement between the United Nations High Commissioner for Refugees and the Government of Country X, Rev. MNW 24/10/01' (UNHCR 2009) <https://www.refworld.org/legal/modellaw/unhcr/2009/en/21585> accessed March 15, 2024.

19 Zieck (n 4) 4–5.

20 ibid 7.

> Co-operation between the Government and UNHCR in the field of international protection of, and humanitarian assistance to, refugees and other persons of concern to UNHCR shall be carried out on the basis of the Statute of UNHCR, of other relevant decisions and resolutions relating to UNHCR adopted by United Nations organs.[21]

This obligation is standard in agreements when UNHCR operates in non-signatory states. The "relevant decisions and resolutions" referred to in the above typically concern the resolutions of the General Assembly, which expand the mandate of UNHCR as well as the many conclusions adopted by UNHCR's Executive Committee.[22] The latter concern issues and norms regarding protection and humanitarian assistance which are often not addressed in any binding legal instrument.

Examples of agreements following this approach are UNHCR's 2005 MoU with Sri Lanka and 2019 MoU with Indonesia. Both MoUs explicitly refer to Article 35 of the 1951 Convention and Article 2 of the 1967 Protocol which elaborate the nature of co-operation of national authorities with the United Nations, as well as to the UN Guiding Principles on Internal Displacement.[23] A starkly different example, containing no normative content concerning refugee protection, is UNHCR's 1979 cooperation agreement with Indonesia which is mainly focused on the privileges and immunities of UNHCR staff.[24] As for the "functions" of UNHCR, Article 1 of this MoU merely states: "The UNHCR Branch Office will exercise functions assigned to it by the High Commissioner in relation to his activities in Indonesia."

Cooperation agreements often do not follow the model agreement in terms of structure and content and may not even have "cooperation agreements" in their title. The 1993 MoU between UNHCR and Saudi Arabia, negotiated in the context of the 1991 Gulf War, does not follow this "model."[25] It is less detailed

---

21 UNHCR 'Model Agreement' (n 18) art 3(1).

22 Zieck (n 4) 263–64.

23 'Agreement between the Office of the United Nations High Commissioner for Refugees and the Government of the Democratic Socialist Republic of Sri Lanka. Colombo, 7 December 2005.' Available in *United Nations Juridical Yearbook 2005* (United Nations 2009) 110.

24 'Agreement between the Government of the Republic of Indonesia and the United Nations High Commissioner for Refugees Regarding the Establishment of the Office of the UNHCR Representative for Indonesia, 15 June 1979.' On file with authors.

25 'Memorandum of Understanding between the United Nations (United Nations High Commissioner for Refugees) and the Government of Saudi Arabia. Jeddah, 22 June 1993.' Registered *Ex Officio* (No. I-30092) as 'Memorandum of Understanding Concerning

and similar in structure and content to that developed for UNHCR Syria at around the same time. UNHCR's 1996 agreement with Kuwait is another example of an agreement that decisively differs from the blueprint.[26] Other agreements may be considerably more rudimentary, not reaching the "threshold of a cooperation agreement in the sense of UNHCR's model cooperation agreement."[27]

Zieck has argued that the cooperation agreements should be considered "not only as part of the conventional law on international privileges and immunities but also as part of … the international refugee law regime,"[28] a view with which we concur. Many of these agreements are registered as treaties with the UN Secretariat, and thus hold an official status. However, even those agreements that are not registered stem from UNHCR's Statute and are therefore derivatively made part of the international refugee law regime. As we explore further below, given that some of these agreements either contradict, or even go beyond, the obligations placed upon states by the Refugee Convention, the de facto fragmentation potentially brought about by MoUs is a cause for concern.

2.2 *Special Agreements*

The second kind of agreement discussed in this chapter is the special agreement. In contrast to the "ideal type" version of a cooperation agreement, special agreements can vary in structure and content. Nevertheless, these types of agreements typically focus on measures which improve the situation of refugees and/or seek to reduce the number of refugees requiring protection.

Special agreements can, for example, be agreements introducing refugee status determination (RSD) procedures, or those governing voluntary repatriation. As for the latter, UNHCR has negotiated special agreements with coun-

the Establishment of United Nations High Commissioner for Refugees Field Offices in Saudi Arabia.' For the Text, see 1725 UNTS 158. Also available in *United Nations Juridical Yearbook 1993* (United Nations 2001) 147; See further Maja Janmyr and Charlotte Lysa, 'UNHCR's Expansion to the GCC States: Establishing a UNHCR Presence in Saudi Arabia 1987–1993' (2023) 33(1) *Middle East Critique* 45.

26 'Co-Operation and Office Agreement between the Office of the United Nations High Commissioner for Refugees and the Government of the State of Kuwait, April 8, 1996.' Available at <https://www.refworld.org/legal/agreements/unhcr/1996/en/24607> accessed March 18, 2024.

27 Zieck (n 4) 297.

28 ibid 7–8.

tries including Pakistan, Vietnam, Sri Lanka, Bangladesh and Eritrea.[29] The agreements can also be used to outline an agreed division of labor between UNHCR and the host government in terms of refugee protection and relief.[30] Importantly, special agreements may, particularly when they focus on protection, compensate for the fact that the host state is not a party to any of the relevant refugee law instruments, and may be lacking national laws on refugees and asylum.[31]

Much like cooperation agreements, as direct by-products of the UNHCR Statute, they add to the content and form of the international refugee law regime, yet they remain understudied. In what follows, we build on the work of Zieck, Kagan and others, to argue that these agreements may have a particularly important role in non-signatory states: they can constitute an alternative protection regime for refugees.

3 Alternative Protection Regimes

Agreements between UNHCR and refugee-hosting states are a notable part of UNHCR's attempts to negotiate and promote what it describes as "protection space" for refugees, which has become central to the agency's presence in non-signatory states. The idea of "protection space" became increasingly widespread in the 2000s and gained further prominence through its central position in UNHCR's 2009 *Policy on Refugee Protection and Solutions in Urban*

29 'Agreement between the Islamic Republic of Pakistan and the Office of the United Nations High Commissioner for Refugees on the Voluntary Return of [Afghan] Refugees, June 9, 1988'; 'Memorandum of Understanding between the Socialist Republic of Vietnam and the United Nations High Commissioner for Refugees [Relating to the Voluntary Repatriation of Vietnamese Refugees], December 13, 1988'; 'Memorandum of Understanding among the Government of the Socialist Republic of Sri Lanka and the Office of the United Nations High Commissioner for Refugees Relating to the Repatriation of Sri Lankan Refugees and Displaced Persons, February 1, 1993'; 'Memorandum of Understanding between the Government of the People's Republic of Bangladesh and the Office of the United Nations High Commissioner for Refugees [Relating to the Voluntary Repatriation of Myanmar Refugees], May 12, 1993'; 'Memorandum of Understanding between the Government of Eritrea and the United Nations High Commissioner for Refugees for the Voluntary Repatriation and Initial Reintegration of Eritrean Refugees, April 16, 1994'.

30 Michael Kagan, 'The UN "Surrogate State" and the Foundation of Refugee Policy in the Middle East' (2012) 18(2) *Journal of International Law and Policy* 307.

31 Zieck (n 4) 286.

Areas.[32] While "protection space" does not have a legal definition, UNHCR understands it to be "the extent to which there is a conducive environment for the internationally recognized rights of refugees to be respected and upheld."[33] Critics of this notion have rightly raised questions over the concept's lack of clarity and non-binding nature, its focus on the institutional space between protection institutions and refugees (rather than refugees' experiences of protection), and how it may devalue the normative strength of obligations toward refugees.[34]

Within this wider context, however, MoUs with host states nonetheless represent one of the more tangible ways to improve protection in non-signatory states. This is a longstanding approach: provisions to compensate for the fact that the host state was non-signatory to the main refugee instruments were, for example, included in the 1954 agreement with Egypt and in the 1963 draft agreement with Lebanon.[35] In these cases, UNHCR was explicit about its hope that the agreements would essentially compensate for much of the protection that would normally be afforded refugees through the Convention.[36] Drawing on the 1954 agreement with Egypt, the 1963 draft agreement with Lebanon included three articles that reflected key norms of the Refugee Convention. The Lebanese government was obligated to i) at the request of UNHCR, issue identity documents, residence permits, and work permits to all refugees on Lebanese territory; ii) issue travel documents to refugees enabling them to travel outside of Lebanese territory; and iii) respect the principle of *non-refoulement*.

---

32 'UNHCR Policy on Refugee Protection and Solutions in Urban Areas' (UNHCR 2009) <https://www.refworld.org/policy/strategy/unhcr/2009/en/69893> accessed March 18, 2024; See also Jeff Crisp, Jane Janz and José Riera, 'Surviving in the City: A Review of UNHCR's Operation for Iraqi Refugees in Urban Areas of Jordan, Lebanon and Syria' (2009) <https://library.alnap.org/help-library/surviving-in-the-city-a-review-of-unhcrs-operation-for-iraqi-refugees-in-urban-areas-of> accessed March 15, 2024.

33 UNHCR (n 32).

34 Martin Jones, 'Moving Beyond Protection Space: Developing a Law of Asylum in South-East Asia' in Susan Kneebone, Dallal Stevens and Loretta Baldassar (eds), *Refugee Protection and the Role of Law: Conflicting Identities* (Routledge 2014) 257; Eveliina Lyytinen, 'Refugees' Conceptualizations of "Protection Space": Geographical Scales of Urban Protection and Host–Refugee Relations' (2015) 34(2) *Refugee Survey Quarterly* 45.

35 'Accord Entre Le Haut Commissaire Des Nations Unies Pour Les Réfugiés et Le Gouvernement Egyptien, February 10, 1954.'; 'Accord Entre Le Gouvernement Libanais et Le Haut Commissaire Des Nations Unies Pour Les Réfugiés, 1963.' Both documents on file with authors.

36 UNHCR F11/S2/B15 (hereafter UNHCR 11/2/15), 'Proposed Agreement for Our Lebanon Office' in 2.3.20 LAN to SUD Privileges and Immunities, November 16, 1962' December 11, 2015.

More recent agreements may also reiterate core refugee protection principles and, as such, create an important link between non-signatory states and the Refugee Convention. Through the 1993 agreement with UNHCR, Saudi Arabia commits itself to providing protection to refugees on its territory.[37] Similarly, UNHCR's 1998 agreement with Jordan contains the Convention definition of a refugee, without the geographic and temporal limitations, and declares Jordan's commitment to international standards of refugee protection, including the principle of *non-refoulement*.[38]

Another example is UNHCR's 1993 agreement with Bangladesh, which establishes that UNHCR shall discharge its "international protection mandate" and ensures UNHCR's access to refugee camps.[39] It also lays out the responsibilities of the Bangladesh government, including ensuring "safety and security for the Myanmar refugees in the camps and outside." Most importantly, the agreement gives refugees from Myanmar the right to "legal assistance provided by UNHCR" and upholds the principle of *non-refoulement* by pledging to go ahead with voluntary repatriation only under "safe and voluntary" conditions. Furthermore, it upholds the refugees' right to exercise their "freedom of option" when it comes to repatriation to Myanmar.

A specific way in which some MoUs contribute to protection is by outlining the roles and responsibilities of UNHCR (and states parties), and thus often enabling UNHCR to carve out space for specific areas of work, which may, in practice, grow over time. For example, while it is UNHCR's policy that states should conduct RSD, and it continues to attempt to "hand over" this responsibility to states,[40] in many non-signatory states UNHCR acts as a "surrogate state" taking on responsibilities including RSD.[41] The 2003 agreement signed with Lebanon's General Security Office concerning the "processing of cases of asylum-seekers applying for refugee status with UNHCR Office," assigns the

---

37 Memorandum of Understanding, Saudi Arabia (n 25).

38 Ghida Frangieh, 'Relations Between UNHCR and Arab Governments: Memoranda of Understanding in Lebanon and Jordan' (LSE Middle East Centre Blog 2016) <https://blogs.lse.ac.uk/mec/2016/09/23/relations-between-unhcr-and-arab-governments-memoranda-of-understanding-in-lebanon-and-jordan/> accessed March 18, 2024; Dallal Stevens, 'Legal Status, Labelling, and Protection: The Case of Iraqi "Refugees" in Jordan' (2013) 25(1) *International Journal of Refugee Law* 1.

39 UNHCR (n 10).

40 Caroline Nalule and Derya Ozkul, 'Exploring RSD Handover from UNHCR to States' (2020) 65 *Forced Migration Review* 27.

41 Michael Kagan, '"We Live in a Country of UNHCR": The UN Surrogate State and Refugee Policy in the Middle East' (UNHCR Policy Development and Evaluation Service 2011) Research Paper 201 <https://digitallibrary.un.org/record/721793?v=pdf> accessed March 18, 2024.

registration of asylum seekers and the undertaking of RSD in specific cases to UNHCR.[42] Similarly, UNHCR's 1998 MoU with Jordan gives it a range of responsibilities, including conducting RSD, interviewing asylum-seekers being held by Jordanian authorities, providing assistance to asylum-seekers in need, and seeking durable solutions for refugees.

Notably, many agreements that contain elements of the Refugee Convention (and the UNHCR Statute) are signed with states that have consistently rejected the possibility of signing the Convention. The flexibility afforded by these agreements, and the fact that they can be tailored to a state's individual concerns, is arguably one of the ways they are made palatable to non-signatory host states.[43] From UNHCR's perspective, when dealing with such states, even agreements that may contain "heavily compromised version[s] of refugee protection" may be preferential to there being no agreement at all, and thus, for example, no legal mechanism to address the *refoulement* of refugees.[44]

That said, MoUs notably have the possibility of binding the host state into observing norms and principles well beyond anything that could be derived from customary international law or even the Refugee Convention itself.[45] Zieck has highlighted how the refugee definition in one of the central agreements between Pakistan and UNHCR is so broad that it may be comparable to the refugee definition contained in the UNHCR Statute or in the regional 1969 OAU Convention Governing the Specific Aspects of Refugee Problems in Africa.[46] This means, according to Zieck, that if Pakistan acceded to the Refugee Convention, the narrower Convention definition of a refugee would entail that "most of the Afghan refugees who sought refuge in Pakistan would not have qualified as [Convention] refugees."[47]

Similarly, MoUs can establish and further the creation of new norms and standards in refugee protection. A 2007 tripartite agreement between UNHCR, Pakistan and Afghanistan reaffirms the voluntary nature of repatriation, adding that repatriation "shall only take place on the agreed principles of

42 Memorandum of Understanding, Lebanon (n 14) art 8.

43 Kagan (n 30).

44 ibid.

45 Marjoleine Zieck, 'The Legal Status of Afghan Refugees in Pakistan, a Story of Eight Agreements and Two Suppressed Premises' (2008) 20(2) *International Journal of Refugee Law* 253.

46 Marjoleine Zieck, 'Accession of Pakistan to the 1951 Convention and 1967 Protocol Relating to the Status of Refugees: Signing on Could Make All the Difference' (2010) 5 *Pakistan Law Review* 1.

47 ibid 5.

voluntarism and gradualism ..."[48] Zieck explains that "'[g]radualism' is a newly-coined term and should be taken to refer to the need to phase the pace of return in recognition of the limitations of the so-called 'absorption capacity' of the country of origin, which to date remains extremely limited."[49]

4 Concerns and Critiques

Thus far, we have outlined how many agreements attempt to – and indeed do – provide alternative protection regimes to the Refugee Convention in non-signatory host states. Nevertheless, the "quality" of protection that MoUs provide, both on paper and in practice, varies significantly. They may all aim – subject to the constraints of a specific context – to increase and improve refugee protection, particularly when compared to an alternative scenario in which there is no legal basis for UNHCR's presence, nor a clear outline of UNHCR and host state responsibilities. Nevertheless, the alternative protection regimes they constitute are often fraught with challenges and inadequacies, on which we now focus. In exploring critiques of these instruments, we argue that MoUs can, in some cases, i) limit refugee rights; ii) lack both refugee participation and transparency; iii) have an unclear legal status and are often hard to enforce; iv) be unreflective of practice on the ground; and v) lead to fragmentation by creating multiple, overlapping agreements.

4.1 *The Limits to Refugees' Rights*

In some cases, the agreements may include clauses that are problematic from a human and refugee rights perspective. These agreements often result from challenging negotiations, influenced by domestic and international geopolitical pressures. The 2003 agreement with Lebanon, for example, fails to mention key protection norms such as the principle of *non-refoulement*. Instead, it establishes a legally peculiar obligation on UNHCR to resettle recognized refugees within a set timeframe, even though UNHCR has no authority to force third countries to accept refugee resettlement. Nevertheless, the agreement

48 'Agreement Between the Government of the Islamic Republic of Pakistan, the Government of the Islamic Republic of Afghanistan, and the United Nations High Commissioner for Refugees Governing the Repatriation of Afghan Citizens Living in Pakistan (2007)' art 6. On file with authors.

49 Zieck (n 45).

only accepts UNHCR's protection role based on the expectation that refugees recognized by UNHCR be resettled within less than a year.[50]

The agreement furthermore states that "Lebanon does not consider itself an asylum country" and that an "asylum seeker" is a "person seeking asylum in a country other than Lebanon."[51] Indeed, the MoU not only legitimized the notion of Lebanon not being a country of asylum, but also helped introduce this approach as a central principle in Lebanon's refugee governance.[52] Ever since, the notion of Lebanon as "no country of asylum" has been incorporated into numerous official documents, and even judicial decisions. The MoU is also concerning because it was concluded between UNHCR and Lebanon's General Security Directorate and not, as is standard practice elsewhere, with the country's Ministry of Foreign Affairs. The agreement, and UNHCR, have been heavily criticized for adopting a perspective, which the General Security Directorate might endorse, of refugees as security threats.[53] UNHCR staff have acknowledged that the agreement fails to fulfil the standards customarily required when negotiating such MoUs, with some even referring to it as a "mistake" on UNHCR's part.[54]

Agreements that have been concluded subsequently also contain concerning elements and/or absences. For example, the 2007 tripartite agreement between UNHCR, Pakistan and Afghanistan, unlike previous voluntary repatriation agreements concerning Pakistan, did not address the fate of those who would still be in Pakistan when the voluntary repatriation program was to be terminated in December 2009. This omission, as Zieck has noted, "seemingly free[d] the host state from any particular obligations with respect to those who will still be in Pakistan at the time."[55] While the human rights entitlements of Afghan refugees remaining in Pakistan certainly have not evaporated, the MoU arguably creates an impression that they have. Discussions like these came to the forefront again in late 2023, when Pakistan's government took a decision to expel all "illegal migrants" from the country.[56]

50 Memorandum of Understanding, Lebanon (n 14) art 5, 9.

51 ibid, Preamble.

52 Maja Janmyr, 'No Country of Asylum: "Legitimizing" Lebanon's Rejection of the 1951 Refugee Convention' (2017) 29(3) *International Journal of Refugee Law* 438.

53 Frangieh (n 38).

54 Maja Janmyr, 'UNHCR and the Syrian Refugee Response: Negotiating Status and Registration in Lebanon' (2018) 22(3) *The International Journal of Human Rights* 393.

55 Zieck (n 45).

56 Arjumand Bano Kazmi, 'Illegal Migrants or Refugees?' *Dawn* (October 15, 2023) <https://www.dawn.com/news/1781102> accessed March 18 2024.

Governments in many non-signatory states – particularly in the Middle East – also do not fully acknowledge the durable solutions set out in the international refugee regime. With local integration not being accepted as a durable solution, UNHCR's agreements with states like Jordan, Lebanon and Kuwait refer to durable solutions only in terms of return or resettlement. The Kuwait agreement, for example, stipulates that UNHCR shall provide "international protection" to refugees and others falling within the scope of its mandate, but also that it shall seek permanent solutions to their problems only by either facilitating voluntary return or "their assimilation within new national communities."[57] Essentially, agreements such as these risk undermining local integration as a durable solution by giving moral, political and even legal authority to a narrow understanding of durable solutions.

On the other hand, UNHCR's 2021 MoU with Bangladesh relating to the island of Bhasan Char lays out a range of protections for the Rohingya refugee population pertaining to services and individual case management by specialized protection actors, continuous registration and documentation of refugees, psycho-social counselling, and community-based protection, all of which are meant to be jointly ensured by the Bangladesh government and UNHCR. This MoU also guarantees refugees access to requisite services to meet their basic needs but does not clarify who is responsible for ensuring them.[58] In a notable and positive step, it also gives refugees on Bhasan Char the permission to engage in livelihood activities. Concerningly, though, the MoU gives Rohingya refugees a minimal right to freedom of movement, restricted to the island.[59] Following criticism likening Bhasan Char to a "prison-like island,"[60] the Bangladesh government began allowing Rohingya

57 'Cooperation and Office Agreement between the Office of the United Nations High Commissioner for Refugees and the Government of the State of Kuwait, April 8, 1996,' art 4. On file with authors.

58 'Memorandum of Understanding between the Government of the People's Republic of Bangladesh (GOB) and the Office of the United Nations High Commissioner for Refugees (UNHCR) (on Behalf of the United Nations Agencies Working on the Rohingya Humanitarian Response in Bangladesh) Relating to Bhasan Char.' Available at <https://myanmar.iiss.org/files/rohingya/2021.10%20%20GoB%20and%20UNHCR%20%20Bhasan%20Char%20MoU.pdf> accessed December 9, 2024.

59 ibid para 2(h). See also, Maja Janmyr and M Sanjeeb Hossain, 'Bhasan Char: Prison Island or Paradise? Are Rohingya Refugees Being Denied Their Right to Freedom of Movement?' *Lacuna Magazine* (May 12, 2022) <https://lacuna.org.uk/migration/bhasan-char-rohingya-refugees-right-to-freedom-of-movement/> accessed March 18, 2024.

60 '"An Island Jail in the Middle of the Sea": Bangladesh's Relocation of Rohingya Refugees to Bhasan Char' *Human Rights Watch* (June 7, 2021) <https://www.hrw.org/report/2021/

residents of Bhasan Char to receive their relatives and to visit relatives living in mainland camps.[61] This implies that host states can improve existing practices without amending relevant provisions in MoUs.

4.2 *Participation and Transparency*

There are also significant concerns about the agreements' transparency, and the (in)ability of refugees to participate in crafting, or to even have access to, the agreements. First, the kinds of MoUs discussed in this chapter are often strictly confidential and not all are registered as treaties (see section on *enforceability*), leading to a lack of transparency concerning their status in international law. This is particularly acute for agreements concluded before 2003, with few officially registered. While UNHCR's internal procedures now require the registration of cooperation agreements, in many contexts other agreements are still confidentialized.[62] For instance, since 2017, at least three MoUs have been signed between the UNHCR and the Bangladesh government on data sharing, voluntary repatriation, and Bhasan Char, all of which remain confidential.[63]

While some historical agreements are available in archives or the UN's treaty database, others are leaked into the public domain. Their contents become available to scholars, lawyers and refugees through research, which does not constitute reliable and straightforward access, especially for refugees living in very challenging circumstances. This means that the very subjects of the agreements – refugees – are left in the dark about the legal frameworks that shape their present situations and possible futures. It is imperative, as we have argued in more depth elsewhere, for refugees to be given access to the agreements and the policies that govern them.[64]

06/07/island-jail-middle-sea/bangladeshs-relocation-rohingya-refugees-bhasan-char> accessed March 18, 2024.

61 'Rohingyas Visit Relatives in Bhasan Char' *New Age* (January 21, 2022) <https://www.newagebd.net/article/161488/rohingyas-visit-relatives-in-bhasan-char> accessed March 18, 2024.

62 Zieck (n 4) 365.

63 M Sanjeeb Hossain, 'Country Report Bangladesh – D4.5 Final Country Reports' (2023) <https://www.asileproject.eu/wp-content/uploads/2023/10/D4.5_Bangladesh_Final-Country-Report.pdf>, accessed December 9, 2024.

64 Maja Janmyr, M Sanjeeb Hossain and Lewis Turner, 'Give Refugees Access to the Agreements That Govern Them | Oxford Law Blogs' (Border Criminologies, April 13, 2023) <https://blogs.law.ox.ac.uk/border-criminologies-blog/blog-post/2023/04/give-refugees-access-agreements-govern-them> accessed March 15, 2024.

In more recent years, in some cases while these very agreements are being negotiated, UNHCR and governments of host states have increasingly committed themselves to facilitating the meaningful participation of refugees in decisions shaping their lives. This is clear, for example, in the UN Global Compact on Refugees (GCR), which recognizes that "[r]esponses are most effective when they actively and meaningfully engage those they are intended to protect and assist."[65] But how can such promises be implemented, without refugees having access to the legal frameworks to which they are subject? How can refugees meaningfully participate in that regime, or advocate for their rights?

4.3 *Legal Status and Enforceability*

Another concern related to transparency centers on the agreements' legal status and enforceability. Both formal and informal agreements may be legally binding or non-legally binding, and most states agree that MoUs can contain legally binding elements.[66] That said, there is little doubt as to the legal nature of cooperation agreements as international treaties.[67] Through the signing of a cooperation agreement, both parties – UNHCR and the host state – can generally be considered to have the intention to create binding obligations under international law. Such agreements are designated precisely as "agreements" and most have the structure of a treaty: a preamble, body and final clauses which also include the entry into force of the agreement, the language to be considered the authentic one, and provisions on interpretation, amendment and termination.[68]

Additionally, many agreements are registered *ex officio* with the UN Secretariat under Article 102 (1) of the UN Charter. *Ex officio* registration means that this Secretariat determines whether or not the submitted agreement qualifies for registration as an international agreement. Letters of Understanding between UNHCR and a host state government – which elaborate general provisions of MoUs to facilitate their implementation – may also be registered in this way.[69] While all *ex officio* registered agreements must be seen as international agreements, because of their similarity in terms of substance, all coop-

65 UNGA, 'Global Compact on Refugees'(United Nations 2018) para 34 <https://www.refworld.org/legal/agreements/unga/2018/en/124198> accessed March 18, 2024.

66 UNGA, *First report on non-legally binding international agreements*, by Mathias Forteau, Special Rapporteur, UN Doc A/CN.4/772 (April 23, 2024) 41; Klabbers (n 3) 66–7.

67 See Vienna Convention on the Law of Treaties (adopted 23 May 1969, entered into force 27 January 1980) 1155 UNTS 331 art 2, para 1(a).

68 Zieck (n 4) 89–90.

69 ibid 287–88.

eration agreements, registered or not, can be considered international agreements in the sense of Article 102.[70]

As for special agreements, these may or may not be considered international agreements. That said, even agreements that are not registered as international treaties or are otherwise considered legally non-binding, may still have legal effect. As the Special Rapporteur on non-legally binding international agreements recently has noted, legal non-bindingness "does not mean that international law is not likely to apply to them in some respects."[71] Indeed, "one of the thorniest and most sensitive questions ... is determining the extent to which non-legally binding international agreements ... would produce or be attributed legal effects in international law."[72] This would mean that even a special agreement could be seen to be, if not legally binding, then at the very least as having the potential to produce or be attributed some legal effects.

There are nonetheless extensive practical challenges to holding governments (and UNHCR) accountable for their commitments in these agreements, particularly regarding access to courts and legal aid. While the agreements often include a provision on dispute settlement,[73] we know very little about how disputes are settled, if they are at all. This is arguably compounded by the agreements' aforementioned lack of transparency vis-à-vis third parties. How can those acting on refugees' behalf attempt to ensure that agreements are implemented when they may not even have access to the full text of the agreements due to them being confidentialized?

There is a striking need for more research into this matter, and into the overall question of how courts in non-signatory states relate to these agreements. Nascent research on this topic suggests that courts in some non-signatory states have begun to explicitly draw on principles embedded within these agreements. In Pakistan, for example, the judiciary appears to have interwoven provisions of domestic and international law with UNHCR-Host State agreements to provide protection to the country's refugees.[74]

---

70 ibid 92.

71 UNGA, 'First report' (n 66).

72 ibid 52.

73 The model cooperation agreement, for instance, contains a clause *inter alia* providing that '[a]ny dispute between UNHCR and the Government arising out of or relating to this Agreement shall be settled amicably by negotiation or other agreed mode of settlement, failing which such dispute shall be submitted to arbitration at the request of either Party.' See UNHCR (n 18) art XV.

74 See *Rahil Azizi v State of Pakistan* (2023) Writ Petition No 1666, Islamabad High Court; *Aamir Aman v Federation of Pakistan* (2020) PLD 533, Sindh High Court; Arjumand Bano

4.4 *Practice and Implementation*

While many of these agreements, for example in terms of the alternative protection regimes that they (aim to) provide, appear laudable and positive, in many contexts the agreements appear to be un- or partially-implemented, not invoked, or overtaken by events that follow their signing yet are not updated. Therefore, in some cases, MoUs arguably do not accurately represent practices on the ground. This, when combined with their questionable enforceability, raises important questions about the extent to which refugees can avail themselves of the protection regimes they ostensibly live under.

In Jordan, for example, the 1998 MoU was signed when only approximately 5,000 refugees and asylum-seekers were registered with UNHCR. The document appears to neither have envisaged, nor have been written for, contexts of prolonged mass displacement like the Iraqi and Syrian crises that followed.[75] The MoU states that UNHCR has one month to examine an asylum claim and then can issue refugee identification documents that will be valid for six months. UNHCR was – very unrealistically – expected to find a solution (ie resettlement or safe, voluntary return) within that six-month period.

In 2014 the MoU was amended, to allow UNHCR ninety days to examine claims, and to issue documents for one year.[76] Importantly, there appears to have been an ambiguity over whether the six months (later one year) was a renewable period, or a one-off. While the government has confirmed it is now a renewable period,[77] for years UNHCR spoke as if it was non-renewable, stating in 2014, for example, that the government would "bend the rules" or "turn a blind eye" to cases where the MoU's timeframes are not adhered to.[78] Therefore while the existence of a timeframe establishes the principle, important to the government, that asylum-seekers' stay in Jordan should be temporary, what it means for refugees in practice is more ambiguous, and appears to have changed over time.

In Lebanon, the 2003 MoU included elements that UNHCR arguably never had the authority or capacity to deliver on, such as its promises of

---

Kazmi, 'Pakistan's Judicial Engagement with International Refugee Law' (2025) *International Journal of Refugee Law* <https://doi.org/10.1093/ijrl/eeaf001> accessed February 2, 2025; Kazmi (n 56).

75 Frangieh (n 38).

76 Samia Qumri and Lewis Turner, 'Refugee Recognition Regime Country Profile: Jordan' (2023) RefMig Working Paper No. 4/2023 68.

77 Lewis Turner, 'Who Is a Refugee in Jordan? Hierarchies and Exclusions in the Refugee Recognition Regime' (2023) 36(4) *Journal of Refugee Studies* 877.

78 Stevens (n 38).

resettlement.[79] Soon after it was agreed, UNHCR and the government disagreed significantly on its interpretation and therefore the MoU essentially broke down shortly after its negotiation.[80] Given the disagreements on the meaning of the (arguably unimplementable) text, the MoU does not offer an accurate reflection of practice on the ground, or of UNHCR-governmental relations. Indeed, UNHCR has struggled ever since to find new ways to formally regulate its cooperation with the government, and today, the legal mandate for UNHCR's work is largely left undefined, allowing for more pragmatism by UNHCR, but also making the organization more vulnerable to governmental interference in its operations.

Despite the 2018 MoU between UNHCR and Bangladesh, which ensured that "any use of information [relating to refugees] for purposes other than assistance and identification or transfer to third parties would need to be approved by UNHCR,"[81] it has been alleged that Rohingya refugees' biometric data, collected during the verification exercise jointly conducted by the UNHCR and the Bangladesh government, was shared by the latter with the Myanmar government without the informed consent of Rohingya refugees.[82] Although UNHCR strongly disputed this claim,[83] research on this topic suggests that Rohingya refugees' data was shared without their informed consent.[84]

4.5 *Fragmentation*

One of the agreements' potential consequences is the fragmentation that they exacerbate. In some contexts, UNHCR's presence and operations in host states may appear to be regulated by different agreements, sometimes simultaneously. For example, Zieck has examined the agreements concluded between Pakistan and UNHCR, showing how each major political change in Af-

---

79 Kagan (n 30).

80 Janmyr (n 54).

81 'UNHCR Bangladesh Operational Update, 23 January – 5 February 2018' (UNHCR 2018) <https://reliefweb.int/report/bangladesh/unhcr-bangladesh-operational-update-23-january-5-february-2018> accessed March 18, 2024.

82 'UN Shared Rohingya Data Without Informed Consent' *Human Rights Watch* (June 15, 2021) <https://www.hrw.org/news/2021/06/15/un-shared-rohingya-data-without-informed-consent> accessed March18, 2024.

83 'Statement on Refugee Registration and Data Collection in Bangladesh' UNHCR (June 15, 2021) <https://www.unhcr.org/news/news-releases/news-comment-statement-refugee-registration-and-data-collection-bangladesh> accessed March 18, 2024.

84 M Sanjeeb Hossain, Tasnuva Ahmad, Mohammad Azizul Hoque and Tin Swe, 'The ejajot of Rohingya refugees in the age of digital humanitarianism' (2024) 73 *Forced Migration Review*.

ghanistan induced the conclusion of an agreement pertaining to the voluntary repatriation of Afghan refugees from Pakistan.[85]

The concurrence of agreements need not necessarily be problematic. The model cooperation agreement even includes a clause stipulating that the agreement supersedes and replaces previous agreements.[86] In theory any such situations could be solved by applying the rules regarding the application of successive treaties relating to the same subject matter.[87] Whether this happens in practice is of course a different question. For example, irrespective of their legal status, the agreements are commonly perceived as "softer" law that more accurately may describe the refugee system as it operates "on the ground" – in contrast to "harder," multilateral treaties. As Kagan has argued, however, the law "from below" may nonetheless be used much more, and thus become "harder" in the process.[88]

Furthermore, different kinds of fragmentation are created in different contexts, depending in part on whether MoUs narrow or expand the kind of protection that is outlined in other legal instruments. For example, in Bangladesh, where the MoU on Bhasan Char contradicts the Refugee Convention, particularly in terms of freedom of movement, the proliferation of MoUs, which may hold the most power in that context, appears to narrow the scope of refugee protection, and MoUs are not in fact overridden by "higher" legal statutes. Like many of the other concerns outlined in this chapter, these (potential) fragmentations are much more challenging when only some agreements and not others are publicly available for scrutiny.

5 Conclusion

This chapter has spotlighted key international refugee law instruments that are rarely subject to sustained academic attention: agreements between UNHCR and refugee-hosting states. In examining both cooperation and special agreements (and the potentially blurred boundaries between them), we have demonstrated how these agreements can form alternative protection regimes in non-signatory host states. The agreements vary significantly in structure, content, depth and, most crucially, in the rights they afford those seeking international protection. While some MoUs offer noticeable limits on

85 Zieck (n 45).
86 UNHCR, 'Model Agreement' (n 18) art 16 (6).
87 Zieck (n 4) 316.
88 Kagan (n 30).

refugee rights (either explicitly or by omission) others go beyond states' obligations under the Refugee Convention. We have therefore demonstrated that these agreements, which form part of the body of international refugee law, have the potential to create regimes that offer meaningful protection to refugees.[89]

At the same time, if agreements are to live up to their potential, and to meaningfully improve refugees' lives, then several key issues need to be tackled, both by the drafters of future MoUs and the implementors of existing ones. Too many agreements are limited in the contribution they can make to refugee protection by content that limits refugee rights, their lack of inclusion of – or accessibility to – the people they are about, their uncertain legal standing and questionable enforceability, the gap between what is promised on paper and implemented in practice, and the multiple, overlapping and potentially contradictory legal regimes they can create.

These agreements – because of their potential to both protect and harm refugees, and because they are severely understudied – should be the focus of much more attention, both within research and within humanitarian policy and practice. Varying in content, they warrant closer, comparative attention by refugee law and refugee studies scholars to understand more precisely how – and which – refugee protection norms are diffused in these contexts. Relatedly, the widespread use of MoUs as alternative protection regimes can constitute a shift away from – or in some cases toward – the protection offered by the Refugee Convention. This should, in turn, merit further scrutiny of the relationships between the agreements and the Convention, UNHCR's attempts (or lack thereof) to get states to accede to the Convention, the role that UNHCR plays in refugee law and politics, and the role of the Convention in today's protection landscape.

Acknowledgements

This work was supported by the European Union's Horizon 2020 research and innovation program under grant agreement No 851121 (ERC Starting Grant 2019). Author contributions for this chapter were equal and names appear in alphabetical order.

89 See also Zieck (n 4) 323.

CHAPTER 11

Universities and UNHCR: Teaching International Refugee Law in Pakistan

Arjumand Bano Kazmi and Sikander Ahmed Shah

1 Introduction

How is international refugee law (IRL) taught in non-signatory states? This chapter addresses this question with a focus on Pakistan. Pakistan has not acceded to either the 1951 Refugee Convention or its 1967 Protocol (together and individually "the Refugee Convention"),[1] and despite hosting one of the largest refugee populations in the world for over four decades, it has not enacted national legislation on refugees.[2] This sets out Pakistan's legal context as a non-signatory state, in which the United Nations High Commissioner for Refugees (UNHCR) holds the mandate to promote IRL and protect refugees.[3]

This chapter explores how and why some of the country's leading universities have recently begun teaching and researching IRL. As this develops, UNHCR is engaging with academics, lawyers, refugee rights activists, state law enforcement agencies, and non-governmental organizations as domestic actors, to advocate, adapt, and contextualize IRL norms. Universities are well positioned to facilitate this process by fostering critical debates and scholarly inquiry that is sensitive to local contexts and by enabling the

1 Convention relating to the Status of Refugees (adopted July 28, 1951, entered into force April 22, 1954) 189 UNTS 137, and Protocol relating to the Status of Refugees (adopted January 31, 1967, entered into force October 4, 1967) 606 UNTS 267.

2 That said, in the absence of applicable national and international standards focusing on refugees, one may draw on a broader body of international and national law to provide protection for refugees in Pakistan. This chapter will highlight some of these, including the principle of *non-refoulement* as well as the Constitution of Pakistan. See Arjumand Bano Kazmi, 'Pakistan's Judicial Engagement with International Refugee Law' (2025) *International Journal of Refugee Law* <https://doi.org/10.1093/ijrl/eeaf001> accessed February 2, 2025.

3 Statute of the United Nations High Commissioner for Refugees, contained in the Annex to UN General Assembly Resolution 428(V) of December 14, 1950. GA res 428(V) (December 14, 1950).

DOI:10.1163/9789004710306_012

gradual incorporation of "foreign norms" into local practices.[4] We therefore situate this chapter within a broader scholarship that focuses on the spread of norms, particularly in IRL.[5]

Although arguably an understudied topic, there is nevertheless a growing interest in IRL teaching in non-signatory states. UNHCR has collaborated with universities in Saudi Arabia in the teaching of refugee law to law enforcement officers from all countries in the Gulf Cooperation Council.[6] Similarly, in Indonesia, scholarship on the social and legal status of refugees and internally displaced persons is advancing with numerous universities now offering courses on refugee law and rights.[7] And in India there have been discussions led by the Jindal Global University on establishing refugee law clinics for Indian law schools.[8] Focusing on Pakistan, the present study aligns with this interest and contributes to the aim of this volume, namely to bring non-signatory states into the ongoing debates about the influence of IRL beyond treaty obligations. By exploring how IRL is taught in this context, we are paving the way for more critical and timely scholarship in this area.

This chapter further contributes to the scholarship on the pedagogy of international law more generally. Al Attar and Chimni, for instance, advocate employing Third World Approaches to International Law (TWAIL) in the teaching of international law; this calls for learning about the "others" of international law and emphasizes "increasing the diversity and localization of knowledge production to promote epistemic justice."[9] The

4 Amitav Acharya, 'How Ideas Spread: Whose Norms Matter? Norm Localization and Institutional Change in Asian Regionalism' (2004) 58(2) *International Organization* 239, 241.

5 These include Acharya (n 4); Leiza Brumat, Andrew Geddes and Andrea Pettrachin, 'Making Sense of the Global: A Systematic Review of Globalizing and Localizing Dynamics in Refugee Governance' (2022) 35(2) *Journal of Refugee Studies*, 827; and IK Roepstorff, 'A Call for Critical Reflection on the Localisation Agenda in Humanitarian Action (2019) 41(2) *Third World Quarterly* 284.

6 Maja Janmyr and, Charlotte Lysa, 'Saudi Arabia and the International Refugee Regime' (2023) 35(3) *International Journal of Refugee Law* 251.

7 Maja Janmyr, 'The 1951 Refugee Convention and Non-Signatory States: Charting a Research Agenda' (2021) 33(2) *International Journal of Refugee Law* 188.

8 Rashmi Raman, *Refugee Law Clinic for Indian Law Schools* (White Paper, 2020) Centre for International Legal Studies, Jindal Global Law School, India.

9 Mohsen Al Attar, 'Must International Legal Pedagogy Remain Eurocentric?' (2021) 11(1) *Asian Journal of International Law* 195; BS Chimni, 'Three Approaches to the 1951 Convention: The Case for a Dialectical Approach' (2024) *Journal of Refugee Studies* 10 <https://doi.org/10.1093/jrs/feae011>. See also Mohsen Al Attar and Shaimaa Abdelkarim, 'Decolonising the Curriculum in International Law: Entrapments in Praxis and Critical Thought' (2023) 34(1) *Law and Critique* 41.

scholarship on teaching migration and asylum law is also witnessing a turn that de-emphasizes teaching in a positivist frame.[10] It calls for reflection on the role of law schools in contextualizing the norms of the Refugee Convention in the curriculum. Accordingly, Jones argues for a transformation in IRL pedagogy that would enable future lawyers and activists to "reimagine refugee law beyond the narrow exceptions to fixity and citizenship," and "pay attention to local legal frameworks, arguments and jurisprudence."[11]

Drawing inspiration from critical legal studies and TWAIL approaches, we aim to present our analysis within these frameworks. In so doing, we uphold the spirit of this volume which emphasizes a wide range of grounded, bottom-up, and empirically rooted approaches. Our study is informed by document analysis, semi-structured interviews, and research observations. Analysis of IRL curricula includes module outlines from the faculties of law and contemporary studies at two national universities in Pakistan – the Shaikh Ahmad Hassan School of Law at the Lahore University of Management Sciences (LUMS),[12] and the Department of Peace and Conflict Studies at the National Defence University (NDU) in Islamabad.[13] We have also examined the research and policy work on IRL at the Department of International Relations, Balochistan University of Information Technology, Engineering and Management Sciences (BUITEMS) in Quetta.[14] 10 interviews were conducted with academics based in these universities and with relevant officials at UNHCR in Pakistan. In addition, proceedings of two multistakeholder

10 See, for instance, Richard Grimes and Simona Travnickova, 'The Theory Behind Effective Learning and Teaching' in Richard Grimes, Věra Honusková and Ulrich Stege (eds), *Teaching Migration and Asylum Law: Theory and Practice* (Routledge 2022). See also International Institute of Humanitarian Law online courses on 'Teaching International Refugee Law for Academics and Trainers' <https://iihl.org/engagement-with-academia-and-specialized-trainers/> accessed June 30, 2024.

11 Martin Jones, 'On Building a Boat (or, Learning How Not to Teach Refugee Law)' in Richard Grimes, Honusková Věra and Stege Ulrich (eds) *Teaching Migration and Asylum Law: Theory and Practice* (Routledge 2022). Also relevant in same volume is Fatima Khan, 'An Overview of the Teaching of Refugee Law at the University of Cape Town, Law Faculty.'

12 The Lahore University of Management Sciences (LUMS) <https://lums.edu.pk/> accessed March 30, 2024.

13 The National Defence University (NDU) <https://ndu.edu.pk/> accessed March 30, 2024.

14 The Balochistan University of Information Technology, Engineering and Management Sciences (BUITEMS) <www.buitms.edu.pk/> accessed May 5, 2024.

national conferences organized by LUMS, and deliberations at a five-day symposium held at NDU, provide a dialogic empirical nuance.[15] Finally, Sikander Ahmed Shah, one of the authors of this chapter, brings his personal observations and experience of developing, introducing, and teaching IRL at LUMS. Research fieldwork was conducted during February and December 2023 in Pakistan, with follow-up interviews conducted remotely during 2024.

The chapter is presented in five parts. After this introduction, Part 2 provides context by examining the legal and policy landscape of refugee protection in Pakistan. The next two parts constitute the core empirical contribution. Part 3 delves into the institutional environment shaping the teaching of IRL. Centering on UNHCR, this section assesses its engagement with universities. Part 4 examines the curricula and pedagogic approaches adopted by LUMS and NDU. Part 5 concludes the chapter with reflections for future research on this topic.

In summary, we highlight the diverse strategies UNHCR has adopted to promote IRL norms through teaching and research in Pakistan's higher education institutions. We show how despite some challenges, UNHCR has formed collaborations with both private and public universities. However, we argue that this approach has so far been predominantly top-down, driven and sustained by UNHCR. The IRL curriculum, as well as related training and advocacy materials, could benefit from a deeper critical analysis of the international refugee law regime.

2 Legal and Policy Context

The historical, social, and political challenges of Pakistan's refugee-hosting experience are well documented.[16] The country has been sought as a refuge

15 Two conferences on IRL curriculum and pedagogy were held at LUMS, Lahore, Pakistan in November 2022 and September 2023. UNHCR provided the financial support and attended the conferences. Academics and representatives from the Higher Education Commission (HEC) and Pakistan Bar Council (PBC) participated. Authors attended these conferences.

16 Notable works include Daniel A Kronenfeld, 'Afghan Refugees in Pakistan: Not All Refugees, Not Always in Pakistan, Not Necessarily Afghan?' (2008) 21(1) *Journal of Refugee Studies* 43; Frédéric Grare and William Maley, 'The Afghan Refugees in Pakistan' (Middle East Institute/Fondation pour la Recherche Stratégique, June 30, 2011) <https://reliefweb.int/report/pakistan/afghan-refugees-pakistan> accessed December 9, 2024; Pierre Centlivres- Demont and Micheline Centlivres-Demont, 'The Afghan Refugee in

by people from Bangladesh, Somalia, Iraq, Iran, Indian-controlled Kashmir, and Afghanistan. The presence of Afghan refugees in Pakistan has led to one of the largest and protracted refugee situations in the world.[17] In the aftermath of the Soviet invasion of Afghanistan in December 1979 and the subsequent civil wars, millions of Afghans fled to neighboring Pakistan and Iran.[18] Ever since, periodic large-scale voluntary repatriation took place and comparatively few resettlements in other destinations were secured. Millions stayed in Pakistan or crossed the border again due to the perpetual violence and economic uncertainty in Afghanistan.[19]

In the early years of Afghan refugee inflow, Pakistan extended a generous welcome, allowing refugees to move freely, run and own private businesses, and purchase private property.[20] Gradually, they considered Pakistan their permanent home and settled across the country including in the urban centers.[21] However, since the 1990s, as the law-and-order situation has worsened through heightened ethnic conflicts and cross-border aggression, the government authorities have implicated Afghan refugees in these events.[22] Consequently, the initial hospitality turned into a hostile experience for thousands of Afghans living in Pakistan, creating an environment of uncertainty that persists to this day.

In 2024, UNHCR estimated that 3.1 million Afghans resided in Pakistan.[23] Over the years, the government has assigned Afghan refugees to various categories to keep track of their population growth, police their movement between refugee villages and urban centers, and monitor their economic

---

Pakistan: An Ambiguous Identity' (1988) 1(2) *Journal of Refugee Studies* 141; Akbar S Ahmed, 'Resettlement of Afghan Refugees and the Social Scientists' (1980) 4(1) *Journal of South Asian and Middle Eastern Studies* 77; Nasreen Ghufran, 'The Role of UNHCR and Afghan Refugees in Pakistan' (2011) 35(6) *Strategic Analysis* 945; Amina Khan, 'Protracted Afghan Refugee Situation: Policy Options for Pakistan' (2017) 37(1) *Journal of Strategic Studies* 42.

17 UNHCR News, 'Afghanistan Refugee Crisis Explained' (July 18, 2023) <https://www.unrefugees.org/news/afghanistan-refugee-crisis-explained/#Afghanistan> accessed June 10, 2025.

18 Gerald Walzer, 'UNHCR Operations in Pakistan in the Early 1980s' (2008) 27(1) *Refugee Survey Quarterly* 40.

19 Kronenfeld (n 16).

20 Centlivres-Demont and Centlivres-Demont (n 16).

21 Kronenfeld (n 16).

22 Khan (n 16).

23 'Pakistan–Afghanistan Situation Refugee Response Dashboard, as of December 2023', Operational Data Portal' (UNHCR) <https://data.unhcr.org/en/documents/details/107878> accessed June 10, 2024.

activities.[24] These categories determine their legal status either as registered with UNHCR and/or state authorities for a fixed duration, or staying in the country as illegal migrants.

As stated above, Pakistan has not ratified the Refugee Convention, nor does it have any national laws concerning refugees. Consequently, the legal status of all refugees in Pakistan is governed by the Foreigners Act (1946), which relates to the entry and residence of foreign aliens or non-citizens.[25] This means that Pakistani authorities deem any foreigners entering the country without proper and valid travel documents as illegal residents and subject to detention and deportation.[26]

However, parallel to this practice, the governance of refugees in Pakistan relies heavily on cooperation between the state and UNHCR and the institutions they jointly support.[27] Given the magnitude of the refugee population, UNHCR maintains a large presence in Pakistan.[28] It works with the state to deliver upon its mandate particularly in providing international protection to refugees and other persons of concern. UNHCR also facilitates and manages periodic voluntary repatriation of Afghan refugees. This has been operationalized through a series of protection and repatriation agreements in the form of UNHCR–host state memoranda of understanding (MoUs).[29] Since 1988, Pakistan has also been an active member of UNHCR's Executive Committee of the High Commissioner's Programme (ExCom).[30]

At the state level, refugees are governed by the Commissionerate for Afghan Refugees, under the authority of the Ministry of States and Frontier Regions.[31] Established in 1979, the Commissionerate works with support

24 Khan (n 16); See also Sanaa Alimia, 'Performing the Afghanistan–Pakistan Border Through Refugee ID Cards' (2019) 24(2) *Geopolitics* 391; and Umar Rashid, 'UNHCR in Pakistan: Analyzing the Global Governance Regime: Repatriation of Afghan Refugees from Pakistan' (2019) 6(1) *LUMS Law Journal* 31.

25 The Foreigners Act 1946 of Pakistan, s 3(2)(g) <https://khalidzafar.com/wp-content/files_mf/1527083634ForeignAct1946.pdf> accessed May 28, 2024.

26 Alimia (n 24); Rashid (n 24).

27 Kazmi (n 2).

28 Walzer (n 18).

29 Marjoleine Zieck, 'The Legal Status of Afghan Refugees in Pakistan, a Story of Eight Agreements and Two Suppressed Premises' (2008) 20(2) *International Journal of Refugee Law* 253.

30 Humanitarian Affairs of the Permanent Mission of Pakistan to the United Nations, Geneva <https://pakungeneva.pk/humanitarian-affairs/> accessed June 10, 2025.

31 Commissionerate for Afghan Refugees (CAR) Government of Pakistan <https://www.govserv.org/PK/Islamabad/106119878583271/Chief-Commissionerate-Afghan-Refugees-Islamabad-Official> accessed June 10, 2025.

from UNHCR on managing voluntary repatriation of Afghan refugees and delivering education and health facilities to those who reside in Pakistan.[32] However, since the return of the Taliban government in Afghanistan in August 2021, the existing policy frameworks and implementation platforms face an impasse.[33] Pakistan has resisted a mass influx of Afghan refugees and forcibly deported thousands of Afghans refugees throughout 2022 and 2023.[34]

This legal and policy context influences the development of IRL teaching in Pakistani institutions. As part of its international protection mandate, UNHCR has a central role in the promotion of IRL and the dissemination of its core principles.[35] To this end, it cooperates with states, civil society organizations, and academic institutions "to encourage the teaching and understanding of IRL."[36] In the section below, we discuss how UNHCR engages with universities, navigates Pakistan's higher education system, and responds to the challenges in the context of a non-signatory state.

3 UNHCR and the Higher Education Sector in Pakistan

Pakistan's leading universities teach IRL and conduct research on the social and legal aspects of refugee rights. This is achieved through UNHCR's proactive involvement. As this section will discuss, however, there are a number of institutional challenges to the promotion of IRL in Pakistan's higher education system. For example, our research suggests that universities offering legal education are often reluctant to include courses on refugee law, arguing that there are no specific laws applicable to the governance of refugees in Pakistan. While this perception is partially accurate, it overlooks

32 Government of Pakistan Ministry of States and Frontier Regions Islamabad, *SAFRON Yearbook 2022–2023* <https://cabinet.gov.pk/SiteImage/Publication/YB-2022-23.pdf> accessed June 10, 2027, 16.

33 Kazmi (n 2).

34 Arjumand Bano Kazmi, 'Illegal Migrants or Refugees?' *Dawn* (Karachi, October 15, 2023) <www.dawn.com/news/1781102> accessed March 18, 2024; Guidance Note on the International Protection Needs of People Fleeing Afghanistan: UNHCR Update 1, issued February 2023 <www.refworld.org/policy/countrypos/unhcr/2023/en/124216> accessed February 20, 2024.

35 Corinne Lewis, UNHCR and International Refugee Law: From Treaties to Innovation (Routledge 2012).

36 ibid 152. Quoted ExCom Conclusion 29 (XXXIV), k,1983.

important legal provisions that nonetheless are applicable to refugee-related matters – these will be discussed in Part 4.

This section explores how UNHCR establishes formal cooperation agreements with universities and provides both financial assistance and subject expertise in curriculum development and research. We begin with a brief explanation of the system of higher education and how UNHCR navigates it by adopting diverse approaches to public and private universities. We then assess the nature of UNHCR's cooperation with LUMS as a private university, followed by its support for BUITEMS, a public institution.

3.1 *Institutional Navigation*

As an extension of UNHCR's mandate to promote the Refugee Convention,[37] UNHCR's representation in Pakistan has for decades collaborated with education institutions in the teaching, training, research, and advocacy of IRL. These activities can be seen, as emphasized in chapter 9 of this volume, as approaches to enroll state actors into the network of international protection of refugees. Importantly, they are seen by UNHCR as a long-term engagement aiming to protect refugee rights. As one senior UNHCR official shared with us:

> Pakistan is not signing the treaty, we know that. But if our ultimate aim is to ensure that refugee rights are protected, and the government always has reservations to the accession of the Refugee Convention, it's not something that will happen easily or any time soon. In a roundabout way, we ensure that we work towards this aim through education about and promotion of the treaty … It is one of those longer-term things which kind of contributes to improving the environment around discussing the refugee issue especially in Pakistan where there's generally a negative sense attached to it.[38]

Until recently, these collaborations were sporadic.[39] One of the earliest was established in 2003 between UNHCR and the Allama Iqbal Open University of Pakistan.[40] An MoU was signed whereby the university undertook to

37 Lewis (n 35).

38 Interview with UNHCR official 1, February 8, 2023, Islamabad.

39 ibid.

40 ibid. See also Jack Redden, 'Pakistani University to Start Refugee Law Course with UNHCR Help' (UNHCR, October 8, 2003) <www.unhcr.org/news/pakistani-university-start-refugee-law-course-unhcr-help> accessed September 5 2024.

offer a three-month course on refugee law in major Pakistani cities and in six Gulf states – Saudi Arabia, Dubai, Abu Dhabi, Oman, Bahrain, and Qatar.[41] The course content was designed with the extensive involvement of UNHCR, and included information about the Refugee Convention and how it indirectly places obligations on states that have not ratified them. The course has since been discontinued.

In the past few years, UNHCR has begun to re-engage with universities.[42] Our research focuses on this re-engagement. We zoom in on UNHCR's collaborations with LUMS and BUITEMS which were initiated in 2019 and 2017 respectively. But it should be noted that UNHCR is also seeking to establish links with other public universities, including the National University of Sciences and Technology and the International Islamic University, both located in Islamabad.[43] NDU does not have a formal collaboration with UNHCR, but it nevertheless teaches IRL. By way of comparison, in Part 4, we will discuss IRL teaching at NDU alongside LUMS.

To better understand UNHCR's engagement with universities, a few words first on the system of higher education in Pakistan: the Higher Education Commission of Pakistan (HEC) governs all higher education institutions in policy formulation, quality assurance, and financial management.[44] Established in 2002, the HEC is a statutory body formed by the government of Pakistan. In addition, the Pakistan Bar Council (PBC) is authorized by the government to oversee the direction of legal education, including the development of a national syllabus for the LLB and other university programs.[45] In the provision of legal education, the roles of these two bodies overlap significantly.[46] All law faculties, whether in public or private universities, are required to observe the HEC and PBC rules in setting up their degree programs. However, only the HEC rules apply to other faculties.

UNHCR must navigate this regulatory framework to promote and introduce IRL in universities. This, however, is not straightforward.[47] There has

---

41 ibid.

42 Interview with UNHCR official 1 (n 38).

43 ibid.

44 Higher Education Commission of Pakistan (HEC) <https://www.hec.gov.pk/english/Pages/default.aspx> accessed November 2, 2024.

45 Pakistan Bar Council (PBC) <https://www.pakistanbarcouncil.com/> accessed June 10, 2025.

46 Sardar Ali Shah, Balasingam Usharani and Dhanapal Saroja, 'Legal Education in Pakistan: An Overview', (2018) 26(2) *IIUM Law Journal* 401.

47 Observations made at the LUMS conference, 'Promoting the Study of Refugee Rights via Curricula Development at Educational Institutions across Pakistan', held at LUMS, Lahore on September 27, 2023.

been resistance from the HEC and PBC to introducing a refugee law course in legal education.[48] Regulated by these bodies, law faculties at various public universities do not feel the need to invest in the teaching of refugee law.[49] To counter this challenge, UNHCR employs two distinct approaches: it establishes formal collaborations with (a) law faculties in private universities such as LUMS; and (b) other, mostly social science, faculties in public universities such as BUITEMS. We now turn to examining these distinct formal collaborations.

3.2 *Private Universities*

UNHCR negotiates different types of formal agreements with universities. While some MoUs focus on broader objectives of establishing cooperation between the concerned parties, others contain specific activities in a project-style approach. As this section will show, UNHCR's cooperation with LUMS constitutes one of the more formal ways of collaborating on the teaching of IRL. This partnership is facilitated by LUMS's status as a private university. Unlike public universities, LUMS enjoys a greater flexibility to formalize collaborations and integrate IRL into its legal education programs. In contrast, and as we shall see in section 3.3, UNHCR's partnerships with public universities typically result in IRL being introduced as a research subject outside law faculties.

The LUMS–UNHCR collaboration is regarded as UNHCR's flagship initiative, dedicated to creating a tailored university course on IRL as part of the law faculty.[50] The course is being promoted as a "gold standard" for adoption by other universities across Pakistan.[51] Over the past decade, LUMS and UNHCR have partnered on various training workshops for law enforcement agencies and government ministries, covering topics such as statelessness and the protection of internally displaced persons.[52] This long-standing relationship fostered trust and close rapport between the two institutions.[53] In 2019, the first MoU between the two was signed to develop and incorporate IRL into the law curriculum. It was negotiated between the university

48 ibid.

49 Interview with academic 3, November 24, 2024, via WhatsApp.

50 Interviews with academics 1 and 3, August 29, 2024, Oslo. Academic 3 was via WhatsApp.

51 ibid.

52 ibid.

53 ibid.

leadership at LUMS and UNHCR's senior representative in Pakistan. The MoU was most recently renewed in February 2024 for another five years.[54]

Referred to as the Cooperation Framework Agreement, the LUMS–UNHCR MoU 2024 seeks to ensure that the IRL course "is consistent with the developments in the field of international law and standards" and is "interdisciplinary considering surrounding aspects of international refugee protection such as social, economic and anthropological dimensions." In terms of the responsibilities of the parties concerned, the agreement requires LUMS to "periodically review" and update the IRL module and teaching materials and maintain the course as its core curriculum "regardless of whether additional funding for course is provided." In turn, UNHCR assists with the updates, advises on refugee law issues, and provides UNHCR expert guidelines and other materials on the application and interpretation of IRL for inclusion in course materials.[55]

UNHCR further undertakes to ensure that LUMS participates in consultative forums that aim to develop provincial and national consensus on the proposed IRL curriculum. To establish this consensus, LUMS agrees to "make efforts to introduce this course to other legal education institutions using its educational reputation and position … in Pakistan."[56] In terms of tangible outputs, UNHCR required LUMS to provide and update an extensively developed module outline of an undergraduate IRL course, a teaching manual, and PowerPoint slides suitable for teaching and training on IRL to multiple audiences.[57] Both UNHCR and LUMS have the right to use these materials in other relevant work.

LUMS academics assert that in signing the MoU, the university preserved its independence in developing the IRL curriculum, while incorporating guidance from UNHCR's legal protection team to shape its content.[58] Thus far, the collaboration between LUMS and UNHCR has progressed fairly smoothly.[59] A LUMS academic describes the nature of the MoU as follows:

> At LUMS, we have a standard procedure for agreeing MoUs with international organizations. Likewise, with UNHCR, we have a broad,

54 Cooperation Framework Agreement Between UNHCR and LUMS, signed February 8, 2024. Copy on file with the authors.

55 ibid. All text quoted in this paragraph is taken from the Cooperation Framework Agreement.

56 ibid.

57 Interviews with academics 1 and 3 (n 50).

58 ibid.

59 ibid.

> principles-based agreement, which is more like an undertaking to support each other. Yes, UNHCR provides us with finances, but these are activity-based funds which we agree with them from time to time within the life of an MoU. Details of these finances are not included in the MoU. The real purpose behind the MoU is to give our collaboration a legitimate status … So, for example, if the state authorities or other international organizations approach us and need our advice or training provision, we could tell them that we work in partnership with UNHCR, we are guided by their expertise, so they will be involved too.[60]

This collaboration arguably aligns with the aims of both institutions. For LUMS, UNHCR's expertise and access to refugee populations across Pakistan are indispensable.[61] With limited academic research on refugee issues in the country and a lack of capacity and resources among academics to collect up-to-date information, UNHCR effectively bridges this gap. At the same time, UNHCR benefits by integrating IRL into legal education, promoting Refugee Convention norms to both lawyers and non-lawyers, and building a network of academic institutions and civil society organizations to advance its mandate and exert influence on the state.

While this cooperation is undoubtedly valuable and mutually beneficial, it also suffers from significant limitations. It is premised on the assumption that IRL offers a comprehensive solution to all refugee issues and therefore must be widely promoted. In a non-signatory context, however, this promotion clashes with the "unequal genealogy" of the Refugee Convention and obscures the depoliticized and Eurocentric foundations of the international refugee law regime.[62] Furthermore, as Cole observes in chapter 9, UNHCR itself has been implicated in exacerbating displacement in the Gulf states and facilitating the forcible return of refugees in Bangladesh. In Pakistan, UNHCR faced accusations of complicity in the 2016 *refoulement* of Afghan refugees.[63] Consequently, the assumption that the Refugee Convention and UNHCR operate as apolitical solutions underpins these MoUs between

60 Interview with academic 3 (n 49).

61 ibid.

62 BS Chimni, 'The Birth of a "Discipline": From Refugee to Forced Migration Studies' (2009) 22(1) *Journal of Refugee Studies* 11.

63 Human Rights Watch, 'Pakistan Coercion, UN Complicity: The Mass Forced Return of Afghan Refugees' (Feb 13, 2017) <www.hrw.org/report/2017/02/13/pakistan-coercion-un-complicity/mass-forced-return-afghan-refugees> accessed August 19, 2024.

UNHCR and LUMS, fostering a reluctance to critically interrogate both the instrument and the institution. In Part 4, we explore how this reluctance is reflected in curriculum design. First, however, we turn to UNHCR's collaboration with public universities.

3.3 *Public Universities*

Faced with limited opportunities to engage public university law schools in the teaching of IRL, as this section will show, UNHCR employs a different approach.[64] In 2017, it formalized a collaboration with BUITEMS, a leading university in Quetta, the capital of Balochistan. The resultant MoU – the "Partnership Framework Agreement" – aims to advance research, advocacy, teaching, and training on refugee issues.[65] This includes the establishment of the International Centre for Refugees and Migration Studies (ICRMS) within the Department of International Relations.[66]

The Partnership Framework Agreement is renewed annually, with activities and objectives tailored to each year. The 2024 agreement, for example, focuses on promoting refugee protection policy and law through public lectures, a crash course on refugee rights, and policy dialogues.[67] These dialogues bring together government ministries, the regional chapter of the Commissionerate for Afghan Refugees, international and national refugee support organizations, and refugees themselves. Additionally, with financial backing from UNHCR, ICRMS provides grants and awards to students from refugee communities and supports emerging scholars specializing in refugee studies.[68]

ICRMS has, in the span of short time, developed as an important partner of UNHCR in the promotion of refugee law and rights.[69] Under the MoU, ICRMS functions as a "center for direct implementation of activities of

64 Interview with UNHCR official 3, November 12, 2024 via WhatsApp.

65 The UNHCR and BUITEMS Partnership Framework Agreement (PFA), Project Workplan, September 2024. Copy on file with the authors.

66 The International Centre for Refugees and Migration Studies (ICRMS) <https://icrms.org.pk/> accessed June 5, 2024. See also UNHCR, BUITEMS launches Centre for Refugees and Migration Studies in Quetta (June 7, 2017) <www.unhcr.org/pk/3483-unhcr-buitems-launches-centre-for-refugees-and-migration-studies-in-quetta.html> accessed June 5, 2024.

67 ibid.

68 Interview with academic 5, November 10, 2024 via WhatsApp.

69 Interview with UNHCR Official 3 (n 64).

UNHCR."[70] The MoU further clarifies this purpose by stating that running activities through UNHCR at the public university not only enhances the organization's visibility but also helps it build stronger connections within the public sector. In other words, ICRMS acts as a gateway for UNHCR's engagement with public institutions. Despite this, interviewees claim that ICRMS's efforts are frequently overlooked by the university's central administration.[71] In addition, and as with other public universities, the law faculty and university leadership at BUITEMS question the necessity of teaching refugee law in Pakistan.[72]

A defining feature of ICRMS is that it addresses both refugee and migration issues. This dual approach contrasts with UNHCR's long-standing stance against conflating the two. A UNHCR official we interviewed posits:

> Refugee protection and laws on it are very specific … they are about a situation where forced displacement is taking place, whereas migration is about all kinds of migrants … We [UNHCR] have to ensure that refugee issues are not diluted into broader migration issues [when deciding the curriculum] … This is a very big challenge that becomes counter-productive for us as a refugee agency.[73]

However, ICRMS argues that including migration is necessary, as focusing solely on refugee issues would fail to account for the region's complex political and social dynamics.[74] Putting the spotlight on refugees who have received Proof of Registration cards from the state and UNHCR would exclude many others categorized differently for political reasons.[75] This may exacerbate existing divisions between refugees, migrants, and host communities, especially considering the shifting demographics and geopolitics of the region. This amalgamation of refugee and migration studies reflects ICRMS's agency in shaping its collaboration with UNHCR.

70 The UNHCR and BUITEMS Partnership Framework Agreement (n 65).
71 Interview with academic 5, November 10, 2024 via WhatsApp.
72 The Department of International Relations, however, offers a full undergraduate module on international law, and may in the future consider teaching IRL as part of it. Interview with academic 4, November 7, 2024 via WhatsApp.
73 Interview with UNHCR official 1 (n 38).
74 Interview with academic 5 (n 68).
75 ibid.

Another aim of UNHCR that until now has been resisted by public universities is to advocate for a national refugee law. In March 2023, a National Refugee Bill was introduced and debated in the National Assembly of Pakistan.[76] Although the bill was never enacted into law, UNHCR played a crucial role in assisting with drafting and building a consensus on its content among politicians, civil society organizations, and academics.[77] On the significance of this development, a UNHCR official states:

> Even if you sign the treaty, in order to apply it … you will have to have a national law … so why not advocate having a national law? We will keep on promoting the treaty, it is our priority within the agency … but we are not going anywhere with that, are we? For the last 40 years, the state has been managing a certain population with administrative measures … They [refugees] are here when they are here … can we afford to continue to manage them on ad-hoc basis? So my view is, my personal opinion, that why don't we start advocating strongly for a national refugee law that meets the international refugee protection standards … and alongside that we continue to promote the accession to the treaty … We can do this through our work with universities.[78]

However, UNHCR's enthusiasm is not shared by public universities, which, as noted earlier, oppose integrating IRL into legal education. Proponents of this stance argue that "future lawyers should focus on mastering and applying existing laws rather than diverting their efforts toward studying imagined laws and policies."[79]

Before moving on to Part 4, where we will examine the curriculum and pedagogy of IRL in Pakistan, it is important to reiterate key points from Part 3. UNHCR promotes IRL by supporting its teaching and research at Pakistan's leading universities. A major challenge is the resistance from higher education institutions to including IRL in legal education. UNHCR resolves this challenge by successfully introducing a dedicated IRL module at LUMS and establishing ICRMS. However, these collaborations remain largely driven and sustained by UNHCR. While there are some indications

76 The National Refugee Bill, National Assembly of Pakistan, March 2023, <https://na.gov.pk/uploads/documents/642a741e1c041_286.pdf> accessed February 18, 2024.

77 Interview with UNHCR official 2, May 29, 2023, Islamabad. Interview with a politician responsible for presenting the Bill in parliament, April 3, 2023.

78 Interview with UNHCR official 1 (n 38).

79 ibid.

of universities asserting agency and independence in their approach to teaching and research on refugee law and rights, their collaborations with UNHCR are predominantly shaped by its influence, expertise, and financial support.

4 Teaching International Refugee Law

This section focuses on the teaching of IRL at LUMS and NDU. We have noted already that LUMS is a private university based in Lahore, collaborating with UNHCR in the teaching of IRL in legal education. NDU, on the other hand, is a public university located in Islamabad. It does not have a formal partnership with UNHCR, but nevertheless teaches IRL at the Department of Peace and Conflict Studies. There is a limitation to our examination of the curricula which should be noted. The information about NDU, in its teaching manual and other documents, is rather limited compared to the detailed account of the LUMS curriculum and pedagogy. However, we include NDU to provide a sense of how public universities would approach IRL teaching in the absence of UNHCR involvement.

We begin by outlining the aims and objectives of the IRL curriculum at both institutions. Next, we examine the course materials and module guides used for teaching IRL, and include a reflection on the pedagogical approaches employed in delivering the subject.

4.1 *Aims and Objectives*

When asked why teaching IRL is important in Pakistan, academics and UNHCR professionals interviewed for this research emphasized that the social and legal problems faced by refugees in the country can no longer be ignored.[80] Given Pakistan's proximity to Afghanistan, where political instability and threats to minorities persist, the repatriation of all Afghan refugees remains unlikely. The dynamics of Pakistan–Afghanistan geopolitics and national security concerns frequently implicate Afghan refugees, creating serious tensions between refugee and host communities. Furthermore, the ongoing climate crisis poses severe challenges to Pakistan, potentially displacing millions internally. Academic institutions, therefore, have a crucial role to play in addressing these interconnected and complex issues.

80 Various interviews with academics in Lahore, Quetta, and Islamabad during fieldwork in Pakistan, and some via WhatsApp.

The Refugee Rights course at LUMS thus aims to grapple "with possible solutions to the challenges explored (mainly legal) with a clear understanding of how complicated the problems are."[81] It intends to foster critical and creative responses from participants on the challenges faced by refugees and states. The "law in context" approach is a key to the course design. As an academic at LUMS explains:

> You see, we couldn't just offer a law course on refugees on which there's no applicable national or international law. We can't possibly ignore this context. No! … But Pakistan has other legal obligations stemming from its ratifications of human rights conventions and our own Constitution guarantees certain fundamental rights to everyone residing in the country. So, we had some idea how we could package a course which focuses on IRL … Our previous work with UNHCR on other things further prompted this idea that we could introduce teaching on refugee-related issues, legal and political … that somehow, we must address this complexity in the context of Pakistan. We did see the need for it and for it to be based at the law school.[82]

At NDU, on the other hand, the Refugee Law course aims to provide a unique overview of international migration and refugee law.[83] It brings insights from Pakistan's experience with refugees and the geopolitics of refugee crises elsewhere, including the movement of Syrian refugees to Europe and the treatment of the Muslim minority in India following the enactment of the Indian Citizenship Amendment Act of 2019. The course description asserts that the legal system on its own cannot address the problem of forced migration unless there is a political will to address the causes of displacement including climate change, labor migration and exploitation, and human trafficking.

4.2 *Curriculum and Pedagogy*

At LUMS, the course was initially titled "The Refugee in International and Pakistani Law."[84] It was later renamed "Refugee Rights" to attract students

81 Cooperation Framework Agreement Between UNHCR and LUMS (n 54).

82 Interview with academic 3 (n 49).

83 'Refugee Law', Module Outline for the MPhil in Ethnicity and Nationalism, 2021, National Defence University. Copy on file with the authors.

84 'The Refugee in International and Pakistani Law', Module Outline, LUMS, 2019. Copy on file with the authors.

from other social science disciplines.[85] It is offered as an elective for senior-year undergraduate students and was developed in close collaboration with UNHCR in 2019. At NDU, IRL is taught as part of the Migration and Refugee Law elective module.[86] This module is offered in the MPhil program in Ethnicity and Nationalism. The module was introduced in 2021.

The Refugee Rights course at LUMS is taught in English and spans a 14-week semester.[87] Intended as a multidisciplinary module offered to undergraduate students from both the law and social science faculties, the module is structured into two parts: the international refugee law regime, followed by the Pakistani legal system. Broadly, the module seeks to familiarize students with the legal frameworks governing refugees at both international and domestic levels. It also endeavors to provide a critical understanding of the key criteria for defining and determining refugee status, alongside historical and multidisciplinary perspectives on the status of refugees in Pakistan. The average size of the class is 35 students per year.[88]

The preliminary weeks focus on the international refugee law regime by introducing students to the texts of the Refugee Convention and United Nations General Assembly (UNGA) Resolutions regarding UNHCR's mandate.[89] Compulsory reading sources include the mainstream IRL texts by Goodwin-Gill and McAdam[90] and Hathaway and Foster,[91] alongside the critical perspective by Chimni.[92] At the outset, students are invited to reflect on the "unequal genealogy" of the Refugee Convention, and on the concept of the "myth of difference."[93]

The subsequent weeks dedicate several sessions to the different elements of the refugee definition. These sessions cover various aspects of how

85 Interviews with academics 1 and 3 (n 50). 'Refugee Rights', Module Outline, LUMS (last updated in 2022). Copy on file with the authors.

86 Interview with academic 6, May 24, 2023, Islamabad. 'Refugee Law', Module Outline (n 83).

87 English is a language of instruction for all degree programs at LUMS. It is also the sole language of instruction for all legal education in Pakistan.

88 Interviews with academics 1 and 3 (n 50).

89 'Refugee Rights', LUMS Module Guide for Teachers (Spring 2023). Copy on file with the authors.

90 Guy S Goodwin-Gill, Jane McAdam and Emma Dunlop, *The Refugee in International Law* (OUP 2021) ch 1.

91 James C Hathaway and Michelle Foster, *The Law of Refugee Status* (2nd edn, CUP 2014) ch 3.

92 BS Chimni, 'The Geopolitics of Refugee Studies: A View from the South' (1998) 11(4) *Journal of Refugee Studies* 350.

93 ibid.

refugee status is determined according to the Refugee Convention, including the problem of ascertaining what constitutes a well-founded fear of persecution and membership of a particular social group. The Refugee Convention, UNGA Resolutions regarding UNHCR's mandate, and UNHCR's *Handbook on Procedures and Criteria for Determining Refugee Status and Guidelines on International Protection under the 1951 Convention and the 1967 Protocol relating to the Status of Refugees*[94] form the compulsory reading. Additionally, students are encouraged to understand and differentiate distinct approaches to defining persecution, including the "subjective," "literalist," and "human rights" approaches.[95] Reading Hathaway and Foster, alongside the UNHCR *Handbook* and case law analysis, the curriculum appears to advocate the human rights approach as it bolsters complementarity between refugee law and human rights law, which is significant to grasp in a non-signatory context.[96] The 1954 Convention on Statelessness,[97] and UNHCR's role in supporting internally displaced persons are also examined.

At NDU, the module has a wider and more interdisciplinary scope, with IRL studied alongside broader debates on migration, asylum, statelessness, and "internationally displaced persons."[98] This last category is kept deliberately broad to cover both refugees fleeing persecution and others who are displaced due to climate crises.[99] The module is taught over a 16-week semester and is delivered in English. On average, 10 students enroll in this course each academic year.

From Week 10 onward, the module gives significant attention to the global refugee protection framework including the study of the Refugee Convention, the principle of *non-refoulement*, European Union refugee laws and international human rights law, with special attention given to the Convention against Torture and Other Cruel, Inhuman or Degrading Treatment

94 UNHCR, Handbook on Procedures and Criteria for Determining Refugee Status under the 1951 Convention and the 1967 Protocol relating to the Status of Refugees, HCR/1P/4/Eng/REV.2 (February 1, 2019) <www.unhcr.org/media/handbook-procedures-and-criteria-determining-refugee-status-under-1951-convention-and-1967> accessed September 4, 2024.

95 'Refugee Rights' (n 89); Hathaway and Foster (n 91).

96 'Refugee Rights' (n 89).

97 For the Convention Relating to the Status of Stateless Persons 1954, see <www.unhcr.org/ibelong/wp-content/uploads/1954-Convention-relating-to-the-Status-of-Stateless-Persons_ENG.pdf> accessed September 4, 2024.

98 Module Outline on 'Refugee Law' (n 83).

99 Interview with academic 6 (n 86).

or Punishment (CAT).[100] The nexus between the Refugee Convention and international human rights law is examined in the context of the conditions of refugees in Pakistan.

Both courses address domestic social, legal, and political dynamics to varying degrees. While the Refugee Convention is studied as an international legal framework, its relevance is contextualized within Pakistan's legal system. This is achieved by highlighting the principle of *non-refoulement*, recognized as a customary norm of international law that must be upheld. In the absence of specific refugee laws in Pakistan, the *non-refoulement* principle is further reinforced through the country's obligations under other international human rights treaties. For instance, Pakistan has ratified CAT, which prohibits *refoulement*.[101] Pakistan is also a state party to other international conventions that safeguard refugees by providing protection to all individuals, regardless of their nationality or statelessness.[102] Among these are the International Covenant on Civil and Political Rights (ICCPR), the International Covenant on Economic, Social, and Cultural Rights (ICESCR), the Convention on the Rights of the Child (CRC), and the Convention on the Elimination of all Forms of Discrimination against Women (CEDAW).

The coupling of the *non-refoulement* principle and international human rights law is particularly relevant in the non-signatory state context. Academics and UNHCR officials believe that domestic legal protection for asylum seekers and refugees in Pakistan can be sought through two avenues: (a) applying the principle of *non-refoulement* in conjunction with obligations under human rights conventions; and (b) upholding the fundamental rights of all individuals as set out by the Constitution.[103] To contextualize this approach locally, the curriculum includes recommended readings on

---

100 Convention Against Torture and Other Cruel, Inhuman or Degrading Treatment or Punishment, adopted December 10, 1984, United Nations General Assembly Resolution 39/46 (entered into force June 26, 1987).

101 ibid article 3.

102 Research Society for International Law (RSIL), 'Pakistan's Domestic Implementation of its International Human Rights Obligations' (2020). Executive Summary of the report at <https://portal.mohr.gov.pk/wp-content/uploads/2020/11/Executive-Summary.pdf> accessed February 20, 2024.

103 Various interviews with academics and UNHCR officials. This assertion is substantiated by including the case law materials where available in the curriculum. Notably, Pakistan's judiciary has respected the importance of the customary status of the principle of *non-refoulement* and acknowledged the application of the norms and principles of international human rights conventions on refugee-related cases. Jurisprudence has linked these with the constitutional guarantees offered to all persons in Pakistan. See Kazmi (n 2).

relevant Pakistani case law. Prominent cases studied in these sessions include *Muhammad Akbar Cheema v Superintendent Jail, Kot Lakhpat* (1994), and *Ghulam Sanai v The Assistant Director, National Registration Office* (1999).[104] The recent landmark judgment *Rahil Azizi v the State* (2023) is also being added to the syllabus.[105] While the body of case law is limited, it plays a crucial role in preparing future lawyers, jurists, and activists to advocate effectively for the rights of refugees and asylum seekers.[106]

At LUMS, the Refugee Rights curriculum includes detailed discussions on refugees and religion.[107] These discussions explore the persecution of religious minorities as a basis for determining refugee status. Students are introduced to Islamic legal principles which give prominence to protecting the dignity and respect of asylum seekers. They are encouraged to discuss the rights of refugees under Islamic law and to critically assess the extent to which these principles are reflected in Muslim states' practices of hosting and protecting refugees. Drawing on scholarly readings and the principles of Islamic law derived from the Quran and Hadith, students are also invited to explore the potential components of an Islamic legal framework for refugee protection.[108]

An interesting aspect of this subject is furthermore the inclusion of former UN High Commissioner for Refugees Antonio Guterres's opening remarks at the 2012 Organization of Islamic Cooperation Ministerial Conference on Refugees in the Muslim World.[109] In his remarks, the High Commissioner acknowledged the Islamic legal principles of refugee protection and highlighted that the majority of the world's refugees are hosted by Muslim countries. He advocated for greater global recognition and support for the contributions of Muslim states to the international refugee law framework. LUMS academics suggest that incorporating Guterres's endorsement of Islamic law and the hospitality of Muslim nations helps sensitize students – most of whom are Muslim – to how a religious duty toward

104 Muhammad Akbar Cheema v Superintendent Jail Kot Lakhpat [1994] P Cr LJ 2362; Ghulam Sanai v Assistant Director, National Registration Office [1999] PLD 18 (Peshawar).

105 *Rahil Azizi v The State and others* (2023) Writ petition No 1666 (2023), Islamabad High Court.

106 Interview with academic 3 (n 49).

107 'Refugee Rights' (n 89) and 'Refugee Law' (n 83).

108 'Refugee Rights' (n 89).

109 ibid.

refugees and asylum seekers is recognized and respected in international legal and policy domains.[110]

In the context of legal education, it is particularly noteworthy that the LUMS curriculum includes a session on domestic "Applicable Law."[111] This session examines the Foreigners Act (1946) and its judicial application to refugees and asylum seekers, encouraging students to critically appraise the law as a colonial construct.[112] Interestingly, this session introduces UNHCR–host state MoUs as key sources for understanding Pakistan's collaboration with the agency in refugee protection. Discussions cover the 1993 Cooperation Agreement and the 2003 Tripartite Agreement.[113] Marjoleine Zieck's work brings scholarly nuance to these readings.[114]

The incorporation of these MoUs into the refugee law curriculum is interesting for many reasons. As noted by Janmyr, Hossain and Turner in chapter 10, MoUs may constitute alternative protection regimes for refugees in non-signatory states even though their legal standing is often unclear. In Pakistan, MoUs are increasingly regarded as part of the domestic legal framework, reflecting the country's evolving legal practices. Elsewhere, Kazmi has demonstrated how Pakistan's high courts have periodically referenced these MoUs in legal reasoning to extend protection to refugees.[115] Incorporating these MoUs into the curriculum and placing them as part of domestic law, we posit, underscores their importance both in academia and in organizations where the course could be utilized for training and advocacy on refugee law. Additionally, making them accessible to a broader audience sets a positive example to other non-signatory states, where UNHCR–host state MoUs are often less transparent and confidentialized (see chapter 10).

While including UNHCR–host state MoUs in the curriculum adds value to understanding the domestic legal context, the role of UNHCR in Pakistan

---

110 Interviews with academics 1 and 3 (n 50).

111 'Refugee Rights' (n 89).

112 ibid.

113 'Cooperation Agreement between the Government of Islamic Republic of Pakistan and The United Nations High Commissioner for Refugees' (1993), copy on file with the authors, and 'Tripartite Repatriation Agreement between UNHCR and the Government of Pakistan and Afghanistan' (2003) generally called 'The Tripartite Agreement 2003' <www.refworld.org/legal/agreements/unhcr/2003/en/106940> accessed December 6, 2023.

114 Marjoleine Zieck, 'Accession of Pakistan to the 1951 Convention and 1967 Protocol Relating to the Status of Refugees: Signing on Could Make All the Difference' (2010), 5 *Pakistan Law Review* 1.

115 Kazmi (n 2).

is only partially addressed. The curriculum lacks a balanced critique of UNHCR's prolonged presence in the country, along with the associated historical and political challenges. As observed throughout this chapter, UNHCR plays a significant role in shaping the refugee protection infrastructure in Pakistan through collaborations with entities such as the Commissionerate for Afghan Refugees, relevant government ministries, and other national and international non-governmental organizations. The refugee agency operates locally through its implementing partners, typically local non-governmental organizations, and closely monitors the developments in case law while engaging with lawyers on refugee-related issues. The curriculum should examine this network, how it has come about, and the role of UNHCR within it in greater depth. It should also focus on how Pakistan influences the refugee agency through its membership and proactive participation at the ExCom, including making routine contributions to Executive Committee conclusions.[116]

5 Conclusion

This chapter has examined recent developments in the promotion of IRL at leading universities in Pakistan. Taking Pakistan's non-signatory status to the Refugee Convention as its premise, we have explored how IRL is being introduced as an academic discipline through both teaching and research, while highlighting key challenges in this process. We have found that UNHCR plays a crucial role in fostering collaborations with private and public universities through MoUs. Lastly, we evaluated the IRL curriculum and teaching approaches at LUMS and NDU.

We contend that these developments have largely been top-down, driven and sustained by UNHCR. Where the IRL curriculum has been developed through UNHCR's involvement, such as at LUMS, there is a need for deeper critical analysis of the Refugee Convention and the broader international refugee law regime. This analysis should include a political and historical exploration of the Eurocentric origins of the Refugee Convention, alongside a more comprehensive examination of UNHCR's legal and political role in its extended operations in Pakistan.

Three key trends emerge from these developments. First, given that Pakistan is unlikely to accede to the Refugee Convention in the near

116 Permanent Mission of Pakistan to the United Nations, Geneva, <https://pakungeneva.pk/topics/humanitarian-affairs/> accessed June 30, 2025.

future, resistance from the HEC and PBC to the inclusion of IRL in the core curriculum of legal education may persist. To address this, UNHCR could continue to strengthen its dual approach of engaging with both public and private universities. While private universities may formally collaborate with UNHCR to promote and integrate IRL into their law courses, UNHCR could continue to focus on expanding its engagement with social science faculties in public universities to support both teaching and research. That said, there remains a serious need to stimulate greater demand for IRL education among academics and students across Pakistan.

Secondly, as teaching and research advances at LUMS and other universities, there is a potential to develop IRL into a more comprehensive and critical subject. This transformation could integrate historical, postcolonial, and TWAIL critiques of the international refugee law regime. Chimni's call to decolonize IRL scholarship and acknowledge the colonial context in which the Refugee Convention was framed and adopted would significantly strengthen such assessment.[117] Furthermore, such a reimagined approach to IRL education could adopt an inclusive and participatory teaching methodology, actively engaging with and addressing the needs of refugee communities.

Lastly, the localization of IRL norms and refugee rights education is likely to continue evolving. This approach involves designing IRL curricula that incorporate a "jurisdiction-specific assemblage of international, national, and local norms."[118] In practice, this requires positioning refugee law education along a spectrum, with IRL norms at one end and local norms of refugee protection at the other. Both sets of norms deserve close attention to ensure they are nurtured and integrated into a broader, more contextualized understanding of refugee rights. Such a spectrum is, in essence, a call for "critical localism" which recognizes "translocal and transcultural entanglements," as advocated by Janmyr and Skribeland in chapter 1 of this volume.[119]

Finally, we acknowledge that our research is merely one first step in initiating a broader study of IRL promotion through universities in the context of non-signatory states. This also means that it remains a work in progress, with many questions warranting further exploration. What should be the scope of UNHCR's involvement in shaping an IRL curriculum and pedagogy that would ensure a balanced critique of an institution existing in the midst

117 Chimni (n 9).
118 Jones (n 11).
119 K Roepstorff, 'A Call for Critical Reflection on the Localisation Agenda in Humanitarian Action' (2020) 41(2) *Third World Quarterly* 284.

of political exigencies and its own utility? How can we foster a bottom-up and participatory approach to developing an IRL curriculum that is informed by and responsive to the voices of refugees and asylum seekers? Lastly, how can we theorize the spectrum along which the relevance of IRL teaching unfolds in non-signatory states? This spectrum would reflect the dynamic ways in which IRL takes shape in these states while they, in turn, would contribute to its evolution.

Acknowledgements

This work was supported by the European Union's Horizon 2020 research and innovation program under grant agreement No 851121 (ERC Starting Grant 2019). We wish to thank Maja Janmyr and Özlem Gürakar Skribeland for their meticulous review and insightful discussions during the writing of this chapter.

Index

www.ingramcontent.com/pod-product-compliance
Lightning Source LLC
Chambersburg PA
CBHW071247230926
51849CB00001B/256